The Psychology of

THINKING

JOHN PAUL MINDA

The Psychology of
THINKING

Reasoning, Decision-Making & Problem-Solving

Los Angeles | London | New Delhi
Singapore | Washington DC

Los Angeles | London | New Delhi
Singapore | Washington DC

SAGE Publications Ltd
1 Oliver's Yard
55 City Road
London EC1Y 1SP

SAGE Publications Inc.
2455 Teller Road
Thousand Oaks, California 91320

SAGE Publications India Pvt Ltd
B 1/I 1 Mohan Cooperative Industrial Area
Mathura Road
New Delhi 110 044

SAGE Publications Asia-Pacific Pte Ltd
3 Church Street
#10-04 Samsung Hub
Singapore 049483

Editor: Luke Block
Production editor: Imogen Roome
Proofreader: Christine Bitten
Marketing manager: Michael Ainsley
Cover design: Wendy Scott
Typeset by: C&M Digitals (P) Ltd, Chennai, India
Printed and bound in Great Britain by Ashford
Colour Press Ltd

Library of Congress Control Number: 2015933377

British Library Cataloguing in Publication data

A catalogue record for this book is available from
the British Library

MIX
Paper from
responsible sources
FSC
www.fsc.org   FSC® C011748

ISBN 978-1-4462-7246-6
ISBN 978-1-4462-7247-3 (pbk)

At SAGE we take sustainability seriously. Most of our products are printed in the UK using FSC papers and boards.
When we print overseas we ensure sustainable papers are used as measured by the Egmont grading system.
We undertake an annual audit to monitor our sustainability.

CONTENTS

PREFACE

The psychology of thinking is a topic that has fascinated me for as long as I've been a psychologist. In fact, even before I became a psychologist I was always interested in the process of thinking. My interests in cognition in general, and thinking in particular, are what led me to pursue a career as a cognitive psychologist.

ABOUT ME

Currently, I am an Associate Professor of Psychology and a member of the Brain and Mind Institute at The University of Western Ontario. As a researcher, I am interested in thinking as it relates to concepts and categories. I run a research laboratory that investigates how people learn new categories and represent them with concepts. My students and I also study how conceptual structure interacts with and affects behavioural outcomes. We have done research on medical expertise and on the kinds of reasoning tasks that physicians engage in. Most recently, my students and I have begun to study some of the effects of context and cognitive fatigue on cognitive processes like categorization.

As an instructor, and as a psychologist in general, I am interested in other aspects of thinking as well. Every year since 2003, I have taught a course on the Psychology of Thinking. In this course, which is aimed at third- and fourth-year psychology students, I cover topics such as concepts and categories, reasoning, decision-making, problem-solving, and expertise. This course has become one of the most popular advanced courses in our calendar, and every year students tell me how much they have enjoyed being able to learn more about this most fundamental of human behaviours.

Over the last few years, I have put together a large collection of content and material for this course. There are many other excellent resources and texts that cover some aspects of the thinking process. There are excellent books on reasoning, on problem-solving, on judgement, and on decision-making. There are excellent textbooks on critical thinking. And there are many good edited volumes on the psychology of thinking. Despite this, I have often wished for a single, comprehensive textbook on this topic, a textbook that would cover the psychology of thinking as an advanced topic in cognitive psychology and is suitable for undergraduates in a psychology programme and maybe even for graduate students as well. I hope that this textbook can fill that role.

THE AIMS AND SCOPE OF THIS BOOK

This textbook is intended to serve as the primary text for an upper-year course on Advanced Cognition and/or the Psychology of Thinking. The topics that I will cover represent a deliberately chosen subset of advanced cognition topics that cohere around a general theme of higher-order cognition and thinking: concepts, reasoning, decision-making, problem-solving, language and thought, expertise, and applied thinking. I have grouped these topics together because they are all aspects of higher-order human cognition. Although many of the components of these topics can be found in other, non-human species (similarity, for example) the topics covered in this text are, for the most part, uniquely human.

A primary goal of this textbook is to provide students with current psychological accounts of the thinking process. The psychology of thinking is a topic that extends much of the information that is typically covered in an undergraduate introductory course on cognitive psychology. In order to provide an overarching structure, I have grouped the topics and chapters together into broad themes. The first theme concerns **the organization of human thought**. For example, a core aspect of how people think involves the comparison of existing states, stimuli, or precepts with past experience. These mental comparisons form the basis of the thinking process, and they involve the computation of the similarity between mental representations or concepts. And because much of this cognition requires access to memory, I devote a chapter to covering those topics, and explaining how they are involved in the thinking process.

A second theme is **general reasoning and thinking**, and several chapters are devoted to how and why people engage in reasoning. Reasoning is at the core of the psychological study of thinking and this text explores deductive reasoning, inductive reasoning, and causal reasoning. Another topic in this theme that is likely to have broad appeal is the interaction between language, culture, and thought. This idea goes back as far as the Sapir–Whorf hypothesis in the middle of the twentieth century and continues to be of interest to psychologists, anthropologists, and linguists.

A third theme deals with the **behavioural outcomes of thinking**. These chapters focus on decision-making, problem-solving, and the role of motivation on the thinking process. I conclude with a chapter on expertise and expert-level thinking, which includes a discussion of the formal expertise of chess, science, and medicine.

The book is organized in a progressive fashion. Some topics, such as similarity, are introduced early on, so that subsequent chapters can refer to these topics. As often as possible, I have tried to cross-reference chapters within chapters. In the earlier chapters, I have tried to make a note of when these topics will come up again. In later chapters, I have tried to make a note of how those topics relate to the things that were covered earlier. Some readers may find the back-and-forth distracting, but my hope is that it will help to bring a sense of cohesiveness to the entire text.

I wrote this book with the intention that it would have a broad appeal within the field of Cognitive Psychology. My hope is that it may also be of interest to instructors and lecturers in other fields, such as Cognitive Science, Business, Education, Medicine, and Philosophy. The intention is that the chapters follow the natural progression for a standard semester or half-year course (10–12 weeks). Each chapter is designed to be covered in a week (as 1–2 lectures or as a single seminar discussion), although some chapters could be split over the course of two weeks.

ACKNOWLEDGMENTS AND THANKS

I have many people to thank. In a very general sense, I want to thank all of the students who have been enrolled in my Psychology of Thinking courses over the past ten years. Every year I learn something new from them, and I learn new things about the literature as I prepare what I hope are interesting lectures. If I did not enjoy teaching and lecturing so much, and in particular teaching about this topic, I never would have written this text.

I also have my own graduate students to thank: Ruby Nadler, Sarah Miles, Sarah Devantier, Rahel Rabi, Emily Neilsen, and Karen Zhang. They all contributed to some of the research that went into parts of this book. They also helped to keep my lab running when I was preoccupied with writing the text. I was able to focus on this because of my trust in their ability.

I also want to thank the editorial staff at Sage Publications. Keri Dickens, who helped with this book from the beginning to the end, provided great feedback and just enough motivation to help me finish. I always appreciated her willingness to allow for the inevitable delays and extensions of deadlines. I want to thank Michael Carmichael, who helped with the initial stages and the proposal. I also want to thank the many reviewers who looked at preliminary versions of each chapter and provided helpful feedback, suggestions, and criticism. To everyone who played a role on the editorial side of things, I especially thank you for your patience with my writing.

Most of all, I thank my family: my wife Elizabeth and my two daughters Natalie and Sylvie. They put up with my occasional grumpiness as the project neared a deadline. They tolerated late nights as I worked on the draft. They sometimes had to put up with my forgetfulness because I was preoccupied with completing this book. They helped with encouragement. For example, if I was sitting at my desk and was reading the news, catching up on email, or catching up on Facebook, my younger daughter would say "Dad, aren't you supposed to be working on your book?".... Sometimes, that's all the motivation you need.

SECTION 1
THE ORGANIZATION OF HUMAN THOUGHT

1 THE PSYCHOLOGY OF THINKING

Thinking is so central to the human experience that it has been described as the essence of being. We are all familiar with the phrase, "*Je pense donc je suis*" or "I think therefore I am." This comes, of course, from Descartes' *Discourse on the Method* (1637) and underscores what is so crucial and compelling about the study of thinking. Humans, like other animals, behave, learn, respond, communicate, and remember. But humans also think. We can discover something new by thinking about it. We can solve problems in the mind, visualize solutions, and arrive at an important decision by thinking. We can be aware of our own thoughts and aware of the consequences of our actions and behaviours.

This book is about the **psychology** of thinking. That might sound redundant, given that psychology is often defined as the study of the mind or of mental activity. In other words, if psychology is not about thinking, what else can it be about? Psychology is a very broad field, encompassing everything from the study of neurotransmitters and basic neuroanatomy to the study of learning and memory to the understanding of mental health and the study of group behaviour. **This book is concerned with the study and understanding of the thought process.** Thinking is usually studied within the broader field of cognition. **Cognitive psychology** has traditionally been defined as the study of information processing and behaviour. This encompasses everything from basic attention and perception to memory, concepts, and thinking. As a topic within the study of cognitive psychology, the psychology of thinking is concerned with complex mental behaviours, such as problem-solving, reasoning, decision-making, and becoming an expert. A good understanding of basic cognition is very useful in understanding the psychology of thinking, but it is not necessary. In other words, if you are reading this book as part of a course on thinking, a course on reasoning and decision-making, or even a business or marketing course, and you have already taken a course on cognition, then you may find some helpful overlap in some of the topics covered. But if you have not taken a course on cognition, I do not think you will have any additional difficulty. I have tried to write this text so that it builds on prior knowledge, although that knowledge is not strictly necessary and you can enjoy and use this book without any prior formal study in cognition.

In this first chapter, I want to describe what thinking is (and also what it is not, for the purposes of this book). I want to consider several examples of thinking, and several challenges to clear thinking. I will also describe some of the ways in which thinking has traditionally been studied.

WHAT IS THINKING?

A basic description

Thinking is mental activity, but it is not just any mental activity. Or rather, thinking and mental activity are not synonymous. For example, basic visual perception, memory consolidation, and coordination of sensory motor activity are all very sophisticated mental activities, but these kinds of behaviours are not usually considered to be thinking. **Thinking is a very specific subset of mental activity that involves working with mental representations, planning and executing behaviours, and the coordination of cognitive resources.** For example, solving an algebra problem, analyzing the themes in a film, discussing the prospects for your favourite sports team, or making a split-second decision about which route to take when a road is closed are all examples of thinking. Daydreaming, fantasy, depressive thoughts, and anxious ruminations are also examples of thinking, although in this book I will deal primarily with thinking as a cognitive phenomenon and will spend less time considering the contents of unstructured thought or the clinical ramifications of thoughts that are difficult to control.

Different kinds of thinking

Thinking can be divided up in many ways, including divisions based on content, effort, the desired outcome, underlying cognitive processes, and function. These kinds of divisions are intuitive but also allow researchers to study thinking at different levels. For example, we must make a distinction between the kind of thought that one engages in when solving an introductory physics problem and the kind of thought that one engages in when catching a fly ball in baseball. For readers not immediately familiar with fly balls, a fly ball is a ball that is hit with a high, slow arc. Catching one is fairly easy with practice and involves being able to predict exactly where the ball will land, and placing oneself in that location (McBeath, Shaffer, & Kaiser, 1995). Solving a physics problem and catching a fly ball both require attention and both have a measurable outcome (passing the exam or catching the ball), and both are essentially physics problems. But solving an introductory physics problem requires sustained attention, the recall and generation of learned facts, the conscious application of those facts, and the ability to engage in some kind of explicit monitoring of the behaviour. This is a conscious and effortful process, even if the solver in question has some experience with physics problems. Catching a fly ball, on the other hand, is a process that often defies verbal description. It is intuitive and does not seem to rely on the recall of facts, but rather on the replay of hand–eye coordination routines. These are both examples of complex thinking, and yet they differ in terms of what psychological processes are active during the execution. A thorough understanding of the psychology of thinking requires being able to differentiate between these two kinds of thought processes, the cognitive processes that underlie them, and to be able to have an adequate theoretical description of thinking that encompasses both kinds of thinking.

Consider another example, the thinking processes behind a game of chess. Playing chess effectively requires the coordination of several cognitive processes and behaviours. One must have sufficient knowledge of the rules, a good recall of the rules, and the correct application of the rules. Playing chess, especially playing chess effectively, also involves recall for common chess positions and recall of previously played games of chess (Chase & Simon, 1973; De Groot, 1965). Playing chess effectively also involves thinking ahead, thinking about what your opponent might do, and developing a strategy for how to react based on what you think the other player will do. This second set of behaviours involves what is known as a **theory of mind**, which means being able to consider the contents of another person's thoughts.

Playing chess can be contrasted with playing a visually oriented video game. Many games, especially the simple, action games found on mobile platforms such as "Angry Birds", place much less emphasis on rule acquisition and retrieval of rules for memory, and place a greater premium on procedurally learned motor responses. As with the previous example (catching fly balls versus solving physics problems), the first behaviour is a conscious and effortful process whereas the second behaviour is an intuitive and procedural process that defies verbal description. Interestingly, both rely on some degree of retrieved memories. In the chapter on expertise in this text, we will discuss at length the degree to which expert chess players rely on rapid retrieval of previously learned patterns. This may share some overlap with the kind of rapid retrieval of previously learned motor responses involved in many visually oriented video games. So although these two kinds of thinking are quite different in many ways, and solve different problems, there are shared underlying mechanisms – in this case, retrieval of prior instances from memory.

We could go on with many other examples, dissecting them to consider what principles of thought and cognition are involved. Writing a paper for a course requires reading and retaining new ideas, considering more than one idea simultaneously, being able to examine the parallels and analogies among ideas, and being able to make use of basic linguistic processes to communicate the idea. Learning to play a short piece on the piano involves the mapping of written notes to motor action, the focus of attention on the sound of the piece, and the coordination of several different motor behaviours. Diagnosing patients involves attending to symptoms, comparing the similarity of the observed symptoms to memory representations of previously seen patients. Looking over many of these examples, we start to see commonalities: focusing attention, making judgements about similarity, considering several ideas simultaneously. These common attributes will eventually become the objects of study for understanding the psychology of thinking.

CHALLENGES TO THE THINKING PROCESS

Thinking occurs on many levels and, as described above, different actions require different levels of thought. In fact, most of the time we either arrive at correct decisions or we arrive at decisions for which there was little cost for an incorrect decision. Furthermore, many researchers argue that humans are quite capable of predicting and judging information even in the face of incomplete and sparse information. For example, a recent study by Tom Griffiths and Joshua Tenenbaum looked at people's ability to make quick judgements about things that they were not experts in, such as how much money a movie might make, a person's lifespan given a quick summary, or how long it takes to bake a cake (Griffiths & Tenenbaum, 2006). They found that most people were able to make predictions that fell closely in line with statistical models of optimal outcome. In other words, people often make really good judgements and predictions even if they are not exactly sure how or why they are doing it. A possible explanation is that people are very efficient at using their existing knowledge, memory, and understanding to fill in gaps and make quick predictions.

But if you have ever arrived at the wrong conclusion, solved a problem incorrectly, or made a bad decision, you've probably realized that thinking can sometimes be a challenge. We make mistakes. Sometimes we have to think about too many things at once, or we do not have all the information needed to arrive at a good decision. The section below considers some of the primary challenges that we face. We will consider many more "thinking challenges" later in this book.

Multitasking

Multitasking is both commonplace and misunderstood. We know that multitasking refers to being able to do more than one thing at a time, like reading and listening to music, talking while cooking, checking Facebook during a lecture, texting and driving, etc. The human brain and mind is designed to be able to divide attention and resources among several input and output channels (Pashler, 1994). What is challenging about understanding multitasking is that most people are aware that it often occurs with some cost to behaviours but at the same time people often assume that it is a necessary action, a positive skill, or both. It would not be uncommon to hear someone claim to be "good at multitasking". But is it really possible to be good at multitasking?

Current research suggests that there is nearly always a cost, and that this cost may even last beyond the multitasking event. For example, Ophir, Nass, and Wagner (2009) created a questionnaire that allowed them to measure light, medium and heavy media multitaskers. In this case, media multitasking refers to using more than one media device or following more than one media stream at the same time. Examples might include studying while watching a show on Netflix, or taking notes in class while checking a Twitter feed, or listening to music while reading. Heavy media multitaskers were those who were more than one full standard deviation above the average score on the questionnaire. Participants in the experiment were asked to engage in a number of tasks that required them to switch quickly between responses and to detect targets in the presence of distractors. If people were really good at multitasking, they might be expected to do well at a task like this, because good performance relies on the ability to switch quickly and to screen out irrelevant information.

This was not the finding, however. Being a heavy media multitasker did not seem to predict better performance on these cognitive tasks. In fact, the researchers found the opposite pattern. They found that heavy or "chronic" media multitaskers performed worse on a test of task-switching ability, likely due to a reduced ability to filter out interference from the irrelevant task set. In other words, the very people who were the heaviest multitaskers and who should have been "good at multitasking" were not really very good at all, and they actually performed worse on a test of actual multitasking. One possible explanation for this counterintuitive result is that heavy media multitaskers have adopted an attentional style that results in greater distractibility. In other words, instead of being better at selectively attending and screening out, heavy media multitaskers were worse because they were constantly switching and being distracted. This does not mean that media multitaskers will suffer on all tasks, but it does suggest that multitasking may not always be a benefit.

BOX 1.1

One of the most prevalent things in many of our lives is the smartphone. For those of us that use or rely on a smartphone, we know the challenges that it presents, and the relative costs and benefits. Without getting into a long list of features and aspects of phones, consider what the smartphone can do to help (or hurt) the thinking process. The positive aspects are pretty clear. People use their phones for communication, texting, as cameras, as clocks, as weather stations, and as a newspaper. As long as the device is connected to a network, users have access to

(Continued)

(Continued)

more knowledge than has ever been possible before. One of the most likely negative effects of having a smartphone is multitasking. Our cognitive systems are designed to process multiple channels of information but there is almost always a cost. As you are reading this now, you may have a smartphone. You may have even thought to look at it right now to see if any text message, emails, etc. have arrived.

Consider another dimension to smartphone multitasking. Not only do people find themselves splitting their attention between several things (e.g., taking notes, listening to a lecture, and checking a smartphone), but you may also find yourself spending energy actively ignoring one of those things. That is, the smartphone uses cognitive recourses when you are checking it or responding to a text, but it also uses cognitive resources when you try to ignore it. As an example, several years ago, I was in the middle of a lecture and my smartphone buzzed because of an incoming text message. Only a handful of people send me text messages (my wife, my kids, etc.) and they would not text me during a class. But this happened to occur at a time when a member of my extended family was in the hospital with a serious condition. The result was that I simply could not concentrate on the lecture, and had to stop to read the text (everything was fine!). The point is that the process of trying to inhibit the urge to read the text message was draining on my cognitive resources.

Heuristics and biases

Another potential challenge to the thinking process is the tendency for humans to rely on heuristics and to show biases when making decisions. A **heuristic** is generally defined as a cognitive shortcut. When people use heuristics they are relying on knowledge to solve a problem or arrive at a solution, rather than a more active thought process. Heuristics are not just guesses, though. Heuristics provide reasonably good solutions or decision outcomes based on personal knowledge. The more extensive the person's knowledge is, the more likely the heuristic will be to provide the correct answer or optimal decision. The advantage of a heuristic is that the solution can be generated quickly. Heuristics are faster than working through a problem, and they are usually correct.

As an example, imagine that you are the designated driver for an evening out with your friends. You want to pick everyone up and drive to your destination in the shortest way possible. One solution to this problem would be to map out the driving distance from your home to the home of each of your friends, and from each friend's home to the homes of your other friends, and then from each friend's home to your destination.

You would then compare every possible permutation and see which of these produces the actual shortest distance. This **algorithm** might be time-intensive but it is guaranteed to find the correct solution. But, in practice, you would probably not carry out this set of calculations. You would rely on a **heuristic** that takes advantage of your general knowledge of the area, and choose a route that seemed to minimize the distances. This would probably also arrive at the same answer (the shortest route). The key difference is that the heuristic only really works well if you have a rich knowledge base to draw upon when making the inferences and generating solutions. And as will be discussed in subsequent chapters, although heuristics might be more efficient, because they are based on specific knowledge, they might produce an incorrect solution if the underlying knowledge base contains false or incomplete information. The reliance on heuristics has long been thought to be a source of cognitive errors (Tversky & Kahneman, 1973, 1974), although more recent work assumes that heuristics are a sign of adaptive cognition (Gigerenzer, Hertwig, & Pachur, 2011). Both of these perspectives will be covered in later chapters on problem-solving and decision-making.

Incomplete or incorrect knowledge

It may seem fairly obvious, but a major source of errors in thinking is an imperfect or incorrect knowledge base. In a sense, this underlies many of the cognitive heuristic errors as well. Consider a very straightforward example: a student is struggling to solve an algebra problem for her homework. If she remembers the correct algorithm, or correct example, the solution should eventually come. However, if she remembers the wrong algorithm, an incorrect example, or can't remember an example at all, the problem will be much more difficult to solve. In general, thinking is more difficult when you are thinking about something that is in an unfamiliar domain. Thinking is more difficult when you are trying to solve a problem that is really novel. Later in this text, in the chapter on problem-solving, we will discuss general strategies for solving problems in cases where the knowledge base is incomplete. At the other extreme, experts are characterized by a very rich and extensive knowledge base. This rich and extensive knowledge base helps experts to solve problems more quickly, make diagnoses more quickly, and make optimal decisions more efficiently.

There are many other examples of how incorrect or incomplete knowledge can affect the thinking process. For example, the general tendency to make judgements and decisions on the basis of information that is available in memory is known as the **availability heuristic** (Chater & Oaksford, 1999; Tversky & Kahneman, 1974). In other words, people tend to make decisions on the basis of the information they have immediately available in consciousness or that is immediately retrievable from memory. More often than not, this heuristic will lead to correct decisions. After all, we have evolved to trust our own memories. However, events that are perceived as being more frequent because of high salience or recency will skew our judgements. People routinely overestimate the likelihood of serious injury due to things like shark attacks, terrorist attacks, aeroplane disasters. These events are tragic when they occur but still occur with very low frequency. However, often the tragic nature of these events leaves them more salient in memory over other mundane events of higher frequency, such as vehicle accidents. As a result, our memory about low and high frequency events is skewed, and this skewed memory representation results in a bias. This bias results in overestimating the occurrence of low-frequency events.

Later in this book, we will cover other types of cognitive errors and bias. In many ways, these errors are a major source of insight into the thinking process. It is also important to note that despite these errors, most people arrive at reasonable conclusions and make good decisions. Herbert Simon, the influential cognitive scientist and artificial intelligence researcher, refers to this as **satisficing** (Simon, 1957). Simon argues that a cognitive system designed to seek optimal performance is likely to be impossible, and certainly undesirable, for most applications. If optimality is difficult or impossible to achieve, then a cognitive system designed to seek optimal performance will fail. A more adaptive approach, one that largely describes human cognitive abilities, is one which seeks a good enough outcome but not a perfect outcome.

THEORETICAL APPROACHES TO THE STUDY OF THINKING

I started this chapter with a reference to Descartes. Interest in understanding thinking goes back much farther than that. Philosophers, theologians, psychologists, and physicians, as well as the average person, have all spent time trying to understand how we think, what we think about, and why we have the thoughts that we do. Since this text is on the psychology of thinking, we will not spend much time discussing the earlier, less psychological accounts. In addition, because this is a book from the cognitive psychological tradition, we will start with early work that directly influenced the cognitive tradition. This does not mean to undermine or negate any of the important work on the role of unconscious motivations in thinking that are associated with the psychoanalytic approach developed by Sigmund Freud. One could easily argue that Freud's work was influential in bringing about a consideration of the complexity of human thought. Furthermore, as we consider what is sometimes known as the "dual process" approach, it may be worth noting some higher-order similarities between the Freudian model of personality (with an emphasis on conflict between fast, intuitive behaviours and slower, higher-order cognitive processes to keep them in check) and the role of a fast, intuitive system versus a slower, deliberative system in thinking and cognition. I am not suggesting that the dual process approach to cognition is analogous to Freudian theories, but rather that both are attempting to describe the same underlying systems of thought.

The Gestalt approach

As discussed above, it is important to understand some of the historical and theoretical developments that led up to our current understanding of human thought. One of the more well-known of these earlier approaches is the **Gestalt approach**. This was one of the primary approaches to the study of thinking in the early part of the twentieth century. The Gestalt approach arose in Germany and was a counter to the **Structuralist** approaches of the same era. Most of us know about the Gestalt laws of grouping. These are perceptual laws that all centre on the idea that humans are biased to perceive whole objects, rather than parts. For example, the **Law of Proximity** states that feature or figures that are near each other will tend to be perceived as belonging to a common object. Likewise, the **Law of Similarity** states that elements or features in a group of objects are perceived as belonging together if the objects are similar to each other. Note that these laws are primarily descriptive, and although they serve as good rules of thumb for describing our perceptual preferences, they have generally been criticized for lacking scientific rigour and for failing to provide sufficient explanatory power. Figure 1.1 shows some basic examples. Although most of these show simple perceptual grouping laws, these laws also suggest a reliance on whole-object perception. By this view, the mind is not a "blank slate" but is designed in such a way as to process information and deal with representations – processed information and representations are the objects of study in the psychology of thinking. And of course, many of the ideas do live on in the contemporary principles of aesthetics and design.

While the perceptual laws of Gestalt psychology have mostly been superseded by more sophisticated theoretical approaches, Gestalt psychology also emphasized several approaches to thinking and problem-solving which influenced subsequent theories of thinking. For example, Max Wertheimer, who was one of the founders of the Gestalt school, considered two broadly

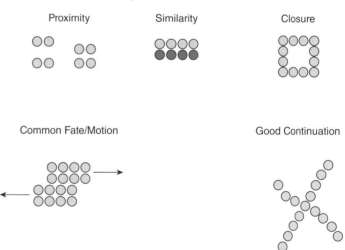

Examples of Gestalt Laws

Proximity Similarity Closure

Common Fate/Motion Good Continuation

Figure 1.1 An example of some of the Gestalt laws of grouping. According to the Gestalt view, we tend to perceive whole objects and show a preference for grouping similar things together.

defined kinds of thinking: **productive thinking** and **reproductive thinking** (Wertheimer, 1959). An example of productive thinking is solving a problem with an insight. Insight problems, as we will discuss later in the chapter on problem-solving, are bursts of ideas, clarity, or correct solutions that often seem to arrive suddenly in the mind. For example, if you are solving a crossword puzzle, you might struggle with a clue and put that one aside while you move on to another clue. Sometimes, the answer to the first clue might seem to arrive suddenly, and might even be accompanied with a feeling of satisfaction and relief. On the other hand, reproductive thinking in problem-solving refers to problem-solving by remembered examples and remembered rules. Although these Gestalt principles of productive and reproductive thinking do not map directly on to current theories, they have influenced more contemporary ideas of algorithmic and heuristic problem-solving.

It might be tempting to regard the Gestalt ideas as an artefact of a less sophisticated time in psychology, but I think that would be a mistake. These ideas do continue to resonate even within our current attempts to understand the thinking process.

The cognitive approach

Most psychology students have read the history of the so-called **cognitive revolution**. This refers to the transition of experimental psychology from a scientific approach that emphasized behaviourism and the laws of learning to the scientific approach that emphasized cognition, mental representations, and information-processing. This revolution did not happen overnight, or even over the course of a few years, but there certainly was a major paradigm shift in the field. Whereas in the 1930s and 1940s a great many university research laboratories would have been designed to study behaviour as a result of learning stimulus response associations, later on in the 1950s and 1960s many university psychology labs were investigating memory as a internal representation, problem-solving as a cognitive process, and thinking.

Most of the topics in this text, and indeed the study of the psychology of thinking, were studied and framed within the cognitive tradition. One of the most influential texts from that era was *A Study of Thinking* by Bruner, Goodnow, and Austin. Published in 1956, this book helped to usher in the modern era of information-processing accounts of thinking. The general thesis of this book was that thinking can be studied experimentally. The book described 30 studies, ranging from investigations of simple rule-learning to the acquisition of complex concepts. Possibly more than any other book, this extensive work laid down the foundations of the modern study of the psychology of thinking (Bruner, Goodnow, & Austin, 1956).

One of the hallmarks of the cognitive approach and of Bruner et al.'s book is the idea that many behaviours are the result of thinking and that thinking is far more than the network of stimulus and response associations that were assumed by many behaviourists. Cognitive psychologists from that era assumed that thinking involved the representation of external and internal events as internalized **mental representations**. There is no set, agreed-upon definition of what a mental representation is, but for our purposes we should define a mental representation as a stable state of activation within a cognitive/neural system that corresponds to an event, object, or idea. Birthday parties, cats, and vaccines are all things in the world. When I think about them, I generally think about them in the same way each time. It is a stable representation. My representation for cats consists of memories and images of my own cat, knowledge about where cats come from, feelings of affection, and likely these are all activated when I think of cats. By this definition, then, thinking is the process by which these internal representations are manipulated. As a result, many of the cognitive accounts of that era emphasized the notion of **symbolic processing**. More contemporary accounts tend to rely less on the idea of mental symbols and the advent of model cognitive neuroscience has allowed theorists to understand thought as a process of changing states of activation, rather that purely symbolic processing. Indeed, many modern self-help and motivational texts routinely refer to "thinking and the brain" or how to "help your brain make better decisions".

Dual process account

Within the field of cognition devoted to thinking, reasoning, problem-solving and decision-making, a long-standing tradition in psychology and in the cognitive sciences is the notion that some cognitive process are fast, somewhat effortless, and not tied to consciousness and that other cognitive processes are slower, more effortful, and more closely tied to consciousness. Although this has taken many forms, the primary version of this theory is known as the **dual process account** or **dual systems theory**. Both terms have been used in the literature. The more common term is the dual process account. In this text, I may use both, though I will usually use dual process. Within this dual process account, the constituent subsystems are almost always referred to with the label "system", thus each of the two systems makes up the dual systems in the dual process account.

The dual process theory assumes that there are two cognitive and neuropsychological systems that underlie the thinking process. Evans (2003, 2008) refers to these as **System 1** and **System 2**, and suggests that these systems differ in terms of evolution, structure, and function. Other theorists have used other terms to describe the two systems, such as **holistic** and **analytic** (Evans, 2003, 2008; Evans & Stanovich, 2013; Nisbett & Miyamoto, 2005; Nisbett, Peng, Choi, & Norenzayan, 2001; Norman & Brooks, 1997; Sloman, 1996). These distinctions can be semantic, but these various descriptions do not always overlap perfectly. In this book, I use the System 1 and System 2 designation as it is the most well-known. Readers should consult Evans (2008) for a comprehensive and critical review of these theories, and I cover the topic in greater detail in Chapter 8.

Most theorists regard System 1 as a cluster of structures and functions that may operate with relative autonomy, and the functions and behaviours ascribed need not interact with other systems. System 1 is generally described as relatively fast, unconscious, independent of general intelligence or working memory ability and operates via associative mechanism. System 1 is also described as the more primitive system. This means that it relies on neural structures that are evolutionarily primitive (e.g., lower cortical structures). As such, System 1 is thought to be shared by humans and non-humans alike.

What kinds of behaviours rely on System 1? When you make a decision with your "gut" it might be a decision that is based on System 1. For example, consider two people who live on the same floor of an apartment building. They may see each other every few days, as each arrives home from work or errands. Initially, neither person may extend a greeting to the other, but at some point (days or week later), one of the persons says "hello" to the other. That is, after many silent meetings, one person makes the decision to greet the other. What thought process led to the decision to extend the initial greeting? Although it is possible that the greeter deliberated about this every morning, weighing the costs and benefits of a greeting and trying to maximize the benefit of saying "hello", a more likely alternative is that the greeting just felt appropriate at that time. After a number of uneventful and silent encounters, the greeter felt that the second person was safe, friendly, or otherwise deserving of a greeting. Put another way, it is probably hard for the greeter to put into words why he or she chose to say "hello" to the other person. It probably just felt right. But behind the right feeling, there is likely to be a whole catalogue of observed behaviour, memories, and associations that helped to tip the scale in favour of a greeting. This catalogue of behaviour is the underpinning of System 1.

When you make a more conscious, deliberative decision, it might be thought to involve System 2 processes more heavily. For example, I recently purchased a new vehicle (not new, but a three-year-old vehicle that was new to me). My current vehicle at the time was an 11-year-old Honda Pilot, and there were a number of problems that were worrying me. I took the car to a dealership for an estimate for several different repairs and the estimate was extensive. I then considered how much I was willing to spend to repair the vehicle and how much longer I thought I might want to drive an 11-year-old car. I reasoned that a newer, similar vehicle might be a better option, and although I had not planned to buy a new car that day, I quickly made a list of costs and benefits, pros and cons, and contacted my wife for a quick discussion. Although there were probably aspects of System 1 reasoning, the decision-making process was one that required a slower, more deliberative approach, a consideration of many outcomes and scenarios, the careful and explicit weighing of evidence, and a conscious decision. This is System 2 thinking.

The dual process approach, though intuitive, has received some criticism as well. In a recent review, Evans and Stanovitch (2013), who are proponents of the dual process approach, outlined what they consider to be some of the primary criticisms and concerns with this theory. For example, one problem is that dual process theorists have offered multiple and vague definitions. At various times they have been referred to as implicit/explicit, associative/rule-based, intuitive/reflective, conscious/unconscious. Individually, these descriptions and dissociations might be workable, but collectively they become more problematic. It is unlikely to be the case that all System 1 behaviours are equally uncontrolled, unconscious, associative, implicit, and intuitive. A second common criticism is that the proposed groupings have not been well aligned. That is, the features for behaviours that are thought to belong to one system are not always observed together. Many researchers have suggested that what might seem like evidence for two separate systems or processes is equally compatible with the view that thinking behaviour operates on a single continuum. In other words, what seems like evidence for a separate System 1 is simply behaviour that is carried out at the less flexible, less conscious part of the thinking continuum.

Aims and scope of this text

A primary goal of this textbook is to provide readers with an overview of the history of the psychology of thinking and also a survey of current psychological accounts of the thinking process. The psychology of thinking is a topic that extends much of the information that is typically covered in an undergraduate introductory course on cognitive psychology. In order to provide an overarching structure, I have grouped the topics and chapters into broad themes. The first theme concerns the **organization of human thought**. For example, a core aspect of how people think involves the comparison of existing states, stimuli, or precepts with past experience. These mental comparisons form the basis of the thinking process, and they involve the computation of the **similarity** (Chapter 2) between mental representations or concepts. This theme also encompasses the structure of mental representations. I have included a chapter on **knowledge representation** (Chapter 3) and a chapter on **concepts and categories** (Chapter 4). This theme also includes a chapter on the interaction between **language and thought** (Chapter 5). This idea goes back to the Sapir–Whorf hypothesis in the middle of the twentieth century and continues to be of interest to psychologists, anthropologists, and linguists.

Each chapter is meant to be able to stand alone, but the theme that holds them together is that these representations and concepts, bound by similarity and shaped by language, are the basic units of thought.

A second theme is general **thinking and reasoning**, and several chapters will be devoted to how and why people engage in reasoning. Reasoning is at the core of the psychological study of thinking and this text will explore **inductive reasoning** (Chapter 6) and **deductive reasoning** (Chapter 7) . I have also included a chapter that covers the influence of **motivation and mood** on thinking (Chapter 8). This chapter also includes a longer and more detailed description on the **dual process approach**.

A third theme deals with the **behavioural outcomes of thinking**. In other words, the topics and chapters comprising Section 3 attempt to answer questions about the how we use our knowledge, concepts, and reasoning ability to make decisions and affect cognitive and practical change. Chapter 9 covers the psychology of **judgement and decision-making**. In this chapter I cover basic heuristics, probability estimation, and theories of decision-making. Chapter 10 covers **problem solving**, and includes a section on creativity as well. I conclude with a chapter on **expertise** and expert-level thinking, which includes a discussion of the formal expertise of chess, science, and medicine (Chapter 11).

2 THE PSYCHOLOGY OF SIMILARITY

> The question "What makes things seem alike or seem different?" is one so funda-
> mental to psychology that very few psychologists have been naïve enough to ask it.
> (Attneave, 1950: 516)

What does it really mean for two things and two ideas to be similar to each other? In many ways, this seems like a trivial question. We know that two dogs can be similar to each other: they are both dogs, they both bark, they have tails, drool, etc. But would they be less similar if only one of them had a tail or if one was large and the other small? And beyond that, how do we make a distinction in terms of how each of these factors affects perceived similarity? Are they similar because they share important features, or are they similar just by virtue of being dogs? In other words, what seems simple to describe at first is actually fairly complex.

In this chapter, I hope to do several things. First, I want to discuss what similarity is. Second, I will show how similarity is involved in the thinking process, and why it is important to study similarity before considering other topics related to thinking. Third, I will consider the ways in which psychologists usually try to assess and measure similarity. Fourth, I will discuss the major psychological theories of similarity and how they work.

WHAT IS SIMILARITY?

For most of us, similarity is a construct that is easy to recognize but often difficult to describe. But I want to start this chapter with an attempt to define similarity. Similarity seems to be a **domain general** construct. This means that it operates according to the same principles whether or not the objects or ideas that are being compared are visual, auditory, lexical, directly perceived, or recalled from memory. If I can arrive at some calculation of similarity by comparing two photos of dogs, it might be pretty much the same as if I saw the dogs in person, or was asked to recall an image from memory. This does not mean that similarity judgements are unaffected by context, but it does mean that similarity as a computation is carried out in the same way regardless of context.

Of course, as soon as we decide that similarity is domain general, and seems to be universal, we also have to account for the incredible flexibility and fluidity that exists in how people understand and rate similarity. For example, if I hold in my hand a Canadian penny and an American penny, I would rate them to be quite similar. Even though they are currencies from two different countries, the composition is similar, their shape is similar, their role within the monetary system is similar (set aside the fact that the Canadian penny has been discontinued and the American penny has not yet been). Suppose I am then handed a Canadian nickel. Does this change my understanding of the similarity between the American and Canadian penny? Are the Canadian penny and the Canadian nickel now more similar to each other? Or are there two kinds of similarity at play? In other words, my perception of surface similarity allows me to rate the two pennies as being similar, but there is also a deeper, more conceptual similarity that allows me to rate the two Canadian coins as being similar. Consider extending the example even further by imagining that I am handed a Japanese yen coin. Functionally, it serves the same role as the penny. Conceptually, it seems an outlier as the other coins are North American in nature. Does it change the similarity among the three North American coins?

There is no set answer to these questions. I bring them up to illustrate that similarity is flexible. There is more than one kind of similarity. We can appreciate similarity between and among objects at different levels.

SIMILARITY AND THE THINKING PROCESS

Similarity plays a role in many core cognitive processes and it is an important aspect of many higher order thoughts as well. Below is an examination of several of these, but the list is not exhaustive.

Object recognition

First, let us consider the process of visually recognizing objects in the world. Quite simply, we are adept at being able to see an object (an apple, for example) and nearly instantaneously, and from a variety of viewpoints, recognize the object, name it, access categorical information, grasp it appropriately, etc. This process of object recognition is often assumed to require an assessment of the similarity between the incoming perceptual representation and the mental representations that have been stored in memory (Biederman, 1987; Tarr, 1995; Tarr, Williams, Hayward, & Gauthier, 1998). Whether we assume that the pattern matching process is done via stored exemplars, stored images, or a stored list of non-accidental properties, there is generally a role for the mental computation of similarity. Objects are recognized (in part, at least) as a function of their similarity to stored patterns of known and previously seen objects. An understanding of similarity is thus crucial for an understanding of the object recognition process. Of course, not all formal theories of objects recognition specify an explicit role for object recognition. This is merely an acknowledgment that similarity plays a role in a general sense.

Memory retrieval

As another example, consider the process of memory retrieval. Semantic memory – memory for facts – is assumed to be organized conceptually (Roediger, 2008). That is, if you are trying to remember something (a name, a place, etc.), the chances are that you will also remember similar things are well. In order to retrieve the right memory, a retrieval cue must contact the most similar representations in memory. This idea underlies many influential models of theories of memory organization and structure. As such, similarity between related memory traces and similarity between a cue and the to-be-remembered item is going to play a role in memory retrieval. Memory retrieval errors are also a function of similarity. We often make errors by retrieving the wrong, but very similar, memory.

Many early cognitive theories of semantic memory demonstrate the importance of similarity with the basic idea of **spreading activation** (Collins & Loftus, 1975). Essentially, spreading activation occurs when a single target concept is activated, and that activation spreads to other related concepts. The degree of spread is influenced by similarity, and may also be taken as an index of similarity. This is typically measured in terms of reaction time in a **lexical decision task**. A lexical decision task is a task in which letter strings that are either words or non-words are presented visually to a subject. The subject is required to respond quickly with a judgement of whether the string is a word or not. Since the error rates are usually very low, the dependent variable is usually the subject's reaction time to respond. If a subject is presented with a target word, such as "FORK", the subject should be faster to correctly identify the word "KNIFE" than to correctly identify an unrelated word like "TRUCK". The fork and the knife belong to the same category, perform similar roles, are used in similar contexts, and are often made of similar material, so we expect the activation to spread from one concept to the next. The faster reaction time is an explicit indication of this similarity.

Other models of memory, such as the instance-based model known as MINERVA2 (Hintzman, 1986; Hintzman & Ludlam, 1980), for example, are built upon the notion that similarity between memory traces is a major component of memory retrieval. In this particular model, memory retrieval functions as a result of the similarity between a probe and many retrieved memory traces. In this model, the probe can be thought of as a cue, or a prompt, requiring the system to recall a memory. This probe contacts as many stored exemplars as it can, but exemplars that are more similar to the probe are retrieved more quickly. A probe that is able to contact many similar exemplars very quickly corresponds to memories that are retrieved easily. A probe that contacts few exemplars, or that takes longer to contact exemplars, corresponds to memories that are less easily retrieved.

In other words, there seems to be an important role for similarity in memory encoding and retrieval. To the extent that memory influences higher-order thinking (a point that is covered in Chapter 3), it is clear that similarity will influence the thinking process.

Problem-solving

Similarity seems to play a role in problem-solving. As an example, consider the process of a student learning to solve elementary algebra equations. At first, the process of keeping the equation balanced might be complicated, and the student needs to keep straight the rules for how to isolate the variable that she is solving. In other words, it is a complex problem to solve and places a significant demand on cognitive resources. Furthermore, suppose that the student is going to be learning several kinds of algebra problems: linear equations with one variable, linear equations with two variables, quadratic equations, etc. Initially, solving each kind takes effort, and keeping each kind of problem straight also takes effort. As the student acquires more skills, she begins to recognize the patterns and rules for each problem type. If a new problem is similar to one that has been solved in the past, then she can use the same set of strategies to solve this new problem. In other words, problems that are similar are solved similarly; a problem-solver can use this assessment similarity to assist in solving problems.

Empirical research has supported the idea that similarity plays an important role in problem-solving. For example, the influential research of Newell and Simon (1972) describes problem-solving as a search through a defined **problem space**. The problem space is simply the arrangement of the current state, the goal, the obstacles to reaching that goal, and the operators that allow one to reach the goal. Solving a problem, then, can be thought of as a process of moving through the problem space from the initial state towards the goal state. How would one keep track of the progress? One possibility is that problem space navigation is a process of tracking the increased similarity between the current state and the goal state. In other words, the problem-solver knows what the goal state or solution state is supposed to look like, and can compare the current state to that in order to determine which action or behaviour to choose next. The topic of problem-solving is covered more extensively in Chapter 10, where the role of similarity will be made more clear, but it is worth introducing the idea now in the context of similarity as a general psychological construct.

One of the best examples of the important role that similarity plays in problem-solving, and one that we will discuss later in the chapter on problem-solving, concerns the role of similarity and expertise in physics. In an influential paper, Chi, Feltovich, and Glaser (1981) asked physics PhD students (experts) and undergraduate students (novices) to sort 24 physics problems into groups and to explain the reasons for their groupings. Novices generally sorted the problems on the basis of surface-feature similarity. That is, they grouped problems according to the literal physics terms mentioned in the problem and the physical configuration described in the problem. Experts, on the other hand, sorted their problems on the basis of deep-feature similarity that were related to the major physics principles governing the solution of each problem. This suggests that experts accessed existing schemata and they used their knowledge of physics to create a solution-oriented sorting. Since the problems were sorted according to these categories, it also suggests that these categories would likely be accessed when deciding how to solve a problem. That is, experts are likely to rely on similarity among problems to help them solve the problems quickly and efficiently.

Similar effects are seen in expert physicians as well (Norman & Brooks, 1997). Specifically, Geoff Norman and Lee Brooks argued that many expert physicians rely on the similarity match between a present case and previously seen cases when making a diagnosis. In fact, the evidence suggests that as physicians progress through training and develop expertise, their reliance on this kind of non-analytic similarity-based assessment increases (Devantier, Minda, Goldszmidt, & Haddara, 2009).

Inductive reasoning

Inductive reasoning typically involves generalizing and making predictions about the future based on past events. For example, you can infer or predict that an apple will have seeds based, in part, on your prior experience of apples. Specifically, if every apple you have ever eaten contains seeds, you can infer than the apple in your hand also contains seeds, even before you take a bite. This is a strong argument because apples are very similar as a group. If you were to make a prediction about the tartness of the apple or its suitability for pies, you might be slightly less certain because not all apples are similar on these dimensions. The point is that similarity is a powerful driving force behind many inferences.

In fact, a complete theory of inductive reasoning is built on the notion that similarity is a primary determiner of inductive strength (Osherson, Smith, Wilkie, Lopez, & Shafir, 1990). The **similarity-coverage** model of Osherson and colleagues assumes that inductions and inferences are based on an understanding of the similarity among the items or concepts being considered in a given argument. Although I will devote an entire chapter to this topic, it is worth describing here in preliminary detail.

Simply put, inductive reasoning is a mental process by which we make predictions about future outcomes based on our knowledge of something. This is predicated in part on an assumption that the future will resemble the past. Consider this example. I cut into a pumpkin and I find a mess of seeds and stringy pumpkin fibres. Every time I cut into a pumpkin I find this. When I see a squash that greatly resembles the pumpkins that I remember cutting (i.e., another pumpkin), I can predict what I will find even before I cut into it. I will find a mess of seeds and stringy pumpkin fibres. Now imagine that I cut into a squash that looks a lot less like a pumpkin – a hubbard squash, for example. Having never seen one, I might still expect to find fibres and seeds, but I might be less confident because the hubbard and the pumpkin are less similar to each other than the pumpkin and the other pumpkins are to each other. In short, the *similarity* between the two items helps to determine the strength of the inductive inference.

Summary

We've reviewed some examples of the role of similarity in thinking, and more will come up. The main point is that similarity underlies just about everything related to thinking. In addition, later chapters will take for granted many of the concepts we discuss here.

THE ASSESSMENT OF SIMILARITY

As the sections above suggest, similarity plays a major role in many of the core cognitive processes that are part of what we call *thinking*. For most of these examples, it is assumed that a person makes a quick and automatic judgement of similarity between concepts, or among category members, or between memories. The similarity judgement has to be fast and automatic in order for memory retrieval to be fast and automatic. But just what is a similarity judgement? What is the character of judged similarity?

The problem is that within many of these processes and theories, similarity is an elusive construct. We still do not have a strong idea of what it actually means for two items to be similar. But subjective similarity and a person's judgement of similarity can be measured. In the following section, I want to review the most common ways to measure and assess similarity.

Ratings task

Perhaps the most straightforward way to measure similarity is simply to ask people how similar two objects are to each other. This would typically be done in a similarity rating task. Subjects would see a series of pairs of objects, concepts, words, etc. On each trial, the subject would indicate on a scale of 1 to 7 how similar these objects are to each other. Usually, "1" corresponds to a label of "not similar at all", and "7" corresponds to a label of "extremely similar" or "exactly the same". For example a Granny Smith apple and a Gala apple might be given a rating of 6; a Granny Smith apple and a plum might be given a rating of 4. It is worth noting that the rating will be influenced by the choice of other items. Granny Smith and Gala apples are similar in the context of fruits, but if all of the comparators are other apple varieties, then the rating would be expected to decrease. The information provided in a task like this is subjective and variable. But in many ways, that is the point. Over many presentations, and with many different subjects, the same two items should generally receive high ratings if subjects agree that, all things considered, the two objects are similar to each other. Correspondingly, if subjects generally agree that two objects are relatively less similar to each other, then the two objects should receive low ratings. Of course, on its own, a ratings task like this is only moderately informative. Later we will discuss more sophisticated models that rely on the information gathered from similarity ratings tasks to gather more in-depth insights into the structure of objects in psychological similarity space.

One of the benefits of this approach is that it is simple and straightforward. Ratings differ between people, and even within a single person's judgement, but on average, there should be some agreement about the relative similarity among objects. However, one of the downsides is that an approach like this does not really tell you how the judgement was made. It offers no additional insight into the underlying conceptual structure. Furthermore, a strict ratings approach will be sensitive to contextual factors, but may not explain them very well. In other words, think back to the example used earlier with the coins from different countries. In one context, the pennies may seem similar to each other; in another context, they may not seem very similar to each other. By just asking for a similarity rating, you only collect information about two things in isolation. Another downside with this approach is that many people find it challenging to assign a single number to a similarity judgement. Or they tend to assign only two or three numbers rather than all seven. Although the rating task is designed to be subjective, it can be difficult from the point of view of participants to really know the difference between a similarity rating of "3" and "4".

Forced choice task

Another way to measure similarity is with a forced choice task. It is called a forced choice task because the subject is required to choose an option. A common variant involves a single target stimulus and two (or more) alternatives. The subject is instructed to choose which one of the two possible alternatives is the best match for the target stimulus. The match is subjective and the subject could be given instructions to choose the stimulus that is "most similar to", "most like", or "goes best with" the target. One advantage of a forced choice task is that it is sensitive to context. In fact, it depends on context in order to force the person to make a decision. Consider again the task of rating similarity among different kinds of fruit. Suppose you present someone with a target that is a red apple and the possible matches are a green apple and a red plum. There are many ways to make the choice (by colour, size, the kind of fruit), and maybe you can even make the case that each stimulus is similar to the red apple target in its own way, but the point is that you have to make a choice. And the idea is that by presenting subjects with many trials, the researcher can (as above with the rating task) gain some insight into a subject's subjective sense of similarity (Devantier et al., 2009; Rips, 1989).

A task like this might be better suited to the more problematic example of the coins from different countries. If presented with a Canadian penny, an American penny, and a Canadian nickel and asked to choose which two are most similar, it is not the overall rating of similarity that matters. In this case, the subject is forced to choose the best possible match, even if he or she does not find it to be especially similar. In this case, all that matters is that two things are more alike than the other two things.

Sorting task

A third way to understand the similarity between things or among things is to ask research participants to sort objects or pictures of objects into groups on the basis of similarity. A task like this is generally carried out with objects or with cards depicting objects. Participants are usually given instructions to sort the objects into as many groups as necessary based on which things best go together. For example, if I were given many different coins of different denominations and local currency, I might choose to sort them on the basis of country of origin, or I might choose to sort them into size groups, or I might opt for a combination of both, depending on how many coins need to be sorted. Unlike the rating task, there is no number assigned to the similarity. Just like the forced choice task, the sorting task takes advantage of contextual effects on similarity judgements.

If a researcher is interested in knowing how objects are grouped together on the basis of similarity, this sorting task is ideal and is commonly used. One downside to a sorting task is that participants are usually not given strict instructions. That means that the analysis of sorting data can be challenging. The researcher must infer from the groups what similarity metric the participant was using.

In Chapter 10 on problem-solving and in Chapter 11 on expertise, I will discuss in greater detail several very interesting studies that attempted to ascertain differences between expert and novice problem-solving skills by asking participants to sort problems into groups or to sort objects into groups based on experience (Chi et al., 1981; Medin, Lynch, Coley, & Atran, 1997).

Summary

Ratings tasks, forced choice tasks, and sorting tasks are useful because they allow the researcher to collect quantitative data about a series or set of stimuli. All three tasks provide some insight into the similarity structure of a concept or the perceived similarity between or among objects. However, those ratings alone don't explain everything about the structure of mental representations. In order to understand how perceived similarity among items affects the structure and the nature of mental representations, we need to address and discuss several theoretical approaches to similarity.

THEORETICAL APPROACHES TO SIMILARITY

We have established that similarity is a crucial construct for many basic tasks, and that the measurement of similarity often involves making explicit decisions about what is usually a fast, implicit process. But so far the actual construct is somewhat elusive. Even the measurements described above presume to be getting at an underlying similarity. The question is: how does similarity actually work? How is it calculated, represented, and used by the mind?

A variety of theories have been developed over the past few decades that explain similarity, and many of them have in common the notion that similarity is essentially the result of feature or attribute comparison. The more features or attributes that two concepts or objects have in common, the more similar these two things are.

For example, one fundamental approach to similarity is commonly known as the **geometric approach**. It is often instantiated as a mathematical framework known as **multidimensional scaling (MDS)**. The general assumption is that the similarity between two things is a function of the psychological distance between them, and that psychological distance is analogous to physical distance. Another way of putting this is that two things that are very much alike, and are described as similar, should be "close" to each other in psychological space. Analogously, two things that are not alike should be "distant" from each other in psychological space. In other words, psychological space operates like physical space. Two objects that occupy nearly the same coordinates in psychological space are similar. Because space is necessarily defined as the distance between things (after all, outer space is just what exists between other things), psychological space is nearly always referred to in terms of distance. So similarity is defined as a small distance in psychological space. That is, the most similar that two things can be is zero distance. There is no distance between them.

The formula for psychological distance (as it can be calculated from a comparison of two objects) is given in equation 2.1. In this equation, the $d(i,j)$ means the psychological distance between two things (i and j) and the assumption is that we are comparing them along of set of relevant dimensions (n). Each dimensional comparison is represented by the absolute value of the difference between them. Crucially, the equation includes an exponent that allows for the comparisons to be made along what is known as "city block space" and "Euclidian space".

$$d\left(i,j\right)=\left[\sum_{k=1}^{n}\left|X_{ik}-X_{jk}\right|^{r}\right]^{\frac{1}{r}} \tag{2.1}$$

The two different metrics are important because different kinds of stimuli seem to show slightly different relationships. **City block space** can be thought of as analogous to locations in a city with a grid pattern of streets. Imagine that you measured the distance between two locations in a city by walking straight along one street, turning a corner, and walking straight along another street. In this case, both measurements contribute to the calculation of the overall distance, not unlike two right-angle sides of a triangle. City block space is generally used when the dimensions of the stimuli being compared or considered have dimensions that are perceptually separable (Attneave, 1950). That is, they can be perceived and processed separately from the whole stimulus.

As an example, consider two objects that differ in terms of size and colour but each dimension can be processed and considered separately: baseballs and softballs, for example. In the United States and Canada, softball is a variety of baseball that tends to be played either casually by many adults or competitively by women and girls. The ball that is used in softball differs in some ways from the ball that is used in baseball. One of the most obvious differences is that the baseball is smaller and white. A softball is a little larger and is usually bright green. Depending on the age of the player, the ball varies in size, such that younger girls play with a smaller ball. In this example, if you are arriving at a similarity calculation among different kinds of baseballs and softballs, you can consider the size separately from the colour. Although both dimensions can be considered when making a similarity judgement, they can each be perceived separately, and each contributes its own value to the distance computation.

If the city block metric is equivalent to the right angles of a triangle, the **Euclidian metric** is equivalent to the hypotenuse. In this case, rather that walking along the right angles of the street, imagine you can pass straight through the building to find the absolute shortest distance between the two locations. Euclidean distance comes into play when the dimensions of the stimuli being compared are composed of perceptually **integral** dimensions. For example, consider the comparison among a whole set of objects of different colours that vary in dimension of *hue*, *saturation*, and *brightness*. The perception of the difference is not difficult, but being able to separately perceive a change in hue alone would not be easy. In this case, the comparisons between stimuli are made using several dimensions that are combined prior to the comparison process.

As a computational technique, MDS is more complicated than what we can discuss within the scope of the chapter, but the basic idea is that if a subject provides similarity ratings (as discussed earlier in the chapter), the MDS algorithm will compute the minimum distance among all concepts and describe these distances along a number of dimensions. The algorithm can specify two or more dimensions, but the best fitting model is the one that maximizes the solutions with a minimum number of dimensions, so typical MDS solutions involve 2–3 dimensions.

Figure 2.1 shows an example of a multidimensional scaling solution for birds. A graph like this would be created by asking participants to rate the similarity between all possible items. In other words, you would rate the similarity between a goose and a duck, a goose and a chicken, a goose and a goose, and a goose and a cardinal, etc. All the possible pairs need to be rated. The MDS solution plots all of the exemplars in multidimensional space. In this case, it is two-dimensional space. If two birds are often rated as being highly similar to each other, they appear close to each other in the MDS solution. Thus goose and duck are physically close to each other in two-dimensional space, just like they are close to each other in conceptual space. What should be apparent from this graph is that the two axes have

An Example of a Multidimensional Scaling Solution

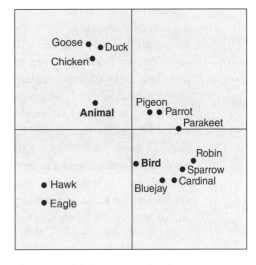

Figure 2.1 This is an example of a multidimensional scaling solution for birds. To generate this, the pairwise similarity among all pairs would have been gathered from raters. The algorithm plots an approximation of the underlying psychological space.

psychological meaning. The x axis seems to correspond to aggressiveness or possibly size. Robins and sparrows are on one side, and hawks and eagles are on the other. The y axis seems to correspond to domestic birds. Geese and ducks and chickens are at the top, and eagles and bluejays are at the bottom. The MDS solution provides a graphical depiction of internal similarity structure of the concept "bird".

The geometric approach makes several fundamental assumptions that are built upon the basic idea that psychological distance approximates physical distance. One of the main advantages of the geometric approach is that it is easily built into a computational system. The computational nature of the geometrical model gives the researcher a way to generate a similarity space for a participant. The computational nature helps to solve one of the problems with gathering basic similarity ratings. Namely, it provides some description of the internal structure of a concept that underlies the similarity ratings that the subject might generate. In fact, the multidimensional scaling solution should allow the researcher to predict the output of a rating task, or the decisions that a subject would make in a forced choice task, or the clusters that might form if a subject were asked to sort objects into groups. Because of this computational advantage, the geometric approach has been built into many models of conceptual structure. For example, in Chapter 4 we will discuss two representational accounts of conceptual structure. One of these accounts, the exemplar model, assumes that categories are represented by the summed similarity among all category members. The other account, the prototype account, assumes that categories are held together by the similarity of category members to a central abstract prototype. Both of these models depend on similarity as calculated by the geometric model (Kruschke, 2011; Minda & Smith, 2011; Nosofsky, 2011).

The geometric model depends on its core assumptions. The fundamental assumption is that objects are represented in a psychological space that is roughly analogous to a physical space. Things that are similar are assumed to be close to each other; things that are dissimilar are assumed to be psychologically distant from each other. Because of this fundamental assumption, the geometric model makes specific assumptions and predictions about the kinds of similarity judgements people make. Although these predictions are quite basic, they can sometimes be shown experimentally to be not always operating in people's judgements. What this means, in essence, is that although MDS and the geometric model work well to explain how people understand similarity relations most of the time, it cannot capture every case. It is a useful tool and a good way to understand psychological similarity, but it is not a complete account. Let's begin by describing a few of these assumptions and predictions. Much of the following was originally discussed by Amos Tversky in his hugely influential paper from 1977 (Tversky, 1977).

The assumption of minimality

According to Tversky, minimality holds that the similarity between an object and itself is the same for all objects. If you measured the physical distance between the coffee cup on your desk and itself, it should be zero, and that should be the same result no matter what you are comparing. Another way of saying this is shown in equation 2.2:

$$d(i,i) \leq d(i,j) \tag{2.2}$$

In other words, the distance between my coffee cup and itself is always less than the distance between my coffee cup and anything else. So if this is true in physical space, it should also be true in psychological space. The similarity of an object to itself (self-similarity) must be nearly zero and the same across other self-similarities. But, as Tversky points out, this may not be true, as the probability of judging two *identical* stimuli is not constant for all stimuli and judgements of similarity will vary, even if by a small amount. To the extent that people make errors in identification or recognition, one underlying possibility is that the minimality assumption does not always hold true.

The assumption of symmetry

The assumption of symmetry is straightforward. The distance between one object and another is the same as the distance between the other object and the first one. In other words, a comparison between two things results in symmetrical relations. Comparison order should not matter. This is true for physical space. If you and a friend are standing at the bus stop, the distance between you and your friend has to be exactly the same as the distance between your friend and you. That is, it is reflexive and symmetrical. Another way to say this is shown in equation 2.3:

$$d(i,j) = d(j,i) \qquad (2.3)$$

Symmetry is a requirement of the fundamental assumption that psychological similarity is analogous to physical distance. If I conclude that a green apple is similar to a red apple, my ratings should not change appreciably when I am asked about the similarity of the red apple to the green apple. In other words, psychological space should have the same qualities as physical space.

But, of course, this is not exactly true. The classic examples come again from Tversky's work. He suggests that the judged similarity between North Korea and "Red China" exceeds the judged similarity between "Red China" and North Korea. The use of "Red China" probably sounds awkward to modern ears, but would have been quite common to subjects in the 1970s and refers to cold-war-era Communist China. Furthermore, most people do not use metaphoric similarity in a way that suggests symmetry. Just as Shakespeare writes that "Juliet is the sun", and not the other way around, we often say that "a child is just like her parent" and not "the parent is just like her child". In short, these violations of the similarity assumption suggest that, for complex stimuli at least, psychological space is not quite like physical space.

The assumption of triangle inequality

Triangle inequality suggests that for three stimuli, the additive psychological distance between two pairs of stimuli must be greater than or equal to the distance between any one pair. Computationally, this is written as:

$$d(i,j) + d(j,k) \geq d(i,k) \qquad (2.4)$$

This assumption is less obvious on the surface than in the two previous examples, but consider the following example (again from Tversky): Jamaica is judged to be similar to

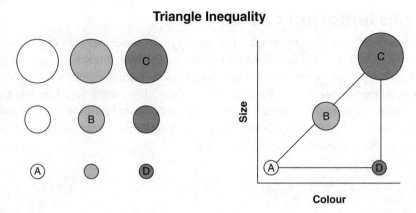

Triangle Inequality

Figure 2.2 Triangle inequality. ABC is a shorter line than ADC but when participants rate the stimuli that are shown, it can appear that the distance from ADC is shorter than ABC.

Cuba, and Cuba is judged to be similar to Soviet Russia, but Jamaica is not judged to be similar to Soviet Russia.

Or consider a less complicated example that works in the other direction. Figure 2.2 shows a set of nine circles that vary in terms of size and colour. In a similarity rating task, some of these stimuli are similar, and others are dissimilar. That is, it is easy to see a similarity between two circles of the same size or two circles of the same colour. It is a little more difficult to know how to rate the similarity between two circles that vary on both colour and size. According to the geometric model, though, these two dimensions should both enter into similarity judgements.

On the right-hand side of the figure is a graph that shows four of these possible stimuli in x–y space, with size as the y axis and colour as the x axis. If psychological space aligns with physical space, then the similarity between A, B, and C should be greater than the rated similarity between A, D, and C. That is, A and B are physically close to each other and B and C are physically close to each other. However, A and D are less close to each other in physical space, and so they should be rated as less similar than A and B. But if you inspect the actual stimuli shown in the left panel of Figure 2.2, you will note that A and D are exactly the same size. And D and C differ in size, but are exactly the same colour. When asked to rate, people prioritize a **dimensional match** and give these pairs higher similarity ratings. The result is that in terms of rated similarity the line going from ADC will seem shorter than the line going through ABC. Geometrically, this cannot be true, but psychologically it seems to be. The implication from a result like this is that psychological space may not always act like physical space (Tversky & Gati, 1982).

The contrast model

One of the biggest problems conceptually with the geometric model is that it only accounts for shared features or mismatched features. It doesn't have a good way to deal with the interaction between these. The contrast model, proposed by Tvserky (1977) includes a way to deal with shared features and distinctive features. According to this model, the similarity between two objects A and B is expressed as a linear combination of the common features shared between the two objects, and the distinctive features unique to each class. Formally, this is given by the following equation:

$$S(A,B) = \theta f(A \cap B) - af(A - B) - bf(B - A) \qquad (2.5)$$

In other words, to calculate the overall similarity $S(A,B)$, one would first arrive at a measure of how many features are shared, and subtract from that features that are unique to A and also features that are unique to B. The contrast model is able to predict asymmetric similarity because the distinct feature multipliers, a and b, are not constrained to be equal. As a result, the impact of distinctive features for one concept may be greater than or less than the impact of distinctive features for another concept. Relating this to Tversky's earlier example of North Korea and Communist China, North Korea would be predicted to be more similar to Communist China than the reverse because we assume to know more about Communist China. China has more salient distinctive features than North Korea, and so asymmetric similarity is predicted. In general, the contrast model is most useful when dealing with the similarity among items when some items are more familiar, more important, or are at different levels of a hierarchy.

The transformational model

One thing that neither model is able to account for is the kind of similarity that exists when two things are linked by non-featural aspects. That is, it is easy to see that two people might be similar, or that two apples might be similar. Both the geometric model and the contrast model can explain these types of similarity judgement. However, these models may not explain the perceived similarity between things like water and steam, or the similarity between a photograph of an adult and a photograph of the same person as a child. Yes, there are shared features between these things. But there is something else that feature-based models are unable to account for. Water and steam are similar to each other because one entity is transformed into the other entity. The relationship is not strictly based on features, but is rather based on the number of steps that it takes to turn water into steam. On that account, ice is closer to water than it is to steam, because the ice to water transformation is one step, and the ice to steam transformation is two steps. Accordingly, ice may be more similar to water than ice is to steam.

The transformational model is based on the notion that there is something similar about two things if one can be transformed into the other. Transformation is actually quite common. We transform water into coffee on a daily basis. We transform water into tea on a daily basis, or transform a slice of bread into toast, batter into cookies, natural gas into electricity. Some of these transformations are small and thus the entities seem more similar to each other. Some transformations can take place in a single step, but the surface features of the two things are very different from each other. Perhaps the best example is the transformation of a monarch caterpillar to a monarch butterfly. Most kids have seen examples of both, and in many schools it is common to have a small aquarium set up containing monarch caterpillars. The children can watch as each caterpillar forms a chrysalis and emerges as a butterfly. This is a remarkable transformation, and although the caterpillar is very different on the surface, we might appreciate that these are still similar. A monarch caterpillar is still somewhat similar to a monarch butterfly.

Although this kind of similarity seems clearly intuitive for things that are known to be transformed, such as butterflies and coffee, it is also possible to show the effects of transformation on fairly abstract stimuli. A study by Imai (1977) provided participants with simple patterns of symbols. Participants were essentially asked to rate the similarity between different patterns. Because the stimuli were created from a static subset of characters, the surface feature similarity was controlled. The only way to reliably make judgements was to base them on different kinds of transformation. Figure 2.3 shows five different kinds of comparisons. The first is identical pattern, where the similarity would be rated very high. The next is a mirror image. The pattern on the left is the mirror image of the pattern on the right. On the left we see five filled circles and three empty circles. On the right we see three empty circles and five filled circles. The next is called a phase shift. Here, you can see that the relative position of the three empty circles has shifted by one position from the pattern on the left to the pattern on the right. The reversal shows a complete exchange of characters from the pattern on the left to the pattern on the right. The most subtle change is the wavelength change. If you imagine the circles as peaks and valleys of a wave, then the pattern on the left has a bigger wavelength than the pattern on the right.

Examples of Stimuli that Vary According to Transformation

Identical	●●●●●○○○	→	●●●●●○○○
Mirror image	●●●●●○○○	→	○○○●●●●●
Phase shift	●●●●●○○○	→	●●●●○○○●
Reversal	●●●●●○○○	→	○○○○○●●●
Wavelength	●●○○●●○○	→	●○●○●○●○

Figure 2.3 An example of the stimuli that were used by Imai (1977) in an examination of transformational similarity.

Participants rated pairs that differed by all of these single transformations as well as pairs that differed by multiple transformations. The main finding was that single transformation pairs were rated as more similar than multiple transformation pairs. The crucial aspect of this result is that the surface features were held constant. Participants had to base their judgements on how many steps were needed to transform one pattern into the next.

SUMMARY

I have placed this chapter on similarity at the beginning of the text because I think that similarity is a construct that is going to affect nearly every other topic that is covered. In Chapters 3 and 4, I cover memory, semantic memory, and the psychology of concepts. All of these topics depend on the assumption that the basic cognitive system calculates similarity among representations. As we discussed at the beginning of this chapter, memories are retrieved because they are similar to a probe. However, memory confusion sometimes results when different representations are too similar to each other. Categories and concepts are held together primarily by inter-item similarity.

Similarity also plays a role in reasoning. As was discussed earlier in this chapter, inductive inferences depend heavily on similarity. In fact, the very core of inductive reasoning is the assumption that future events will resemble past events. That assumption can only be made with the understanding that the system making the prediction can calculate similarity. Similarity plays a role in problem-solving as well because problems can be solved on the basis of how similar they are to previously solved problems. I discuss the role of analogy in problem-solving in Chapter 10. In this case, the assumption is that problem-solvers are able to appreciate an analogous similarity between two different domains and to use that similarity to solve novel problems.

Finally, similarity plays an important role in the psychology of expertise. Experts are those who have studied and worked in a specific domain for many years. As a result, experts have a rich knowledge base upon which to draw when confronting new problems and decisions. One of the primary ways in which they draw on that new knowledge base is to calculate the similarity in deeper ways than novices. In other words, a novice might appreciate the similarity among objects based on how they look; an expert might appreciate the similarity among objects based on how they are used, or on how they might be used in a specific context.

The study of similarity may seem like an aspect of cognition that is not directly related to the psychology of thinking, but I would argue that a complete understanding of the psychology of thinking requires an appreciation of the complexity of similarity within a cognitive system.

3 KNOWLEDGE AND MEMORY

In the previous chapter, I argued that similarity is a psychological construct that underlies many other cognitive processes. In order to make predictions, refer to prior knowledge, and retrieve memories, a cognitive system needs to be able to assess the relative degree of similarity between representations. In this chapter, I discuss knowledge and memory. Most of the other cognitive processes and thinking processes that will be covered in this book rely on and are affected by a person's knowledge and the way in which the knowledge is structured. In other words, people use their memories to solve problems. People rely on memory to assess a situation, make judgements, and make decisions. People use their memories to make inferences and predictions. People rely on short-term, working memory in order to simultaneously consider contrasting alternatives. Indeed, experts are defined as experts because they have a rich knowledge base and useful, accessible memories.

As the memory literature and the concepts and categories literature have often been separated, I will discuss these two domains separately. Concepts and categories will be covered in Chapter 4. A central theme of this chapter is the idea that *the nature and structure of internal representations influence thinking.*

HOW DOES MEMORY INFLUENCE THINKING?

In 2014, several players for teams in the NFL in the United States were accused, arrested, or otherwise implicated in high-profile cases of domestic violence. Domestic violence is obviously a very serious issue, and may seem even more so when someone in the public sphere is implicated. In these cases, there was considerable media coverage and also wide availability of photographs and videos of the incidents. A major survey found that nearly 70% of Americans endorsed the opinion that the NFL has a "troubling epidemic of domestic violence" (Morris, 2014).

The problem with this opinion is that it may not reflect actual rates of domestic violence in the NFL. Several analyses of criminal and non-criminal cases (Figure 3.1) found that the rates of domestic violence among NFL players is significantly lower than the rates of domestic violence among the general population (Morris, 2014). In other words, the available data do not support the conclusion that NFL players are in the midst of a domestic violence epidemic. It is true that several players were implicated in high-profile cases, but those were single events, highly salient, and very memorable. In this case, the available memory may be influencing judgements about the base rates.

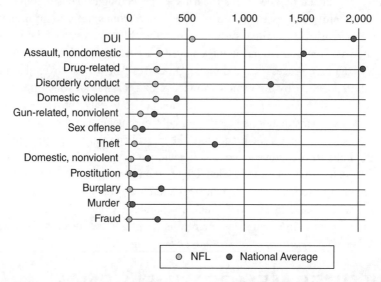

Arrest Rates for NFL Players from 2014

NFL Arrest Rates

Arrests per 100,000 per year, NFL players vs. all men ages 25 to 29

Figure 3.1 Shown are the arrest rates for players in the NFL, compared to arrest rates for the general population in the United States. This figure was originally published on the web by the popular site fivethirtyeight.com.

So why do people feel comfortable in making these incorrect judgements? The best explanation comes from a well-known thinking heuristic known as the **availability heuristic**. The idea, originally proposed in the early 1970s by Daniel Kahneman and Amos Tversky (Kahneman & Tversky, 1979; Tversky & Kahneman, 1974) is that people generally make judgements and decisions on the basis of relevant memories that they retrieve. In other words, when being asked to assess risk, or make a judgement about a likelihood of occurrence, you search your memory and make your decision on the basis of the available evidence. Most of the time, this heuristic produces useful and correct evidence. But in other cases, the available evidence may not correspond exactly to evidence in the world. This is especially true for high-profile or salient events. The actual base rate of the occurrence of domestic violence among NFL players is not widely known and is probably difficult to obtain anyway. Furthermore, the rates of domestic violence among the general population and among other subgroups are also not well known, and certainly these individual events are rarely reported in national media. However, if a very high-profile case is discussed in the news, popular media, and social media, it can skew our perceptions of the base rates. In other words, if you are asked about whether or not there is an epidemic of domestic violence in the NFL, and you immediately remember two or three high-profile cases that just occurred, that available evidence is going to be used in your judgement, and is likely to result in you estimating a higher occurrence than is actually true.

Kahneman and Tversky showed many examples of this. One of their most well-known examples deals with people's estimates of common words. Subjects were asked to imagine sampling a word (of three letters or more) at random from an English text. In other words, imagine taking a book, opening it up, and choosing a word at random. They were then asked to judge the likelihood that this randomly selected word either starts with the letter "R", or that the word has the letter "R" in the third position. When tested, subjects generally estimate the likelihood of "R" in the first position as being higher. This is an incorrect judgement, but consider how you would make that estimation. You would search your memory for words with "R" in the first position, and with "R" in the third position. If you have ever tried to search your memory for words with a given letter in the third position, you know that it is really difficult. We just don't search our memory for words that way. Apart from a psychology experiment, or when we are completing a crossword puzzle, it simply isn't done. And so subjects rely on their available memory to make the judgement, and their available memory consists of many words that begin with the letter "R" and not so many words with "R" in the third position. Using this available memory, they arrived at an incorrect likelihood judgement.

There are many other examples of how this availability heuristic affects our judgements. We may overestimate the likelihood of disaster, risk, or calamitous events, such as aeroplane accidents, terrorist attacks, and shark attacks. We may underestimate the risk of danger from common things, such as food allergies, vitamin poisoning, and carbon monoxide. Furthermore, other researchers have suggested that we have a very poor perception of things like violent crime. The psychologist Steven Pinker has argued that in many ways, the early twenty-first century is the most peaceful, least violent era of recorded human history (Pinker, 2011). Death by violent means, whether criminal, political, or in warfare, is much lower than in earlier eras. This might be true even if we take into account current affairs, terrorism, warfare, and genocide. Yes, there is still violence in the world, but Pinker would argue that, despite this, we still live in a peaceful era. However, most people do not share that opinion. Or even if we do share that opinion, it is still apparent that violence and warfare occupy a considerable amount of news coverage.

There might be many reasons why we don't perceive our current era as being peaceful. First, we do not have direct experience of other historical eras. Or if we do, our memory is not as fresh. In terms of the current era, we often do not know the base rate of violent actions. If a violent death occurs in our neighbourhood, or in our city, it is highly salient to us. We may perceive crime rates as being much higher than they actually are because our news media will report on these things but do not report on incidences of non-violence. Another way of saying this is that a tragic event like a school shooting warrants significant coverage, but at the same time there will be no coverage of all the millions of children who attended school that day and were not victims of violence.

Phenomena like the availability heuristic indicate that higher-order thinking abilities, such as judgement, reasoning, and decision-making, are highly dependent on memory. In most cases, a heuristic like this produces reliable and adaptive judgements, but occasionally can be shown to produce errors. Clearly, if we are going to understand the psychology of thinking, we need to understand its relationship to the cognitive psychology of memory.

HOW DOES MEMORY FUNCTION?

Memory is a very broad term and is used in so many different connotations that before turning to theoretical and psychological accounts, I want to discuss first the basic ways in which the memory system functions. Most of these constructs apply to both short-term and long-term memory as well as semantic memory and episodic memory.

There are many ways to describe memory. Indeed, there is considerable evidence for the existence of different memory systems. Despite this variety, there are some basic ways in which memory functions within the context of a cognitive system. For example, we can divide the core operations into three areas: encoding, storage, and retrieval.

Encoding

Encoding is the term that is most often used to describe the way in which information is put into memory. Once an object, item, or event has been attended to (or, in some cases, even if it is not being attended to: more on that later), it is a valid candidate for encoding into memory. The encoding process creates a mental representation based on the amount of effort and the amount of detail that was processed via attention. For example, suppose you are shopping at a farmer's market for winter squash. Each squash you see is given some low level of processing so that what is encoded into memory is the experience of seeing many squashes. This relatively shallow encoding will result in relatively weak memory traces. However, if you happened to see a squash that was unusually shaped, or very large, or that really caught your attention in some way, you might encode with more effort and detail, and this would likely result in a stronger memory trace for that specific squash.

Memory storage

A second function of memory is the **storage** of these encoded memory traces. At the fundamental level, representations are stored as patterns of activation and connectivity among neurons. But for our purposes, we need to discuss memory storage at a slightly higher, more abstract level. Much of the general knowledge we have about the world and about objects and things in the world is stored and manipulated conceptually. That is, the representation for dog is conceptually close to the representation for cat, and although it might be difficult to determine exactly which neurons are implicated in each representation, the conceptual proximity suggests some degree of neural overlap. Concepts and categories will be discussed in greater detail in Chapter 4.

To continue with our example from the farmer's market, a conceptually organized memory storage system allows you to predict that you would find other squashes, pumpkins, and maybe other root vegetables for sale at the same locations. Similarly, you might also have an entire **script** or **schema** for how to behave and what to expect at a farmer's market. We will discuss scripts and schemas later in this chapter, but for now a good definition of a schema is: *a mental representation that contains general information for how to think, behave, and what to expect in a common situation.*

Memory retrieval

The final function of memory is **retrieval**. As sure as a representation is encoded and stored, there needs to be a set of cognitive processes that retrieve the correct memory traces when required. Often, this is where we observe mistakes and errors, and indeed the literature on memory retrieval has often tended to focus on these. But of course a mistake in retrieval does not necessarily mean that a breakdown in the retrieval processes actually caused the error. The mistake or breakdown could have been made during the initial encoding phase, but the error may only be apparent during the failure to retrieve. Let's continue with our example of the farmer's market. Suppose you arrive at the market and you can't remember what you were trying to buy there. This retrieval failure could be a result of a failure to encode the initial list items. On the other hand, you might be reminded of what you intended to buy when you see the butternut squash at the stand of one of the vendors, indicating that the proper cue resulted in the retrieval of the correct information.

VARIETIES OF MEMORY

Consider the example we have been discussing so far, that of shopping for food at a farmer's market. Think about all the ways in which memory is implicated. Before you even leave for the market, you might think about the items you want to buy. This involves analyzing the contents of your memory for what you might need, what you might be out of, and what you would like to buy. And unless you write a list, it also involves creating a new representation, a mental list of things you'd like to buy. You have to remember how to get to the market. You have to remember why you are at the market. You have to remember what you wanted to purchase. While you are shopping, you are identifying objects based on their similarity to stored category representations and stored object representations. Each of these encounters with an item may activate existing memory traces or lay down a new memory trace. You may even activate a general memory representation in the form of a schema or a script that lets you know how to act and what to expect. All the while, you have to remember what you wanted to purchase, you have to remember where your money is, how much you have left, and what else you still need to buy. This list of behaviours is not even complete because we can imagine how memory is involved in some of the smaller sub steps of the behaviours we listed here. In other words, encoding, storing, and retrieving memory representations underlie nearly every aspect of the farmer's market shopping experience.

Memory is such a big term and such a big idea that it is useful to begin our discussion by describing how it can be segmented and how it has been studied. Memory is *not* a single process. There are many different ways to divide and analyze memory. Perhaps the most useful way to think about kinds of memory is to consider divisions based on content, the encoding process, the retrieval process, the amount of effort required to encode and store the memories, and the duration of the memory. There are many more than that (Roediger, 2008), but this will do for our purposes.

Short- and long-term memory

First, memory is often divided in terms of the duration. Most accounts of memory assume that there are **sensory** and **short-term** memory systems which can process information actively for short-term use. The working memory system is one that is closely tied to active, conscious processing. There are many varieties of **long-term** memory, which are discussed below. These memories are stored with no particular limit on their duration, although of course many memories can be forgotten or can weaken over time.

Short-term memory is usually distinguished from long-term memory by duration, but also in the way it functions. The most common theory of short-term memory is the **working memory model** of Alan Baddeley (Baddeley, 2003, 2012; Baddeley & Hitch, 2004).

Baddeley's working memory assumes that there is a system of neurological structures that work to process immediate sensory information. The working memory system acts as a buffer so that the information can be maintained, processed further, or discarded.

As shown in Figure 3.2, Baddeley's model is **modality specific**. It assumes that there are separate neural circuits for auditory information and visuospatial information. Auditory and verbal information is handled by a system called the **phonological loop**. Visual and spatial information is handled by a system called the **visuospatial sketchpad**. The coordination is handled by a central executive. The **central executive** allocates resources, switches between systems, and coordinates switching between and among representations within a system. Baddeley's model is not the only model of working memory, but it is one of the most well-known. Other theories of working memory still make the assumption that some information is auditory in nature, other information is visuospatial in nature, and that different neurological subsystems are recruited to handle these different modalities (Oberauer, 2009).

According to Baddeley, the phonological loop is a phonological or acoustic store that is connected to inputs from the auditory cortex. A memory trace in the phonological loop will fade after about two seconds unless it is maintained or revived via an articulatory control process known as **subvocal rehearsal**. This is sometimes referred to as the **inner voice**. As an example, think about how you can remember a short piece of information (a number or a short phrase) while you repeat it to yourself.

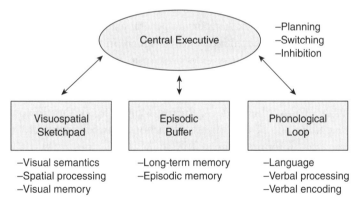

Figure 3.2 A diagram of Baddeley and Hitch's working memory model. The phonological loop handles auditory and verbal information, the visuospatial sketchpad handles information in visual and spatial modalities, and the central executive coordinates resources between the two subsystems.

This inner voice (verbal working memory) is an important component of thinking. At a very basic level, verbal working memory is needed to formulate basic hypotheses, to read a problem, to frame a decision, to test alternatives, and to consider the outcome of one's behaviours and actions. In other words, active thinking requires an active working memory. Active thinking requires language comprehension, reasoning, planning, and problem-solving. Success in all these activities has been shown to be highly correlated with measures of working memory capacity (Oberauer, 2009). Visuospatial working memory operates in an analogous way to verbal working memory, except the assumption is that the visuospatial working memory system recruits visual and motor areas of the cortex in order to maintain representations with primarily spatial characteristics. This has also been shown to be highly correlated with thinking ability (Shah & Miyake, 1996).

Most models of working memory, including the Baddeley model, assume a role for either a central executive or executive functions. In the standard version of working memory the central executive coordinates resources between the two subsystems. Other models of working memory place a greater emphasis on the independent operation of the executive functions. Executive functions are usually defined as **domain-general** characteristics such as task switching, inhibitory resources, and selective attention (Miyake, Friedman, Emerson, Witzki, & Howerter, 2000).

A domain-general process is one that is available for other acts of cognition and thinking, regardless of the modality or the domain. In Chapter 2, similarity in the calculation of inter-item similarity is often seen as a domain-general cognitive function. Similarity operates in the same way for memories and for stimulus judgements. Executive functions may have a similar characteristic. **Task switching** is the act of switching attention from one behaviour to another. Design operates at many different levels of cognition and across many domains. **Inhibition** is another domain-general characteristic. An executive function of inhibition allows the cognitive system to ignore irrelevant perceptual features or irrelevant or unnecessary thoughts or emotions. As an example, the ability to inhibit the processing of irrelevant dimensions has been shown to facilitate hypothesis testing and has been shown to be beneficial for learning new concepts and categories (Lewandowsky, 2011; Miles, Matsuki, & Minda, 2014; Rabi & Minda, 2014). Furthermore, executive functions seem to be one of the biggest distinctions between higher-order thought in young children and higher-order thought in adults (Gathercole, 1999; Rabi & Minda, 2014; Thompson-Schill, Ramscar, & Chrysikou, 2009; Zelazo, 2004).

Because executive functions seem to play such a large role in higher-order thought, many researchers have proposed that executive functions are the primary intellectual component of working memory (Kane et al., 2004). Under this proposal, executive functions serve as a domain-general working memory, and seem to be the primary determinant of general intelligence. In other words, the lower-level components, such as the phonological loop and the visuospatial sketchpad, may not be contributing to higher-order thought to the same degree as the executive functions. In these theoretical treatments, executive function availability and capacity are core determinants of thinking and reasoning ability.

Declarative and non-declarative memory

As far as content is concerned, a very broad division is based on the declarative and non-declarative distinction (Roediger, 2008; Roediger, Marsh, & Lee, 2002; Tulving, 2002). Practically speaking, **declarative memory** is usually thought to be the kind of memory that one can declare the existence of. In other words, it is memory for ideas, facts, events, places, personal characteristics, etc. Within this hypothesized declarative memory division, a distinction can also be made for the existence of **semantic** memory and **episodic** memory. We will discuss both of these in greater detail later in this chapter. For now, let's define semantic memory as memory for known facts and episodic memory as memory for events that are personally relevant and that have some degree of mental time travel.

Distinct from declarative memory, **non-declarative memory** includes memory for things that are difficult or impossible to declare the existence of, such as **procedural memory** and **motor memory**. For example, when you are sitting in class and taking notes by hand, at some fundamental level you have to be able to remember how to draw the individual letters on the page. This is a motor memory, and although it is still a very important aspect of memory, it is one that you have very little control over. If you try to think carefully about how to draw the letters, you might slow down, you might even make mistakes. This procedural memory or non-declarative memory resides in different areas of the brain from declarative memory and generally serves different functions. For the most part, we will deal more with the declarative memory store than the procedural memory store. In terms of thinking and its relationship to memory, the procedural store is less relevant.

Semantic memory: memory for facts

Many years ago, when my younger daughter was learning to speak, we happened to be at an auto shop and I was getting the oil changed in my vehicle. She must have been about a year and a half old and her vocabulary was pretty limited. The auto shop was laid out so that you could see into the repair area through a window. We watched as they drove my vehicle onto the lift and raised it up so that the mechanics could inspect the brakes and tires, and change the oil. As soon as the car went up, her eyes widened and she said "UP!" Of course I reinforced that and I said "Yes, the car is up". Then they brought it down a bit to rotate the tires and she said "DOWN!", and I reinforced that as well. I think the car went back up again and then it went down all the way, and she pointed excitedly, saying "up" and "down". We left and drove back home and she kept talking about up-and-down. The next day, we drove past the auto shop and I asked her if she remembered the car at the shop. And she replied "up" and "down".

The reason I like this story is that it highlights the formation of two kinds of memories related to the same event. On the one hand, she was beginning to understand the concept of "up" and the concept of "down", and how they are mapped onto the words. These concepts would eventually become so entrenched as to be automatic in their usage and retrieval. But before she could get there, she also formed a very specific memory of *our vehicle* going up on the lift at the mechanics shop on a specific day. That event was its own personal memory, but it also contributed to the overall knowledge of the concept of up-and-down.

The distinction between a specific event and general knowledge is one that was made most strongly by the psychologist Endel Tulving (1972, 2002). Tulving distinguished between **semantic memory**, which is memory for facts and general knowledge, and **episodic memory**, which is memory for the past, memory with a personal connection, and the temporal dimension. My daughter's concept of up-and-down reflects the beginning of her semantic memory for those concepts. But the way in which she learned it, relating the event to something that happened to her, is an episodic memory. It is a memory for a specific episode in the past.

A Hierarchical System of Knowledge Representation

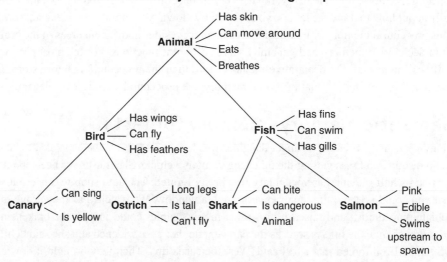

Figure 3.3 An example of one of the most common versions of a hierarchical knowledge representation. Each single node is connected to other basic notes for elementary propositions. Some connections are featural in nature, such as "canaries are yellow", and other connections are categorical in nature, such as "canaries are birds". Information at one level of the hierarchy is inherited by subordinate levels.

Semantic memory is usually thought to be organized conceptually. We will discuss this in the next chapter with respect to concepts and categories. But there are other approaches to how memory is organized. The grandparent of semantic memory organization is the hierarchical approach first described by Collins and Quillian (Collins & Quillian, 1969, 1970; McCloskey & Glucksberg, 1979). Their insight was that some degree of hierarchical structure imposed on knowledge representation would result in an efficiency (Figure 3.3). Knowledge is organized in this system as a hierarchy within a spreading activation system. Individual nodes represent concepts and facts, and links between these nodes represent relationships between concepts. Crucially, attributes of the higher-order node (e.g., ANIMAL) are true of lower-order nodes (BIRD, FISH, etc.). The subordinate facts and concepts inherit properties of the superordinate nodes.

Support for this hierarchical model usually comes in the form of sentence verification tasks or lexical decision tasks. In the **sentence verification task**, subjects are given a statement and are asked to verify if the statement is true, and they answer yes or no. In these tasks, the important dependent variable is the reaction time to say yes or no. The questions themselves are usually straightforward enough so that the subject in the task can answer yes or no correctly. For example, if asked "Do canaries sing?", subjects can answer yes and the answer yes comes quickly. However, if asked "Do canaries have skin?", people still answer yes, but researchers found that for questions like this, it takes a little bit longer. The reason, according to Collins and Quillian, is that the information about canaries and singing is stored at the same node in the same level of the hierarchy. In order to access the information about canaries and skin, activation needs to spread to the superordinate "animal" level of the hierarchy, where a feature "has skin" is represented. The semantic distance between "canaries" and "sings", "canaries" and "skin" is reflected in the difference in reaction time. As a result, this hierarchical structure affects the way in which people think about concepts, think about the properties of concepts, and answer questions.

The basic hierarchical model is not perfect. A strict hierarchy does not deal well with **typicality effects**. When people are asked to verify properties about "robins as birds", they may respond more quickly than when asked to verify properties about "penguins as birds". This is because robins are more typical. More problematic is that some concepts seem to bypass the hierarchy altogether. Medin and Smith refer to these as **nested concepts** (Smith & Medin, 1981). People generally respond to statements about robins as birds more quickly than they respond to statements about robins as animals. This is in keeping with the standard hierarchical model. The reverse is true when asked to verify the birdlike properties of chickens versus the animal-like properties of chickens. For most people, a chicken is a better example of an animal than it is of a bird. In this way, chicken seems to skip the near superordinate of bird, and is connected more strongly to the far superordinate of animal. Although this might make sense intuitively, it is difficult to reconcile with a strict hierarchy.

Later attempts to explain spreading activation tended to do away with the hierarchy. Collins and Loftus (1975) suggested that information is represented in a spreading activation network. Nodes of related concepts are linked by associations. The strength of association is represented by the length. Activation spreads through this network. John Anderson's ACT–R model (1990) also emphasizes associations between nodes and the spreading of activation. Both of these approaches eliminate the hierarchy and both still account for results like sentence verification. In addition, as we will see later in this chapter, this idea of spreading activation also predicts certain kinds of memory errors. These memory errors underlie many of the thinking errors that I will discuss as well.

Episodic memory

Unlike semantic memory, episodic memory seems to have some degree of temporal processing. That is, episodic memory is a memory for a specific episode or episodes that happened to you in the past (Tulving, 1972, 2002). Examples of this might include major life events, such as a sixteenth birthday or a family vacation. Examples also include mundane events, such as what you had for dinner yesterday. Tulving refers to this as "mental time travel" and suggests that this ability is only seen in humans. Additionally, Tulving suggests that episodic memory is evolutionarily recent and late-developing, and seems to rely on both the left and right prefrontal cortex areas.

Intentionality

Memory can also be divided in terms of how the information is initially encoded. Recall that encoding refers to the deployment of attention and the creation of a mental representation. Here we can create a distinction in terms of intentionality. Some encoding is **intentional**, while other encoding is **incidental**. For example, intentional encoding might include studying information for an exam or trying to remember an email address. In keeping with our example of shopping at a farmer's market, intentional memory is committing a list of things to buy to memory. This is intentional encoding because you intend to store and later recall the information. This contrasts with incidental encoding, which refers to learning by association or exposure. For example, you probably know the melody and words of many popular songs that you didn't necessarily intend to encode, store, and recall. It's just that hearing them in various locations and in different scenarios has allowed you to learn them incidentally. Incidental learning is also important for certain kinds of non-declarative memory. For example, learning the rules of the grammar of your native language happened incidentally when you were young. Caregivers and adults spoke to you, asked questions, and addressed you using grammatical structures, and you began to acquire some of these grammatical structures without explicit instruction.

Effortful and non-effortful memory

A related construct is **effort**. Some information is going to require more effort to store and possibly more effort to retrieve. New information – for example, information that you are studying as part of a class – may require more effort than familiar information. Information that is more coherent requires less effort than information that is less coherent. Information that is contained within a narrative or an organized schema will require less effort to encode and retrieve than information that is relatively unstructured (Kintsch, 1994). On the other hand, some memories can be retrieved automatically. Many procedural memories are retrieved automatically and without much awareness. When you are shopping at the farmer's market, for example, seeing the butternut squash triggers an automatic retrieval of the memory for that item on your shopping list.

Implicit and explicit memory

A distinction that is very similar to the distinction of effort is the **explicit/implicit** distinction. Declarative memories are often explicit in nature. That is, when you are studying information for an exam, you put effort into encoding it and you engage in an explicit recall. You are explicitly trying to recall the information. But the overall thinking process also has a role for implicit retrieval. Let's go back to our example of shopping at the farmer's market. You have purchased your butternut squash and you then decide to purchase some fresh onions and some garlic, thinking that the squash roasted with onions and garlic will be delicious. You may have in mind the finished dish for a recipe, but it may not be an explicit process that retrieves that memory and influences your decision. Rather, the decision to buy the onions and garlic happens quickly as a result of implicit retrieval. Implicit retrieval means that memory influences your behaviour even if you are not consciously aware that it is happening. Many examples of the effects of memory on thinking and judgement (like the availability heuristic) are the result of the influence of information that was retrieved quickly and without much conscious awareness.

EXPECTATIONS AND PROCESSING EFFECTS

Expectations can affect recall

Our memory and knowledge for things affects our ability to think about them and to make decisions. Consider a straightforward example. If you think about your university classes, or college classes, many of them involve studying and learning information that you will later need to recall during an exam. Two common forms of examination are the multiple-choice exam and the written-essay exam. Do your expectations for how you will be tested and examined affect the way in which you attempt to learn the information? Do you study differently for a multiple-choice exam than you do for an essay exam? When I ask my students this question in class, nearly all of them indicate that they do study differently. After all, a multiple-choice exam involves recognition memory. You are given a statement and you need to recognize and retrieve the correct answer. You need to be able to eliminate plausible alternatives. As such, when preparing for this kind of exam you are likely to emphasize exact terms to maximize the likelihood that you will recognize the correct answer and minimize the likelihood that you will falsely recognize one of the distractors as being correct. On the other hand, when you are preparing for an essay exam, you know that you will be asked to elaborate on information and recall it, often without a reliable cue. You may not need to recognize a correct answer and distinguish it from distractors, but you may be asked to look for underlying themes and a deeper understanding of the information. So we are likely to agree that we prepare differently for these two kinds of exams.

But what would happen if you prepared for an essay exam but on the day of the exam the instructor indicated that you would be taking a multiple-choice exam instead? What if you prepared to write a multiple-choice exam and were informed that you were going to be writing an essay instead? When I ask students in a class, most of them indicate that they would be very unhappy with either surprise. They also indicate that they think their performance on the unexpected exam would suffer relative to how they would have done in the exam they expected and studied for.

Barbara Tversky and several other researchers investigated this very idea (Lundeberg & Fox, 1991; B. Tversky, 1973). A subsequent meta-analysis (Lundeberg & Fox, 1991) found that across many different studies, students usually performed better when they were tested with the kind of exam they were expecting. In other words, expectations affected the encoding strategy. When the encoding strategy matched the expected retrieval for exam mode, performance benefited. When there was a mismatch, performance suffered.

These studies on test preparation are in line with a long tradition of research that looks at the amount or depth of processing that goes into acquiring information and how that processing affects the nature of the representation that is stored (Craik & Tulving, 1975; Tulving, 1972, 1983, 2002). Another way of saying this is that the way in which you think about an idea, object, or event when you are learning about it affects the information you are able to store as part of the representation.

Levels of processing

The great example of the effects of processing effort and depth on memory comes from an early study in the 1970s by Craik and Tulving (Craik & Tulving, 1975). In their work, they argued for the role of different **levels of processing** on memory storage. They suggested that incoming stimuli (e.g., things that are being processed and learned) are subjected to a series of processes. **Shallow processing** refers to processing information at the sensory and surface level. **Deep processing** refers to processing information in terms of semantics and meaning. In general, they argued that deeper processing brought about better recall of the information in subsequent tests.

In one study (Craik & Tulving, 1975), subjects were asked to learn words in various encoding conditions. All subjects learned the same list. In the structural condition, subjects were asked to say yes or no to the question "Is the word in capital letters?" Half of the words were presented in capital letters and the other half were presented in lower-case letters, so the answer was always yes or no. It should be immediately apparent that this question does not require the learner to spend much effort thinking about the word and what it means. In fact, you can easily do this task with words you don't even know, with non-words, with your eyes out of focus, etc. You don't even need to be able to read the word to answer this question correctly, only to notice the presence of capital or lower-case letters. In another condition, the phonemic condition, subjects were asked to answer the question "Does the word rhyme with_____?", and this blank was filled in with the word that either rhymed or did not rhyme with the target word that they were trying to learn. In this case, subjects needed to read the word and think about how it sounded in order to answer the question correctly. In a third condition, the semantic condition, subjects were asked to answer a question about the object using the word itself. In other words, the solution required sentence verification. In this condition, in order to answer the question correctly, subjects needed to think about what the word actually meant.

When the participants were later tested with a recognition test, the subjects who learned in the semantic condition performed the best. It seems that attending to the meaning of the word encouraged deeper processing, a stronger representation, and better performance on a memory test. This is a robust finding, and has been replicated and extended in a number of different studies and labs. Even when subjects were not told that this was a memory test, engaging in the deeper processing required by the semantic condition still resulted in fairly good performance on the recall task. Other experiments controlled for the amount of time subjects spent processing the initial word, and even when they were made to process the words for longer durations in the shallow conditions, performance was still better in the deeper, semantic conditions. The central message is that memory for information can be strengthened when the information is given considerable, effortful thought.

MEMORY ERRORS

The seven sins

We have discussed how deeper processing results in better recall and possibly in more elaborate memory traces. In addition, we also discussed how activation spreads among nodes and related concepts. From this, we can conclude that a rich contextual setting and strong semantic associations will result in better memory. Which is true. But there is a bit of a downside here. The very things that seem to help memory to function in the most adaptive way possible – strong associations, rich prior knowledge base, a strong conceptual coherence among the items to be learned – may also encourage errors.

A nice summary was provided by the memory researcher Daniel Schacter (1999). He published an article in *American Psychologist* called "The seven sins of memory" in which he lays out seven key ways in which the very features that allow our memories to work so well also guarantee some kinds of errors. The seven sins are transience, absent-mindedness, blocking, misattribution, suggestibility, bias, and persistence. All seven have implications for how thinking can be affected by and even undermined by memory failures.

The first two, **transience** and **absent-mindedness**, are really just everyday memory failures. Information fades over time, or information is not encoded strongly, because the learner does not allocate sufficient resources. As an example, you probably remember many times when reading a text for a class that you kind of "space out" and forget what you just read. That kind of absent-mindedness results in a memory failure. In order to work properly, memory often requires some degree of attention. The third sin, **blocking**, essentially means a temporary retrieval failure or lack of access. This might be due to spreading activation in a semantic memory network. As the activation spreads to many concepts, they all receive some activation and it is difficult to determine which one is the correct fact. This is seen most strongly in the so-called "**tip of the tongue**" phenomenon. This is where you are asked a question and you know you know the answer but you cannot generate the answer. In many instances, you can almost feel yourself saying the answer. It's as if some of the information is present, including the information needed to speak the word, but not at high enough levels to be activated.

Misattribution and **suggestibility** are both errors that also arise from the highly associated aspects of semantic networks. In the case of misattribution, an error comes about when a person remembers the fact correctly but may not be able to remember the correct source. Imagine being asked to learn a list of words and then falsely remembering a word that may not have been on the list because it is highly associated with the words that are on the list (we will discuss this specific case in greater detail below). This is an error, and one that is perfectly understandable given a spreading activation account of memory.

Suggestibility is the tendency to update for past events based on current descriptions. Memory is malleable and suggestible. Finally, **bias** and **persistence** both reflect our own intuitions about our memories. We often show a bias to assume that what we remember reflected events that actually happened. In other words, we trust our own memories. And with good reason. If a false memory or an error arises from a feeling of remembrance that comes from having a highly associated semantic network, it is reasonable to assume that we are remembering something that happened rather than just responding to a state of activation that does not reflect the past.

Our memories often have the unfortunate characteristic of being persistent when we don't want them to be. Traumatic events, unhappy events, and other events that we would like to forget are often difficult to forget because of their initial salience or emotional content, or because of intrusive recollection and rumination. Every time we think about that unfortunate event we strengthen the initial trace. Dwelling on an unfortunate event in the past is likely to make that memory trace all the stronger.

These seven sins are fairly broadly defined, and are all examples of memory errors that come about because of a structured semantic memory. Let's go back to our example of the farmer's market. Imagine that you have entered the market, you have examined the fruits and vegetables available at one of the stands, and you have moved on to another stand. Your friend who is with you asks if the first vendor had lemons for sale. *Did they have lemons? Did you actually see lemons or do you just think you saw lemons?* They may have had lemons, as they had other fruits. But you may find yourself not being 100% certain that you actually saw lemons there. Perhaps you are just inferring the presence of those lemons based on your knowledge of produce vendors in general. In other words, your semantic memory representation of a produce vendor may have a lemon feature. That feature will be activated when you visit the produce stand, even if you don't explicitly see the lemons. It is a spreading activation effect.

The DRM task

Seeking to demonstrate the ease with which false memories can be created, psychologist Henry Roediger explored an interesting paradigm, which is now known as the Deese, Roediger, McDermott paradigm, or the DRM task (Roediger & McDermott, 1995). In the canonical version of the task, subjects are presented with a list of words that they are instructed to remember. In the most well-known example, subjects might see the words: *bed, rest, awake, tired, dream, wake, snooze, blanket, doze, slumber, snore, nap, peace, yawn, drowsy*. Crucially, note that the word "*sleep*" is not in this list, and yet all of these words are connected to the concept sleep. In the DRM task, subjects were given several lists of words like this, and were asked after each list to recall as many words as possible. After six lists, they were given a recognition task which included words from the study lists, new words, and the critical target words that were not on the list but were highly associated (e.g., sleep).

False recognition of the target words was prevalent in the subjects. Indeed, in subsequent investigations, subjects were convinced that the target word had been presented. In versions of the task when subjects were asked to indicate a distinction between whether or not they remembered the word or whether they just knew the word, most subjects indicated that they explicitly remembered seeing that word.

This is clearly a memory error. The word, though highly associated, was not present. Subjects who indicate remembering it are demonstrating a source misattribution error.

Spreading activation among all of the related words results in high activation of the target words, and this is strong enough to result in a false memory.

Change blindness

If you are having a conversation with a stranger, and you look away for a moment, you assume that when you look back the same person will be there talking to you. Evidence suggests that the assumption is so strong that if the person were to change places with someone else, you wouldn't even notice. This failure of memory and attention is known as change blindness. The phenomenon was originally noted by Daniel Simons (Simons & Chabris, 1999; Simons & Levin, 1997, 1998). One version of the study involved two experimenters, a research assistant, and a subject. One of the experimenters would approach a subject on the campus with a map and ask for directions. While the subject was giving directions to the experimenter, two researchers carrying a door or large board would walk in between the researcher asking for directions and the subject. The door was positioned such that the subject would not be able to see the two researchers carrying the door, and for a brief time would not be able to see the researcher asking for instructions. As they were walking by, one of the carriers switched places with the person asking for directions. Once they passed, the subject would be left talking to a different person – the researcher who was initially carrying the board. In nearly every case, the subjects did not notice they were talking to another person. They carried on giving instructions as if they hadn't even noticed. Later questioning revealed that few of them noticed the change.

Other versions of the study involved a more controlled setting. A subject walks into a research lab and approaches a counter where a researcher stands with a consent form. The researcher gives a consent form to the subject and the subjects reads and signs it, and hands it back to the researcher. The researcher then pretends to duck down in order to file the form. At the moment when the researcher is out of view, they switch places with another researcher who then stands up and continues with the introduction to the study. Most subjects don't notice the change and don't even notice that anything unusual happened.

In both of these cases, subjects are said to be blind to a change. This represents a failure to encode the present situation strongly enough. It also suggests a reasonable expectation that a current situation will not change arbitrarily. But the implications for memory and thinking are clear. If you cannot trust your memory to let you know when something is changed, you may not be able to trust your memory for details in longer-term situations. This would be especially salient in eyewitnesses to crimes. If a subject doesn't notice a research assistant switching places, they may not be able to notice enough details about a perpetrator in a crime to be able to reliably identify them. I will discuss other failures of eyewitness testimony in Chapter 5 on language and cognition.

MEMORY AND EXPERT PERFORMANCE

An extensive semantic memory network is also a crucial aspect of thinking and expertise. We have already discussed briefly, and will discuss in greater detail in Chapter 11, how experts often transition from a reliance on rules, the textbook method, and algorithms, to retrieved examples. This is seen very strongly in medical diagnosis (Brooks, Norman, & Allen, 1991; Norman & Brooks, 1997). Geoff Norman and Lee Brooks have argued that expert medical diagnosis and clinical reasoning depends on the expert clinician having a rich, highly interconnected knowledge network. Whereas residents and novice physicians may start out basing diagnoses on textbook examples and diagnostic rules, experts are more likely to base their diagnoses on how much the current patient resembles a previously seen patient. Experts have likely diagnosed and interacted with many patients and so they have a rich knowledge base upon which to draw these inferences and make these diagnoses. Thus, errors in memory may result in errors in diagnosis.

An interesting example of how expert medical doctors use memory to assist in diagnoses comes from several studies undertaken by Lesgold and colleagues (Lesgold, Feltovich, Glaser, & Wang, 1981). They were interested in the cognitive processes that underlie the reading and interpretation of x-rays by radiologists. If you have never seen an x-ray, it is pretty easy to get the overall gist of what you are looking at if there is something familiar to you, such as a skull or a bone. But for any kind of detail, it can be very challenging. Radiologists are physicians who have been trained to interpret medical images like x-rays. In one of Lesgold et al.'s studies, they asked experienced radiologists and medical school students to examine x-ray images for two seconds and asked them to provide a diagnosis. In other conditions, the experts and novices were given longer periods of time to examine the x-rays. One of the interesting things they discovered was that the expert radiologists quickly developed a schema for what they were looking at. In other words, experts didn't need to process aspects of the image that were familiar to them. If they were seeing an x-ray of a lung, they could rely on their own memory representations for what lungs look like and fill in the gaps from memory rather than directly from perception. That way, they could compare the image with the schema and examine pathological differences. Novices have a less well-developed schema and weaker memory representations for x-ray images of lungs, so the novices needed to spend more time processing the actual image because they were not able to rely on an internalized memory representation for lung x-rays. This decreased their ability to notice pathologies.

A possible caveat to this expert advantage might be that if experts are expecting a certain pathology to emerge, and rely on memory representations to fill in the details, they may miss other abnormalities. In fact, this is what researchers found (Norman & Brooks, 1997).

Strong memory representations usually confer an advantage to experts, but occasionally result in errors when the memory representations get in the way of unusual abnormalities.

Schema theory

The previous discussion of memory representation, knowledge structures, and memory systems emphasizes how knowledge is stored and represented. However, as we are primarily concerned with how memory is involved in the thinking process, it is useful to have a conceptual framework that addresses the interaction between representation and other thinking behaviours, such as problem-solving, and hypothesis-testing. One theory that addresses this interaction is schema theory. For our purposes, we can define a memory schema as a general-purpose knowledge structure that encodes information and stores information about common events and situations. This representation is used for understanding events and situations.

For example, let's consider again the idea of going to a farmer's market. We have already discussed all the ways in which memory is involved, and we have mentioned the possibility that the shopper may have a script or schema for how to behave and what to expect in a farmer's market. Assuming that you, as the shopper, have been to farmer's markets or city markets before, you have encoded information about each event, you have stored episodic memories, semantic memories, and have retrieved and used these memories during the event. The schema is the conceptual framework that allows these memory representations to generate expectations. When you arrive at the market, you expect to see several produce vendors, you expect someone to be selling fresh cut flowers, and you expect the majority of the transactions will be conducted with cash rather than credit.

Seen in this way, a schema is not a semantic memory representation *per se*, but rather it is a representation of how memory should be used in thinking. In the Lesgold et al. (1981) studies with radiologists, the researchers concluded that the expert radiologists activated several pathology schemas. They activated a general-purpose knowledge structure that, in addition to containing semantic memory and visual memory, also contained a set of expectations and predictions. The expert radiologists can use schemas and memory to fill in the details of the x-ray even if they didn't actually see them. They expect certain things to be there. Similarly, you don't need to see the cut flower vendor at the farmer's market; you may expect him to be there, and if asked later, you might respond affirmatively even if you did not actually see him.

Sometimes, however, activated schema will cause a person to miss features that are inconsistent with that schema. We mentioned already that expert radiologists might miss other novel pathologies that are not consistent with a diagnostic schema and a set of diagnostic expectations. This is referred to as premature closure in diagnosis

(Voytovich, Rippey, & Suffredini, 1985). But this general idea was demonstrated many years ago by the pioneering work of Bransford and Johnson (1973). In one study, they showed that people often miss key features in a text if those features do not fit with a schema. Subjects were asked to read the following paragraph, which was given the title, "Watching a peace march from the 40th floor".

> The view was breathtaking. From the window, one could see the crowd below. Everything looked extremely small from such a distance, but the colorful costumes could still be seen. Everyone seemed to be moving in one direction in an orderly fashion and there seemed to be little children as well as adults. The landing was gentle, and luckily the atmosphere was such that no special suits had to be worn. At first there was a great deal of activity. Later, when the speeches started, the crowd quieted down. The man with the television camera took many shots of the setting and the crowd. Everyone was very friendly and seemed glad when the music started.

It is a pretty straightforward paragraph, and it probably conforms to our schema of being in a city, watching some sort of demonstration or parade or civic action. As a result, we can probably imagine or fill in details that may or may not be actually present in the text. Crucially, we might miss the sentence that states *"The landing was gentle and luckily the atmosphere was such that no special suits had to be worn"*. This sentence has nothing to do with watching a peace march. It does not conform to the activated schema for an urban environment or a demonstration. As a result, when subjects were asked to answer questions about the paragraph they had read, they often did not remember this sentence. The conclusion is that we miss things that are inconsistent with a schema.

It would be a mistake, however, to assume that we always miss things that are not consistent with the general schema. For example, I am sure you have a schema that reflects your expectations of a standard college or university lecture. You might be sitting in the seat, with your notebook or laptop, and an instructor is at the front of the class with a whiteboard, a chalkboard, or PowerPoint slides. If the instructor stopped in the middle of the lecture, unplugged her laptop, and threw it across the classroom, that scenario would not fit with your schema, but it would be so jarring that it would be very memorable. Clearly, very shocking or surprising deviations from the schema will be memorable.

Other research suggests that details that may not be consistent with the schema are still encoded, but may not become part of the primary representation unless a new schema is introduced. Consider a now classic study by Anderson and Pichert (1978). Subjects in the experiment were asked to read a passage about two boys walking through a house. In addition, they were given a context to the paragraph before reading it. One group of subjects was told to imagine that they were a house burglar. Another group of subjects was asked to consider the passage from the perspective of a potential homebuyer. They were then asked to remember details about the following passage:

> The two boys ran until they came to the driveway. "See, I told you today was good for skipping school," said Mark. "Mom is never home on Thursday," he added. Tall hedges hid the house from the road so the pair strolled across the finely landscaped yard. "I never knew your place was so big," said Pete. "Yeah, but it's nicer now than it used to be since Dad had the new stone siding put on and added the fireplace."
>
> There were front and back doors and a side door which led to the garage which was empty except for three parked 10-speed bikes. They went to the side door, Mark explaining that it was always open in case his younger sisters got home earlier than their mother.
>
> Pete wanted to see the house so Mark started with the living room. It, like the rest of the downstairs, was newly painted. Mark turned on the stereo, the noise of which worried Pete. "Don't worry, the nearest house is a quarter of a mile away," Mark shouted. Pete felt more comfortable observing that no houses could be seen in any direction beyond the huge yard.
>
> The dining room, with all the china, silver and cut glass, was no place to play so the boys moved into the kitchen where they made sandwiches. Mark said they wouldn't go to the basement because it had been damp and musty ever since the new plumbing had been installed.
>
> "This is where my Dad keeps his famous paintings and his coin collection," Mark said as they peered into the den. Mark bragged that he could get spending money whenever he needed since he'd discovered that his Dad kept a lot in the desk drawer.
>
> There were three upstairs bedrooms. Mark showed Pete his mother's closet which was filled with furs and the locked box which held her jewels. His sisters' room was uninteresting except for the colour TV, which Mark carried to his room. Mark bragged that the bathroom in the hall was his since one had been added to his sisters' room for their use. The big highlight in his room, though, was a leak in the ceiling where the old roof had finally rotted.

Not surprisingly, subjects recalled more information that was consistent with the context of the schema they were given. If you were told to read the paragraph with the context of a burglar in mind, you would remember things about famous paintings and coin collections, a closet full of furs, and the side door that was always open. If you were asked to read this from the context of a prospective homebuyer, you might think about the bathroom addition, the leak in the ceiling, and a newly painted downstairs. These are schema-consistent details. However, the researchers then asked subjects to consider the paragraph that they had already read from the perspective of the other context. Subjects who read it from the perspective of a burglar were then asked to reconsider (but not reread) it from the perspective of a homebuyer and vice versa. Subjects recalled additional detail when asked to re-inspect their memory from the alternative context. The implication seems to be that the information was encoded and processed but because it did not fit a schema initially it was not recalled as well. When given a reorganizing context or reorganizing framework, new details were recalled. Our memories, it seems, are quite flexible.

SUMMARY

Memory, which we often think of as storage of past events, allows us to predict the future. When you encounter a new situation, a new person, or a new object, you immediately assess its similarity to previously encountered things. You may recognize an event or a person as being familiar, even if it is a novel situation. If I recognize that this new but familiar event shares a similarity with a previous event, I know what to expect. I know how to behave towards this new event because it is similar to something I have experienced before. I can predict the future with some reasonable certainty based on similarity to previously stored memories. That is an incredibly powerful aspect of human thought. This is the basis of induction, decision-making, and problem-solving.

4 CONCEPTS AND CATEGORIES

Concepts provide structure to the mental world. We rely on concepts to make predictions, to infer features and attributes, and to generally understand the world of objects, things, and events. The study of concepts, categories, and thinking is one that emphasizes how categories are created and learned, how concepts are represented in the mind, and how these concepts are used to make decisions, to solve problems, and to drive the reasoning process. Figure 4.1 shows a hypothetical arrangement among lower-level perceptual responses, structured representations, and higher-order thought processes. At the lower levels, information has not been processed and is essentially in a raw, primitive form. Primitive representations are things like edges, colours, basic shape, phonemes, etc. These primitive representations receive input from the sensory system (the retina, the cochlea, etc.). In order for the cognitive system to be able to plan and make decisions, these primitive

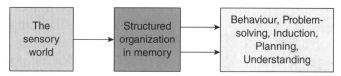

Categorization and knowledge: organize the sensory world into meaningful, usable mental structures.

The sensory world → Structured organization in memory → Behaviour, Problem-solving, Induction, Planning, Understanding

Fundamental cognitive mechanisms are recruited to bring structure to the sensory world.

Figure 4.1 A hypothetical arrangement that shows the role of concepts on other thinking behaviours. The outside, sensory world is structured according to features, similarity, and rules. We use this conceptual information to make decisions, to reason, and to solve problems.

representations need to be processed and structured in some way. In the previous chapter, the discussion was on memory and how thinking is influenced by memory. This chapter discusses the implications of mental representations that have a significant degree of structure. It examines thoughts and ideas that are similar to each other, representations that share activations and overlap at the neural level, and representations that have sufficient structure and coherence to afford prediction, inference, and utility. In other words, this chapter is about concepts.

In this chapter, I use the word **category** to refer to the objects, things, or events in the outside world that can be structured into groups. I use the word **concept** to refer to the mental representation that denotes that category. Categories are groupings of things, natural or otherwise, that exist outside the mind. Concepts are how we represent these groupings. Sometimes the concept reflects the category fairly well, but this is not always the case.

There are Many Kinds of Coffee Mugs

Figure 4.2 A selection of images of coffee mugs retrieved from a Google image search on "coffee mugs". Although there is great variety, we can still perceive some coherence. Very typical coffee mugs might seem to be better members of the category.

As an example of how categories of things might be organized and represented as concepts, consider Figure 4.2. This is a collection of coffee mugs and cups that were collected from a Google image search on "coffee cups". These are all readily identifiable as coffee cups. Some are more obvious than others. Some have more standard features than others, and others have novel features, like a gun handle or a shelf for your biscuits (which is a great idea). When we learn to classify these objects and to recognize them as members of the coffee mug category, we learn to ignore some of the idiosyncratic and unique features, and rely on the most typical and predictive features. But this process is not as straightforward as it seems, as many of the most common features (like being a cylinder) might also be found in members of other categories (e.g., a drinking glass, canister, jar, etc.). We might also notice that even those features which are strongly associated, like a handle, are not necessary for being a member of this category. Coffee mugs should be a really simple, straightforward category, but there is still a fair amount of complexity and variability. Despite this, most of us have formed a reliable concept of what coffee cups are and we are likely to have very little difficulty making a classification decision quickly and easily.

With something simple and straightforward, such as a category like coffee mugs, it hardly seems to matter. After all, as long as you can put your coffee in it, it should qualify as a member of the category. But the formation of (or lack of) stable concepts and category boundaries can have very serious consequences. As an example, consider acetaminophen, the pain reliever commonly found in Tylenol and other over-the-counter headache and cold medicine. If you were asked to say what category you thought acetaminophen was a member of, you might say "medicine" or something like that. You would not say "poison", and yet acetaminophen toxicity is a very serious issue. Every year many people die from taking too much acetaminophen. A recent review found that acetaminophen poisoning was the most common cause of acute liver failure in the USA. It accounts for several hundred deaths a year and causes many more thousands of calls to the emergency room (Hodgman & Garrard, 2012). It turns out that acetaminophen has a very narrow therapeutic window. Exceeding the maximum recommended dosage, even by a modest amount, can result in toxicity, hospitalization, and even death. This is exacerbated by the fact that acetaminophen is found in many over-the-counter medications (like cold and flu medications), so it may not be easy to tell if you have exceeded this dosage.

So acetaminophen is correctly classified as a medication, but with that comes the incorrect assumption that it may be safer than it is. Categorizing something allows you to make predictions and assumptions. But in this case, categorizing acetaminophen as a safe, benign, over-the-counter medication may lead to errors. I do not wish to give the impression that acetaminophen is unsafe in general or that it should be avoided. Taken as directed, it is a very safe and effective medication. But certainly the consequence of categorizing it as always safe would be incorrect.

Categories allow people to make quick and usually accurate judgements (e.g. coffee cup or not), but occasionally they come with a cost of misclassification (e.g safe medication or poison).

WHY DO PEOPLE CATEGORIZE THINGS?

Why do people seem to rely on mental categories for thinking? A related question is why do we, as humans, seem to have the concepts and categories that we do? One possibility is that humans form categories (and form concepts) that reflect the natural structure of the world. That is, I have a fairly good concept of dogs and cats because there is a natural distinction between the two groups. Cats and dogs may live together but they are not the same. Cats and dogs are likely to fall into different categories whether we have name-able concepts or not. Another possibility is that humans form concepts to help achieve goals. Below, I consider several key reasons why people group things into categories and represent these groupings and concepts.

Stimulus generalization

People categorize things in part because of a natural tendency to **generalize**. Stimulus generalization is present in all species and it means that an organism can extend a learned behavioural response to a whole class of stimuli. This would be seen even in the most primitive organisms. In the nineteenth century, William James noted that:

> ...creatures extremely low in the intellectual scale may have conception. All that is required is that they should recognize the same experience again. A polyp would be a conceptual thinker if a feeling of "Hollo! thingumbob again!" ever flitted through its mind. (James, 1890)

This notion suggests that generalization, and with it the tendency to categorize and group memories into clusters, is an inherent aspect of a functional cognitive architecture. And as was discussed in Chapter 2 on similarity, these generalizations are going to be guided by similarity, such that the response rates of a behaviour to a new stimulus will be a function of how similar a new stimulus is to a previously seen stimulus. Roger Shepard referred to this as the universal law of stimuli generalization (Shepard, 1987).

Efficiency

Another reason that people categorize things is efficiency. A concept is a reduction in the amount of information to be retained about a whole group of things. One way to describe a category is as a **behavioural equivalence class**. This means that although a group or class of things may be different and many in number, we behave towards them in the same way. For example, my cat knows the sound of a can of food being opened. Although there are many different cans, and probably some of these sound different, the cat behaves in the same way towards the sound. The individual and unique characteristic of each can does not matter. The cat has efficiently represented a whole universe of food-can sounds with a single behavioural response. So it is with many of our own concepts. We are capable of representing similar things with one core representation. This can be referred to as **cognitive efficiency**. Theories of conceptual representation may differ in terms of how much information is stored in the conceptual representation, and how much information is lost. Most theories of conceptual representation assume that the concept stores general information, with greater cognitive efficiency than many unique individual representations. This distinction will be discussed later in the chapter.

Concepts are natural

Another reason why people categorize things is that the world of objects and things may be somewhat self-categorizing. That is, it may be that there are regularities in the world, both physical and functional, and that our job as inhabitants of the world is to learn about these regularities. This idea goes back at least as far as the ancient Greek philosopher Plato. Plato suggested that, as learners, we "*cut nature at its joints*" when we represent the natural world. Plato was probably talking about how a hunter or a butcher might prepare an animal for eating. It is easier to cut the animal where the joints are, rather than just hacking it apart. That is why we have chicken breast, wing, and drumstick, rather than wings that are cut in half. There are natural ways to cut up an animal. Those natural ways exist whether or not humans decide on that. And so you can imagine that humans form the categories they do based around already existing natural boundaries. We have a concept for fruit, for chickens, and for coffee mugs, because these things are similar to each other in the world. As we engage with the natural world we have no choice but to categorize and conceptualize it along those lines.

If we consider all of these things – the tendency to form generalizations, the possibility of an efficient central representation, and natural groupings that are present in the world – it seems that categorization is practically inevitable.

THE FUNCTIONS OF CONCEPTS

The preceding section described the formation of concepts as a natural and efficient process. In this section, I address the following questions: What are some of the functions of having concepts? How do concepts and categories affect the thinking process?

How to react

Fundamentally, a concept is a cognitive representation that can influence how a person reacts. Just like my cat, who formed the behavioural equivalence class for canned food (see the section on 'Efficiency' above), the concept can encapsulate experience and drive behaviour. Once an object is classified as a member of a category, we can behave towards it as a member of that category. For example, a hubbard squash is a large, light green, winter squash about the size and shape of a rugby football (Figure 4.3). It is somewhat unfamiliar to most people, but once a person is assured that it is a member of the winter squash category, they can behave accordingly. And how do most people react to winter squashes? Pie is a common reaction. That is, you can try to bake a pie that will more or

Hubbard Squash

Figure 4.3 A hubbard squash. On the left, a whole hubbard squash. On the right, hubbard squash cut in half.

less taste like a pumpkin pie, or at the very least you can look up a recipe for a hubbard squash pie that will taste like a pumpkin pie (it is actually better, in my opinion). You know how to cut into the squash, how to prepare it, and where to buy it. There are many other examples: a concert that is classified as classical music encourages a different attitude or style of dress than one that is classified as folk music. A wine that is classified as a desert wine encourages it to be consumed in a specific way and probably not with a steak.

This idea – that categories help you know how to behave or react – might also have troubling consequences on the thinking process as well. This tendency is at the root of many negative racial, ethnic, and occupational stereotypes. We might (even unconsciously) adjust our behaviour when speaking to a person from our own ethnic group, as opposed to a person from a different ethnic group. We adopt different manners when visiting the physician than when talking with the receptionist at the same office. We harbour different attitudes towards some racial groups relative to others. Much of the research and literature on stereotyping and racial prejudice falls within the context of classical topics in social psychology, and suggests that these categories can bias attitudes and perceptions in subtle and implicit ways (Gawronski & Bodenhausen, 2006; Gawronski, Peters, Brochu, & Strack, 2008).

Predictions and inferences

Categories are also used for prediction. Prediction is related to the guiding of behaviour but is more specific. In Chapter 6, I discuss how categories can guide an even more specific kind of prediction known as an **inductive inference**. When an object or an item is classified as belonging to a certain category, we can use the category to make predictions about other attributes that might not be immediately present, but that we know to be associated with the category. Consider again the hubbard squash. On the outside, it is pale green, lumpy, and oblong. But upon reliably classifying it as a winter squash, you might predict correctly that it will be orange on the inside, and will be filled with stringy fibres and seeds (Figure 4.3). This prediction is guided directly by category-level knowledge.

Communication

Categories are also an effective way to communicate information to other people. When we learn to generalize over a whole class of objects, we are usually averaging or summarizing our experience over multiple exposures or many interactions with a stimulus. But obviously, this direct, associative experience cannot be transferred to others. The most effective way to communicate with others is by referring to a known concept or category. For example, rather than relate the long process by which you discovered that the hubbard squash was a winter squash and that it also has yellow-orange flesh, stringy fibres, and seeds, you can just tell your friend that the hubbard squash is a winter squash. Granting the other person some knowledge of the squash's category membership gives that other person access to all the category level information. This idea relates the information denoted in **concepts** with the information denoted by **words**, and so some of the discussion on category learning and communication will also be covered in Chapter 5 on language and thought.

Problem-solving

Concepts and categories also play a role in problem-solving. People often engage in problem-solving strategies and heuristics that involve finding the correct solution from memory. Rather than solve a problem by working through the solution process, or applying a general strategy, the problem-solver may search for the correct solution in memory (Chi et al., 1981). Finding this solution in memory will necessarily involve comparing the current problem to representations of similar, previously solved problems. The idea of concept-based problem-solving occurs in many domains. Expert chess players access store representations for categories of moves (Gobet & Simon, 1996). Expert physicians are known to rely on the similarity of patients to previously seen patients (Devantier et al., 2009; Norman & Brooks, 1997). In addition, there seems to be high agreement among expert physicians about how they form concepts of the reasoning tasks that they access upon seeing a patient (Goldszmidt, Minda, & Bordage, 2013). We will discuss more about the role of conceptual representations on problem-solving in Chapter 10 and among experts in Chapter 11.

THEORIES OF CONCEPTUAL REPRESENTATION

In what we have discussed so far, categorization seems to be a naturally occurring behaviour. In this section, I want to answer the following questions: How are categories represented in the mind as concepts? What cognitive mechanisms play a role? How much information is stored or lost when a concept is formed?

Psychologists have described category representation in terms of several, broadly defined theoretical approaches. The first class of these theories is sometimes called the

classical view of concepts. This view emphasizes featural rules that delineate the category and thus define the concept. This includes the theories known as the **semantic network** and **hierarchal** approaches (Collins & Quillian, 1969, 1970; McCloskey & Glucksberg, 1979), which were discussed in the previous chapter on memory. These theories emphasize the similarity relations within and between categories and also the organization of concepts in memory. The second theoretical approach to the study of concepts is sometimes called the **probabilistic view**. Like the hierarchical view, this theory also emphasizes the importance of similarity within and between categories, but does not rely on a strictly definitional approach (Smith & Medin, 1981). Finally, researchers have argued for the role of knowledge and naïve theories about the world in what is known as the **theory view**. These approaches have been instantiated in several different ways, and each makes a number of core claims about how much unique information about an individual object is retained in the conceptual representation and how much unique information is lost in favour of general, category-level information. The following sections consider each of these in turn.

The classical view

The classical view is often described as "classical" because this is the way that theorists understood conceptual representation from classical times. In addition, we can think of this view as emphasizing categories as **strict classes**. There are two core assumptions in the most rigidly defined version of this theory. First, central to this theory is the idea of necessary and sufficient conditions as qualifiers for category membership. Second is the claim that categorization is absolute, and all members of a class are of equal standing. This view probably seems far too rigid to be a realistic view, but it did seem to be the underlying theoretical framework that guided work on concepts and categories for most of the early era of psychology, and in many ways is still present in folk classification ideas (Murphy, 2002).

To understand the nature of these claims, consider a square. A square is defined as a shape with four equal sides and four right angles. As long as the shape has these attributes it is a square, and indeed the attributes are generally enough to allow the shape to be called a square. That is, each of these is necessary and, together, they are sufficient for category membership. So the definition of the square can be said to consist of these jointly necessary and sufficient conditions. In addition, once a shape can be said to possess these features and can be deemed a member of the square category, it is difficult to imagine how anything else would increase or reduce the validity of that classification. That is, given that four equal sides and four right angles is enough to be a square, it guarantees an equality of being a square. All squares are equal.

BOX 4.1

The classical view has difficulty explaining **family resemblance**. This is the idea that members of a category or a class resemble each other but do not share one single defining characteristic. A family resemblance can be applied to real members of a family. Imagine a large family that gathers on holidays. It might be readily apparent to an observer that many of the family members look similar. Perhaps many have a certain hair colour or the same kind of eyes. But it is very unlikely that there would be one trait that could identify the family members perfectly. We can imagine many categories like this: cats, carrots, candy, and Cadillacs. Each member will be similar to many other members, but maybe not similar to all other members.

The classical view came under close scrutiny in the middle of the twentieth century regarding its failure to account for family resemblance. The philosopher Ludwig Wittgenstein (1953: 31) wrote:

> Consider, for example, the proceedings that we call games. I mean board games, card games, ball games, Olympic games, and so on. What is common to them all? Don't say, "There must be something common, or they would not be called games" – but look and see whether there is anything common to all. For if you look at them you will not see something common to all, but similarities, relationships, and a whole series of them at that.

In other words, the category of games is readily identifiable and its members possess many similarities, but the claim is that we cannot identify a single, defining feature. Wittgenstein's claim helped to usher in the modern understanding of concepts as family resemblance groupings. The idea was picked up by Eleanor Rosch in her paradigm-shifting work in the 1970s and 1980s. Rosch's work is discussed in this chapter.

It is possible to imagine other examples of categories with this definitional structure – even numbers are numbers that are divided by two, a US quarter is a certain size and shape and is produced by a government mint – but beyond some basic examples, the definitional account starts to break down. For example, if you were to draw a square on a sheet of paper, right now, you might draw something that looks like a square, but it won't have the required four equal sides. That is, they are probably not exactly equal in your drawing. And yet you would still call it a square, even if the sides were not exactly equal.

More intriguingly, even something as basic as even numbers might not be as clear. A study by Armstrong and colleagues found that people reliably rate "2" and "4" as better examples of even numbers compared to numbers like "34" and "106" (Armstrong, Gleitman, & Gleitman, 1983). This is troubling for a definitional account of concepts because it suggests that even when exemplars of a category should be equally good members, people are still displaying an effect of typicality.

In fact, the **typicality effect** is problematic for any definitional or rule-based account of concepts. In general, a typicality effect occurs when people rate some category exemplars as being better or more typical category members than others. A simple example would be to consider the dog category. Medium-sized, common dogs, such as a labrador, a retriever, or a German shepard, might be viewed as more typical and as better examples of the category. Smaller, hairless dogs or very large dogs, while still being just as much dogs as the labrador, might be viewed as less typical. It is easy to imagine the typical examples: red apples, a four-door sedan, a 12-ounce coffee mug with a handle, the Apple iPhone. The typical items seem to come to mind almost automatically when asked to describe members of a concept.

The typicality effect was investigated systematically by Eleanor Rosch (Rosch & Mervis, 1975). For example, in one study, Rosch and Mervis asked subjects to list all the attributes of common categories (such as tool, furniture, clothing, vehicle, etc.). What they found was that some exemplars possessed more attributes that were also shared by many of the other members of the category. Other exemplars possessed relatively fewer of these common attributes. These highly typical exemplars were often the first ones to come to mind when subjects were asked to list exemplars. They were also likely to be rated higher in typicality (Malt & Smith, 1982). In other words, these highly typical exemplars seemed to have a privileged status. This is slightly problematic for a classical view of concepts because a strictly definitional account predicts that these typical exemplars should not receive any behavioural privilege. Yet Rosch and Mervis showed that highly typical exemplars, those that seemed to share many features and attributes with other category members, were classified and named more quickly. If people show a preference for typical exemplars, then they may not be relying on a definition or a set of necessary and sufficient conditions.

Hierarchies and the basic level

The basic idea of a hierarchical organization has existed in psychology for decades. One of the original, and most influential, models was the semantic hierarchy of Collins and Quillian (1969, 1970). This model was discussed at length in Chapter 3 with respect to semantic memory, but the same model applies to a discussion of concepts and categories as well, so I want to refer to it again. The idea, seen in Figure 4.4, is that concepts at each node can inherit properties from the nodes above (this is the same figure that was used in Chapter 3). Nodes below can either be a member of a subordinate category ("is a" links) or properties ("has a") links. The early research with this model suggested that common tasks, such as sentence verification, reflected the influence of hierarchically represented concepts.

For example, in one study, participants were asked to read sentences that spanned different levels and were instructed to respond true or false as quickly as possible. For example, the sentence, "A canary can sing" is a property verification sentence that spans zero levels (P0), because a canary *can* sing. The sentence "A canary can fly" spans one level (P1), and "A canary has skin" spans two levels (P2). According to the hierarchical model, participants should take longer to verify a P2 sentence because the relevant information is stored at a different level. It takes some measurable amount of time to mentally travel from one idea to another idea at another level. If you are thinking about a canary, you have activated your canary concepts and you have ready activation for category features. If "skin" were one of these things, then you might imagine that the property was already activated and you should respond very quickly to the question. But it takes longer to verify that property.

A Hierarchical System of Knowledge Representation

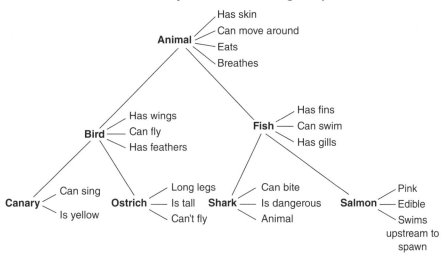

Figure 4.4 An example of one of the most common versions of a hierarchical knowledge representation. Each single node is connected to other basic notes for elementary propositions. Some connections are featural in nature, such as "canaries are yellow", and other connections are categorical in nature, such as "canaries are birds". Information at one level of the hierarchy is inherited by subordinate levels.

So yes, a canary does indeed have skin, but skin is not a property that is often associated directly with canaries. It is stored with the properties of animal, and every subordinate member of the animal category inherits this property. In order to answer that question you have first to activate "canary is a bird", then "canary is an animal" and "animals have skin". So only then will you have activated the mental representation that allows you to answer the question about the canary's skin. On the other hand, since "canary" and "sing" are close associates, they are stored at the same level and the answer is thus retrieved quickly and easily. The results from Collins and Quillian's study supported this, and participants took on average 200 milliseconds longer to verify the P2 sentences compared to P0 sentences. Similar results were found with category membership sentences, such as "A canary is a bird".

This suggests that information for some categories might be stored or accessed hierarchically. This theory has accounted for a wide variety of data, although there are many examples of how people might violate the general assumptions of this as well. In some cases, the strength of stored associations might interfere with a hierarchical representation. The most well-known example is a variant of the typicality effect, whereby people respond faster and more readily to questions about typical instances, such as "robin" or "canary", than to less typical instances, such as "chicken" or "flamingo" (Smith, Shoben, & Rips, 1974). More recent research has investigated whether or not people can store new information in hierarchies by teaching participants novel, artificial categories of information that could be represented in a hierarchy (Murphy, Hampton, & Milovanovic, 2012). Although participants did sometimes show evidence of hierarchical representations, they tended to learn features in an associative way or learned to retrieve whole exemplars. Murphy and colleagues suggest that while hierarchical representation may be one of many ways in which concepts are stored, many other concepts are likely to be stored via feature lists and feature comparisons.

One important aspect of a hierarchical scheme is the nature of each level. Even in a loosely organized hierarchy, each level has some fundamental characteristics that distinguish that level from others. As an example, consider the hierarchical representation shown in Figure 4.5. At the top level, also known as the **superordinate** level, the concepts (PLANT, ANIMAL, VEHICLE) tend to not overlap very much in terms of features and attributes so that the **between-category similarity** is relatively low: animals do not usually look or act very much like plants. But at the same time, **within-category similarity** is also fairly low: there are a wide variety of plants and not all look or act alike. Fir trees, sugar beets and a cactus are pretty dissimilar, but are clearly all members of the plant kingdom. Because the similarity and feature overlap is low all around, similarity itself is not a particularly useful cue in terms of predicting category membership. In other words, you cannot really use featural overlap and similarity to classify the fir tree as a plant because although it might be similar to other fir trees it is not similar to most other plants. At the

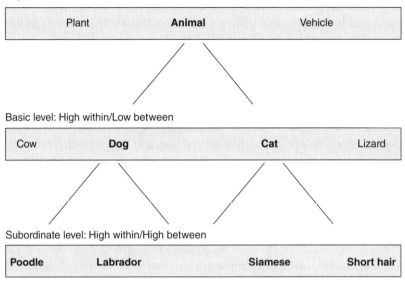

Hierarchical Representations

Superordinate level: Low within/Low between

Plant	**Animal**	Vehicle

Basic level: High within/Low between

Cow	**Dog**	**Cat**	Lizard

Subordinate level: High within/High between

Poodle	**Labrador**	**Siamese**	**Short hair**

Figure 4.5 Another example of hierarchical representation in categorization. Shown are a hypothetical superordinate, basic, and subordinate category levels. Similarity within and between category members varies at each level. Primary object identification and classification occurs at the basic level.

bottom level, known as the **subordinate** level, there is a high within-category similarity (poodles look like other poodles) and also a fairly high between-category similarity (poodles look a fair amount like labradors). Again, because similarity and feature overlap is fairly high, it is not a very reliable predictor of category membership. Furthermore, to the extent that people do use feature similarity to make these classifications, it will need to take into account very specific features and often features that are unique. Corgis (as a dog breed) have a specific look but their most noticeable features are likely to be those that are readily identifiable dog features.

The middle level, referred to as the basic level, is a special case. Here, within-category similarity is high but between-category similarity is low. Although members of the DOG category tend to look a lot like other dogs, there is not nearly as much overlap between members of the DOG category, the CAT category, the LIZARD category, and other members of the animal category. The basic level category is the level which maximizes within-category similarity while simultaneously minimizing the between-category similarity. Because of this, similarity and/or features are a reliable cue to category membership. Dogs have a dog shape and are maximally similar to other dogs and do not have as much similarity overlap with other categories. The same is true for trees, cars, tables, hammers, mugs, etc.

Basic level categories are special in other ways too. In the 1970s, Eleanor Rosch and colleagues (Rosch, Mervis, Gray, Johnson, & Boyes-Braem, 1976) observed that basic level categories are the most abstract level, at which the objects from a category tend to have the same shape, the same motor movements, and tend to share parts. Because the contrasting categories can be easily compared, and similarity is a predictive cue, basic categories also show a naming advantage. That is, if you were shown a picture of a Granny Smith apple, you would likely respond by naming it as an APPLE, and not as a FRUIT (the superordinate) or a GRANNY SMITH (the subordinate). Also, with respect to naming, basic level categories are learned earlier by children, and they are listed first when subjects are asked to list members of a superordinate category. In general, the work of Rosch and many others has shown that although objects are classifiable at many different levels, people seem to operate on and to think about objects at the basic level.

Of course not all objects categories are classified at the basic level all the time. People with extensive experience in a domain might operate instinctively at a more subordinate level (Harel & Bentin, 2013; Johnson & Mervis, 1997; Tanaka & Taylor, 1991). As an example, imagine that you were an apple expert – you were an orchard owner – and, as in the previous example, you were shown a picture of a Granny Smith apple; unlike the novice, who would be expected to respond with the world "Apple", the expert might be expected to respond with "Granny Smith Apple". Several studies have borne out this result. For example, Johnson and Mervis (1997) conducted several studies on classification and attribute generation with bird experts, fish experts, as well as novices, and they found that although the basic level still retained a privileged status, subjects' expertise acted to increase access to categorical information at the subordinate level and even at the sub-subordinate levels for advanced experts. Other researchers have found the same kinds of effects with a broad assortment of categories (Harel & Bentin, 2013; Tanaka & Taylor, 1991). In other words, if you are an expert, your basic level is actually a subordinate level.

Probabilistic views

The classical view and related hierarchical view, although fairly apt in terms of explaining some aspects of human conceptual ability, also fall short in other ways. The aforementioned criticisms of Wittgenstein (see Box 4.1), the prevalence of typicality effects, and the strong reliance on non-critical features all suggest that there needs to be a better way to describe concepts.

One possibility that comes directly out of Rosch's work is the idea that category membership is probabilistic. Rather than being based on a set of necessary and sufficient conditions and residing within a strict hierarchy, a concept is thought to represent a category of things that are grouped together with shared features and overlapping similarity. In this account, broadly referred to as the **probabilistic view**, category membership is not definite. Rather, categorical representation is graded. Graded membership means that the category members vary in terms of how well they fit into the category. Category members are occasionally misclassified but at the same time, highly typical category members are rarely mistaken and are considered to be good examples of the target category.

For example, consider a really common category like a "dog". Whereas it may be impossible to decide on a set of necessary and sufficient conditions, it is straightforward to arrive at a set of **characteristic features** for the dog category. Dogs usually have tails, they usually bark, have four legs, they usually have fur, etc. If one of these features is missing it may reduce the typicality of that dog but it doesn't disqualify them from being members of the dog category. A small Chihuahua may be hairless and much smaller than many other dogs, but we don't consider it a member of a different category. You may have seen a dog with a missing leg, but even though it doesn't have the characteristic feature of "four legs" we don't consider it to be any less of a dog.

However, it is possible to imagine that some dogs possess most of the characteristic features: they are medium in size, have four legs, have a tail, and bark. A golden retriever might be a good example of a highly typical dog that has many of these characteristic features. It is also likely that a dog like this might be classified as a member of the dog category just a little bit faster and more readily than a small, hairless Chihuahua. The probabilistic view would argue that both are members of the dog category, but the golden retriever is more typical, and therefore a better example. If you are going to make a misclassification, you have a higher probability of making a mistake with Chihuahua than with golden retriever.

In the probabilistic views, the typical exemplars or category members are recognized more quickly because they share more features with other category members. In a sense, the typical category member is closer to the centre of the category. And an analogous effect might be observed with the exceptional category members. A very atypical member of a category (like bats as atypical mammals or even as atypical birds if your category for "bird" is based on observable features) is really an outlier. It really is the case that the bat is a lousy member of the mammal category. It looks like a bird, acts like a bird, and cannot see very well. A probabilistic categorization system would assume that bats will be misclassified and will present people with some difficulty. It is plausible that our own inability to classify them readily corresponds to the fact that bats are often feared. Perhaps we fear the bat because they do not fit into a simple, basic category very easily.

But how is this graded typicality structure, which is inherent in the categories, represented in the mind as a concept? The probabilistic view can be instantiated in a number of ways. Traditionally, there have been two opposing accounts. The **prototype theory** assumes that the category is represented by a central tendency known as a prototype. The **exemplar theory** assumes that the category is represented by many stored memory traces, referred to as exemplars. Both of these accounts make similar predictions, but they differ in terms of how much individual information is stored versus how much categorical information is stored. I discuss both accounts below.

The **prototype view** assumes that a category of things is represented in the mind as a prototype. The prototype is assumed to be a summary representation of the category. This can be either an average of the totality of the category members, some kind of list of frequently occurring features, or even an ideal (Murphy, 2002). According to this view, objects are classified by comparing them to the prototype. An object is classified into the category with the most similar prototype to it.

Although Rosch's work on family resemblances inspired prototype theory, the strongest evidence for a prototype representation comes from experimental research with prototype abstraction. One common paradigm, which dates back to the late 1960s and early 1970s, attempted to show how people can abstract a prototype from experience

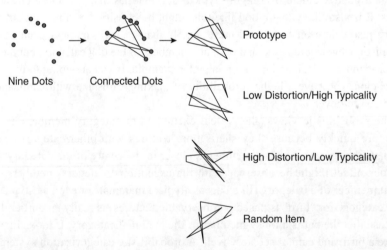

Random Dot Polygons

Nine Dots   Connected Dots

Prototype

Low Distortion/High Typicality

High Distortion/Low Typicality

Random Item

Figure 4.6 An example of some of the kinds of random dot polygons used by researchers like Posner and Keele (1968) and many others. The original prototype is made by selecting 9 coordinates on a screen or an XY space. Subjects are usually trained on distortion of the original shape. Subjects are typically not shown the prototype during training.

with individual stimuli. The basic paradigm asks participants to view a set of novel, visual stimuli until they have formed a conceptual representation of the training set. Later, participants view additional stimuli and then classify them as members (or not) of the category that they just learned about. These are novel, somewhat arbitrary categories, but they do have some internal structure and the task is designed to allow participants to discover the internal structure in an unsupervised manner, similar to how natural categories might be learned.

Subjects are asked to view 40 (or more) training exemplars like those shown in Figure 4.6. Each one of these polygons is generated from a single configuration of nine dots on the screen. The dots can be connected with a line to form the polygon (as shown in the three figures at the very top). This original configuration is the prototype that is used to generate all the other stimuli. In order to generate test stimuli, the researcher relies on an algorithm that jitters the location of each of the dots or points on the figure. In order to create an object that looks a lot like the prototype but not quite, the algorithm would move the location of each dot just a little bit. The resulting shape resembles the prototype but is not exactly the same as the prototype. Think of the Big Dipper constellation with the stars being analogous to the dots in this figure. If you move those stars a little bit, the constellation would still resemble the Big Dipper, but would be just a little bit different. Using this algorithm, the researcher creates a set of stimuli that are all similar to the prototype, but not exactly like it.

In a standard version of the task, participants view the training stimuli over many trials. Each time they see an image, they are asked to study it for a few seconds until they see the next image. After many presentations of images, it is assumed that participants have abstracted something about the whole category of images that they have just experienced. As an analogue, imagine that you did not know anything at all about song birds: you have never seen any birds at all, either live or in picture form. Now imagine that someone shows you several hundred pictures of songbirds. Even if you never knew anything about this category, you would probably abstract something about the category from viewing these pictures. The nine-dot polygon task works in roughly the same way.

After training, and after category abstraction, participants are tested with additional stimuli. Some of these test stimuli are copies of the same stimuli the subjects were trained on, but others are new examples. In keeping with the bird example, this would be like being shown pictures of some of the birds you studied along with new birds that vary in terms of similarity to pictures of the training birds. The test examples include many new stimuli with high similarity to the prototype, new stimuli with low similarity to the prototype and new random patterns that have no connection to the original prototype. Crucially, some of the new test stimuli are the actual prototype of the category. This is the original pattern that was used to create the stimuli, but it was never actually presented during the learning phase. If subjects abstracted a prototype from their exemplar experience, then

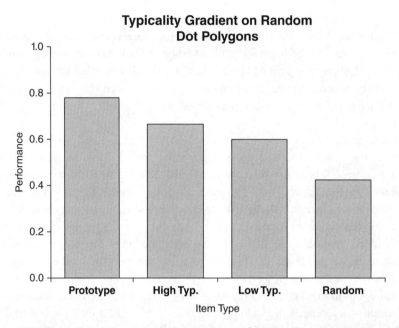

Figure 4.7 This figure shows the average dot pattern performance by control subjects from Knowlton and Squire (1993) along with the subjects in two papers by Reber and colleagues (Reber, Stark, & Squire, 1998a, 1998b). The performance on the prototype pattern is best, followed by performance on high typicality items, low typicality items, and random items.

they should be able to recognize the prototype during the test phase, even though they never saw that original prototype. If we measured participants' responses to each kind of stimuli, we should find a pattern in which the (previously unseen) prototype and the high typicality exemplars are strongly endorsed as being category members whereas the low typicality exemplars are not endorsed.

Across many studies and experiments, this is exactly the pattern the has been found. Figure 4.7 shows the performances of subjects from several different experiments (Minda & Smith, 2011). What is clear is that performance on the prototype items, which were never seen during the learning phase, is quite strong and exceeds the performance on other new stimuli. In addition, a clear typicality gradient is seen for all new items such that typical items, those with some higher level of similarity to the prototype, are endorsed more strongly that those with lower typicality. The ubiquity of this pattern across many dozens of studies has supported the idea that, for some kinds of categories, learning new categories involves a prototype abstraction process (Knowlton, Ramus, & Squire, 1992; Minda & Smith, 2011; Smith, 2002; Smith & Minda, 2002; Smith, Redford, & Haas, 2008).

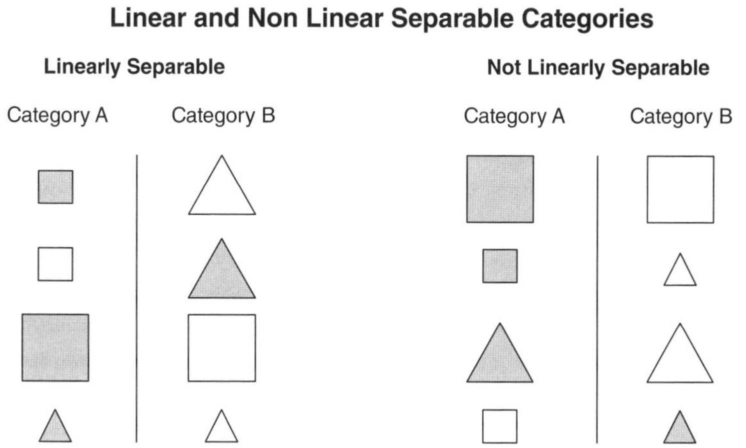

Linear and Non Linear Separable Categories

Linearly Separable			Not Linearly Separable	
Category A	Category B		Category A	Category B

Figure 4.8 An example of simple categories that can either be linearly separable or non-linearly separable. In both cases, each category contains four objects out of eight possible objects. Objects differ along three dimensions of size, colour, and shape.

An alternative to the prototype account is **exemplar theory** (Hintzman, 1986; Hintzman & Ludlam, 1980; Medin & Schaffer, 1978; Nosofsky, 1986, 1987). In this account, we assume that categories are represented in the mind as exemplar traces in memory. In other words, there need not be an additional abstraction, as in the prototype model, but instead the similarity among memory traces for the individual things allows us to treat them as members of the same category. Rather than classify an animal as a "dog" because of its similarity with an abstraction, we classify it as such because it is similar to many things that we have already classified as a dog.

This is an approach that has strong appeal because it eliminates the need for an abstraction process during acquisition. Because decisions are based on similarity to individual items stored in memory, the exemplar approach makes many of the same predictions that the prototype model makes. In some cases, the exemplar model makes some predictions that the prototype model cannot make. One example is known as **linear separability** (Medin & Schwanenflugel, 1981; Minda & Smith, 2011; Smith & Minda, 1998; Smith, Murray, & Minda, 1997). A category set that is linearly separable is one for which some linear function (a line, a plane, or even a more complicated function) can partition the objects into the correct categories. Consider a collection of eight objects that vary by size, colour and shape, and imagine partitioning them into two groups (Figure 4.8). If you have a set of small, red, square objects and a set of larger, white, triangle objects, these can be separated linearly by partitioning the space along those three dimensions. Note that the set of linearly separable categories shown in Figure 4.8 do not have a perfect rule, but the objects share a family resemblance with each other. However, if you have a category set with all of the red objects and the small white square in one category and all of the white objects and the small red triangle in the other, it would not be possible to defend a linear boundary. Thus, this set is considered to be non-linearly separable.

One thing that should be immediately clear from Figure 4.8 is that both categories seem equally learnable. Neither have very strong family resemblance but neither set looks particularly difficult either. In experimental settings, the non-linearly separable categories are no more difficult to learn than the linearly separable categories (Medin & Schwanenflugel, 1981; Nosofsky, 1987). However, the prototype model cannot learn non-linearly separable categories, but an exemplar model, relying on the assumption that classification is based on remembered exemplar traces, can. And research has generally confirmed this prediction (with some caveats that will be discussed later) (Nosofsky, 1987, 1992, 2011).

Although the example above seems contrived, there are at least two things that are worth considering. First, contrived or not, people do not seem to have any special difficulty with these non-linearly separable categories. This suggests that the cognitive mechanisms that support category learning are not necessarily hampered by the non-linear nature of the category partition. Second, think about a category like mammals, for which dolphins are a clear outlier. They do not share many overt features with other mammals, and share considerable properties with members of the fish category. To the extent that natural and artifactual categories may exist in many forms, it seems reasonable that we may not be constrained to just learn prototypes, but also rely on exemplar learning to deal with these kinds of irregular categories (the exemplar process might be well suited to many regular categories as well).

As mentioned earlier, there are some limits to how well people can learn non-linearly separable categories. Several studies have found that as category size and complexity increases, so does the reliance on a linear reparability constraint (Minda & Smith, 2001; Smith & Minda, 1998; Smith et al., 1997). In this case, not only did subjects find the linearly separable categories to be easier to learn, but they also learned to classify the prototype and high typicality items very well, and simultaneously misclassified exceptional items (think of someone always classifying the dolphin as a fish). This pattern is more consistent with the prototype approach, and Smith and Minda (1998) argue that for many categories, prototype abstraction plays an important role, especially in the early stages of acquisition, before the learner can learn the specific exemplars for exceptional stimuli.

In summary, there is considerable evidence that people make use of many different kinds of representations when learning new categories. Depending on the nature and structure of the category to be learned, people may rely on learning rules, abstracting prototypes, or learning exemplars.

The theory view

The classical and the probabilistic views are very much concerned with how new concepts are learned and represented, but a common criticism is that much of the research that has supported this theory has tended to rely on artificial concepts and categories (Murphy, 2002; Murphy & Medin, 1985). An alternative is often called the **theory view**.

According to proponents of this view, concepts and categories are learned in the context of pre-existing knowledge and one's own naïve theories about the world. For example, when I am learning about a new kind of winter squash (like a hubbard squash, for example), I am not just seeing squashes, classifying them, and receiving feedback. Rather, I am relating them to what I already know. I might note that it is like a pumpkin, and so I already expect certain features to be presented. The pre-existing knowledge helps to activate and prioritize features.

This view also suggests that attributes and features may be correlated (Murphy & Medin, 1985). For example, with respect to the category of birds, many common features, such as "has wings" and "flies", co-occur very often. These features might be said to be correlated. According to the theory view, we understand these correlations as being meaningful. That is, we don't just recognize the correlated structure; we understand why the features are correlated. Having wings allows you to fly. On the surface, this interpretation is very straightforward and intuitive, and yet neither the prototype model nor the exemplar model is readily able to account for knowledge about future correlations.

Furthermore, because the theory view relies on knowledge about objects and concepts, rather than just similarity, it may be able to account for some curious findings in which people often seem to ignore their own similarity judgements. In a study by Rips (1989), subjects were asked to consider a 3-inch round object and two possible comparison categories, that of a quarter and a pizza, as shown in Figure 4.9. One group of subjects was asked to make similarity judgements, and to rate the similarity between the 3-inch round object and either the quarter or the pizza. Not surprisingly, subjects rated the 3-inch round object to be more similar to quarter. However, when subjects were asked to indicate which category they thought the 3-inch object belonged in, they overwhelmingly chose pizza. There are two reasons for this.

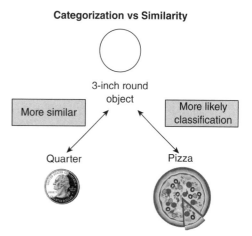

Categorization vs Similarity

Figure 4.9 An example of an experiment by Rips (1989) in which participants were asked about the similarity between the three-inch round object and a quarter and the same object and a pizza.

The first is that pizza has much greater variability than the quarter. Although three inches is a very small pizza, it could plausibly be a member of that category. The quarter category has very little variability and also has some very specific characteristics. Quarters must be made of quarter material and must be minted by the appropriate government authorities. They have heads and tails. In short, although they may be more similar in size to the 3-inch round object, people are unable to classify the 3-inch round object as a member of the quarter category because they know what it means to be a quarter. Only quarters can be quarters and only subjects with that knowledge would be able to make that judgement. As with the case of correlated attributes, a prototype or an exemplar model, both of which emphasize similarity, would not handle this result easily. The theory view does.

SUMMARY

Thinking – solving problems, arriving at conclusions, and making decisions – relies on well-structured mental representations. Concepts allow us to predict things, to infer missing features and to draw conclusions. If we perceive something that fits into an existing concept or category, we have access to most of the important things we know about the objects by virtue of the concepts. Once an object is classified as a member of a category, the object can inherit or take on properties that are associated with the many other objects in the same category. Concepts are the result of organized memory and as such concepts allow memories to be used effectively to guide behaviour. The previous chapters (on similarity and memory) were both about basic, fundamental cognitive processes and mechanisms. But the study of concepts offers a way to understand how knowledge and memory are optimized for adaptive thinking. Concepts allow memories and knowledge to be used efficiently and effectively at the service of other kinds of thinking.

In subsequent chapters, we will see the importance of concepts in thinking. For example, in Chapter 5 on language and thinking, one of the key ideas deals with the linguistic boundaries that define one set of things (basic colours or household objects, for example). Induction (Chapter 6) involves the use of concepts to make inferences and predications on the basis of category membership. Deductive logic (Chapter 7) often involves drawing a conclusion or evaluating a drawn conclusion about a whole class of things: a categorical argument. Categories and concepts play a role in problem-solving and decision-making in terms of providing a frame. Concepts provide the coherence to our experience, which is needed for thinking.

5 LANGUAGE AND THOUGHT

So far in this book I have been discussing the structure of mental representations and how these representations might affect the thinking process. The chapters on similarity, attention, semantic memory, and concepts were all concerned with this topic. You probably have a good idea about how complex thought and cognition depend very much on having well-formed mental representations. In this chapter, however, we are going to take a much closer look at how this interaction between representation and behaviour works. Specifically, this chapter will examine the interaction between language and thinking.

The psychology of language is a great place to start because language is a uniquely human behaviour. Of course, other animals communicate with each other. Sophisticated communication is seen in bees, for example, as bees rely on a system of dances and wiggles to communicate the location of nectar to other bees in the colony (Frisch, 1967). When a honey bee returns from a nectar location, it performs a dance that corresponds precisely to the direction it flew and how long it was flying. The bee is not thinking. The bee has little choice in terms of whether or not to do the dance. The bee would perform this dance even if no other bees were watching. Song birds obviously have a well-developed and highly evolved system of mating and warning songs. These bird songs are unique to each species and require exposure to other bird song in order to be acquired. Dogs communicate with barks, growls, yelps, and the wagging of tails. And anyone with a dog knows that dogs respond to human language and non-verbal cues. Even my cat *sort of* responds to some verbal and non-verbal cues.

These are all sophisticated means of communication, but we do not consider these to be "language" *per se*. Unlike human language, communication in these non-human species is fairly limited and direct. Bee dances have only one function: signalling the location of food. Bird song has a set function related to mating and even though birds require some exposure to other birds song, a bird can only learn its own song. Highly intelligent birds, like the African Grey parrot, can learn to mimic the language of humans, but they are not using human language to carry on casual conversation or to advance an agenda. Even dogs, which are capable of very complex behaviours, are really not able to use communication abilities to consider new ideas, to solve complex problems, and to tell stories. The great apes, specifically bonobos and orangutans, are known to be able to learn complex symbol systems. But they are not using language to direct their behaviours in the way that humans can. In other words, non-human communication and "language-like behaviour" is used primarily to engage in direct communication or as a response to an external stimuli. Non-human language-like behaviour is not tied to thinking in the way that human language is. In this way, human language is remarkable and unique.

BOX 5.1

Some great apes have learned to use communication systems that are very close to a simple natural language that might be seen in humans. The most famous of these are Kanzi, a male bonobo, and Koko, a female western lowland gorilla. Kanzi learned to communicate from observing his mother as she was being trained on a symbolic keyboard communication system. Sue Savage-Rumbaugh has studied Kanzi for decades and, to date, her research team has provided fairly consistent evidence that Kanzi uses his language productively. It is estimated that he has a vocabulary and syntax comparable to a human toddler, and he continues to acquire new phrases, concepts, and uses for his language. Kanzi's abilities far outshine any of the other bonobo chimpanzees in his colony.

Unlike the symbolic keyboard that Kanzi uses, Koko the gorilla communicates via a sign language. Koko has been shown to express herself with this sign language. Her primary trainer, Francine Patterson, has indicated many other complex cognitive behaviours as well.

Despite these successes, the study of language acquisition in great apes has met with a fair amount of criticism and scepticism. The strongest criticism is that despite the clear cognitive sophistication of these apes, the vast majority of their communication is not arbitrary and productive, but consists of direct requests and responses. In other words, unlike humans, great apes do not seem to spend much time engaging in small talk. A more serious criticism concerns the relationship between the teacher/trainer and the animal. Critics have pointed out that many of Koko's communicative successes could be the result of interpretation on the part of Koko's teacher. This in no way detracts from the clear intellect that both Koko and Kanzi display, but it does suggest that even in these most extraordinary cases their language use is still quite limited. You can read much more about this controversy in an excellent, critical article published in *Slate* magazine in 2014 (Hu, 2014).

One of the big questions that psychologists interested in this field want to answer is *"Do we think in language?"* Like many of the other questions that we have been trying to answer, this one is simultaneously trivial and nearly unanswerable. On the one hand, of course we think in something like a natural language. We plan what we are going to say, we ruminate over things that have been said to us, we consider alternatives, we plan actions and think about how these actions will affect things around us. Most of this kind of thinking takes place in explicit conscious awareness with a heavy reliance on an "inner voice" (a part of the working memory system that was covered in Chapter 3). On the other hand, many of our actions and behaviours are influenced by non-conscious computations, and are the result of System 1 thought (Evans, 2003, 2008; Evans & Stanovich, 2013). Rapid, intuitive decisions are made without much or without any influence of the inner voice. For the most part, the influential, **dual-system approach** that we discussed in Chapter 1 (also known as the **default-interventionist** approach) is built on the idea that non-conscious or intuitive processes drive many thinking behaviours, and these often need to be overridden by conscious, linguistically influenced thought.

WHAT IS LANGUAGE?

It is clearly beyond the scope of this text to answer definitively the question of what language is and is not. That is not only too big a topic, but it is an entire field of study. But we do need to have some basic definition of human language in order to understand the interaction between language and thinking.

Early in the history of cognitive psychology, the linguist Charles Hockett described 13 characteristics of human languages (Hockett, 1960). This list of design features is a reasonable starting point. Figure 5.1 shows the complete list of the 13 characteristics, along with a brief description of each feature. These are all features of human language that suggest a unique and highly evolved system designed for communication with others and also with the self (e.g., thinking). Let's consider a few of them in more detail. For example, language is a behaviour that has **total feedback**. Whatever you say or vocalize you can also hear. You receive feedback that is directly related to what you intended to say. According to Hockett, this is necessary for human thinking. It does not take much imagination to consider how this direct feedback might have evolved into the internalization of speech, which is necessary for many complex thinking behaviours.

Language is also **productive**. With human language, we can express an infinite number of things and ideas. There is no limit to what we can say, what we can express, or, for that matter, what we can think. But this can be achieved within a finite system. We can say things that have never been said before, yet the English language has only 26 letters. There are about 24 consonant phonemes in English and, depending on the dialect and accent, there are roughly 20 vowel phonemes. Even when allowing for every variation among different speakers and accents, it is clear that this is a very limited set of units.

Thirteen Design Features (from Hockett, 1960)

Vocal/auditory channel	Communication involves transfer between the vocal and auditory apparatus.
Broadcast transmission/directional reception	The signal can be sent out in many directions, but is perceived in one direction.
Rapid fading, transitoriness	The verbal signal fades quickly.
Interchangeability	A speaker of a language can reproduce any message he or she can understand.
Total feedback	The speaker hears everything he or she says.
Specialization	The vocal apparatus used in speech is specialized for speech production.
Semanticity	Language has semantic content.
Arbitrariness	The signal need not refer to a physical characteristic of the referent.
Discreteness	Language is composed of a discrete, finite set of units.
Displacement	Language can refer to things that are not immediately present.
Productivity	The finite set of units is capable of producing an infinite set of ideas.
Traditional transmission	Language is transmitted by traditional teaching, learning, and observation.
Duality of patterning	A small number of meaningless units combined to produce meaning.

Figure 5.1 This is a list of design features for a natural language. The list is not exclusive, but provides an excellent overview of what language is and is not, and what language can do and what it cannot do.

However, the combination of these units allows for almost anything to be expressed. The phonemes combine into words, phrases, and sentences according to the rules of the language's grammar, to produce an extremely productive system. Contrast this with the kind of communication that non-human species engage in. Birds, bees, and canines are very communicative, but the range of content is limited severely by instinct and design.

Another characteristic of human language is that it is somewhat **arbitrary**. There does not need to be a correspondence between the sound of a word and the idea that it expresses. There is a small set of exceptions, words that are meant to sound like the idea, but this is a very limited subset. For the most part, the sounds that we use to express an idea bear no relationship to the concrete aspects of the idea. They are, in fact, mental symbols that can link together percepts and concepts.

To summarize, for our purposes, language is a discrete, arbitrary, and productive system of symbols that are used to express ideas, to communicate, and to engage in many kinds of explicitly governed thought.

UNDERSTANDING LANGUAGE AS COGNITION

Language is a remarkably complex set of behaviours. At its core, the challenge of understanding language as a cognitive behaviour is trying to understand how humans are able to produce language such that an idea or thought can be converted into speech sounds that can then be perceived by another person and converted back into an idea. Communicative language is essentially a "thought transmission system". One uses language to transmit an idea to another person.

The linguistic duality between ideas and how they are expressed is often described as a relationship between the surface structure of communication and the deep structure. **Surface structure** refers to the words that are used, spoken sound, phrases, word order, written letters, etc. The surface structure is what we produce when we speak and what we perceive when we hear. **Deep structure**, on the other hand, refers to the underlying meaning and semantics of a linguistic entity. These are the thoughts or ideas that you wish to convey via some surface structure. These are the thoughts or ideas that you try to perceive via that surface structure.

One of the challenges in terms of understanding this relationship between surface and deep structure is that very often a direct correspondence seems elusive. For example, sometimes different kinds of surface structure give rise to the same deep structure. You can say "*This class is boring*" or "*This is a boring class*" and the underlying deep structure will be the same despite the slight difference in surface structure. Human language is flexible enough to allow for many ways to say the same thing. The bigger problem comes when the same surface structure can refer to different deep structures. For example, you can say "*Visiting professors can be very interesting*". In this case, a deep structure that follows from this statement is that when your class is taught by a visitor – a visiting professor – it is sure to be interesting because *visiting professors can be interesting*. Another deep structure that comes from exactly the same statement is that attending a party or function at a professor's house is sure to be an interesting event because *visiting professors can be interesting*. The surrounding context makes it easier, but also suggests a challenge when trying to map surface structure to deep structure.

Ambiguity in language

Language is full of ambiguity and understanding how our cognitive system resolves that ambiguity is an incredible challenge. I recently saw a headline from the Associated Press regarding a story about commercial potato farmers. It read "*McDonald's fries the Holy Grail for potato farmers*". It may look funny, but most of us are quickly able to understand the deep structure here. They are not frying the Holy Grail. Rather, the headline writer uses the term "Holy Grail" as a metaphor for something that is often elusive, but ultimately an incredible prize. In order to understand this sentence we need to read it, construct an interpretation, decide if that interpretation is correct, activate concepts about the Holy Grail, activate the knowledge of the metaphoric use of that statement, and finally construct a new interpretation of this sentence. This usually happens in a few seconds and will happen almost immediately when dealing with spoken language – an impressive feat of cognition.

Often, when the surface structure leads to the wrong deep structure it is referred to as a **garden path** sentence. The garden path metaphor itself comes from the notion of taking a walk in a formal garden along a path that either leads to a dead-end or to an unexpected or surprise ending. And that's how garden path sentences work. The most well-known example is the sentence "*The horse raced past the barn fell*" (Bever, 1970). When most people read this sentence, it simply does not make sense. Or rather, it makes sense right up to the word "*barn*". As soon as you read the word "*fell*", your understanding of the sentence plummets. The explanation is that as we hear a sentence, we construct a mental model of the idea. Various theories have referred to this as sentence parsing (Frazier & Rayner, 1982), or constraint satisfaction (MacDonald, Pearlmutter, & Seidenberg, 1994). The details of those contrasting theories are beyond the scope of our discussion, but the central issue remains that the representations are constructed as we hear them. As soon as you hear "*The horse raced*" you construct a mental model of a horse that was racing. You also generate an expectation or inference that something might come after. When you hear "*past*" you generate a prediction that the horse raced past a thing, which turns out to be "*the barn*". It is a complete idea. So when you hear the word "*fell*" it does not fit with the semantics or the syntactic structure that you created.

However, this sentence is grammatically correct and it does have a proper interpretation. It works within a specific context. Suppose that you are going to evaluate some horses. You ask the person at the stable to race the horses to see how well they run. The horse that was raced past the house did fine, but *the horse raced past the barn fell*. In this context, the garden path sentence makes sense. It is still an ill-conceived sentence, but it is comprehensible in this case.

Linguistic inferences

Very often we have to rely on inferences, context, and our own semantic memory in order to deal with ambiguity and understand the deep structure. The same inferential process also comes into play when interpreting the deeper meaning behind seemingly unambiguous sentences. We generate inferences to aid our understanding and these can also direct our thinking. For example, in the United States a very popular news outlet is the Fox News Network. When the network launched in the early 2000s, its original slogan was "*Fair and Balanced News*". There is nothing wrong with wanting to be fair and balanced: that is an admirable attribute in a news organization. But think for a minute about this statement. One possible inference is that if Fox News is "fair and balanced", then perhaps its competitors are unfair and unbalanced. It may not explicitly say that, but it may not hurt Fox News' reputation if you make that inference on your own.

In 2003, I was a postdoctoral fellow and was attending interviews at many universities, seeking a faculty position. I was interviewed at many places in the United States, which made sense because I was born and raised in the United States, I went to school in the United States, and I was a postdoc in the United States. But like most prospective academics, I considered positions in many geographic areas, including Canada. One interview took place in March 2003 at the University of Western Ontario (which is where I work now). March 2003 also happened to be the month when the United States launched what it called the "*Shock and Awe*" campaign in Iraq. Not only was this a very big news event, but I followed it more closely than I might have otherwise done because the campaign began on the very day that I left the United States and flew to Canada for my interview. On the one hand, I felt a little awkward being outside the country and being interviewed at a Canadian institution when my own country's government had just launched an attack that was still controversial. On the other hand, it gave me a chance to see news coverage of this event from a non-US perspective. Remember that in 2003, although many people were getting news from the internet, it was still relatively uncommon to read or see coverage from media in other parts of the world. Most of us received our news via television.

One of the things that struck me as being surprising was the terminology used by most newscasters in the United States versus the terminology used by newscasters in Canada. In the United States, media referred to this as the "*War in Iraq*". In Canada, the newscasters were referring to it as the "*War on Iraq*". That single letter change from "*in*" to "*on*" makes an incredible difference.

In the former case, you are fighting a war against an enemy that just happens to be in Iraq. The war is not against the country of Iraq or ordinary Iraqis, and indeed you might be helping Iraqis fight a war that they wanted to fight anyway. I think that is exactly how media outlets in the United States wanted this to be perceived.

The Canadian government did not support this war, and the news outlets referred to it as a war on Iraq, suggesting that the United States had essentially declared war on another sovereign country. One could argue that neither term was exactly correct, but the only point I wish to make here is that how the war was being discussed is going to have an effect on how it is perceived. It was not at all uncommon (at the time) for many Americans to feel that this was a well-justified military exercise that ultimately was about fighting international terrorists who happened to be based in Iraq. In other words, the US did not declare war on Iraq; the war was just being fought there. How we describe things, and how we talk about them, can absolutely influence how others think about them.

Memory

The interaction between thought and language is complex, and many studies have shown that language use affects the structure and nature of mental representations and the output of many thinking behaviours. Let's consider a classic and well-known example. The eyewitness testimony research conducted by Elizabeth Loftus in the 1970s shows that language use can affect the content of episodic memory (Loftus & Palmer, 1974). In a series of studies, Loftus investigated how memory can be manipulated and affected by the questions that are being asked. In the most well-known example, subjects were shown videos of car accidents and were asked about these accidents in follow-up questions. The general procedure might be close to what happens when the police are interviewing eyewitnesses about an event.

The accident that subjects were shown was relatively straightforward. It depicted two cars intersecting on a city street. After watching the video, subjects were asked to estimate how fast they thought the cars were going when they intersected. But they were not asked with the term "*intersected*". Subjects instead were asked with one of five words: "*collided*", "*smashed*", "*bumped*", "*hit*", or "*contacted*". In other words, all of the subjects saw exactly the same video and were asked about it with the same question, except for the use of a different verb.

When subjects were asked to estimate the speed, not surprisingly those who were asked about how fast the cars were going when they "*smashed*" into each other estimated higher speeds than those who were asked to say how fast the cars were going when they "*bumped*" or "*hit*" each other. That one word change seemed to have an effect on subjects' memory. All subjects saw the same video and the language manipulation did not occur until afterwards. So the initial encoding of memory should have been the same. But when the memories were retrieved and subjects were asked to make an estimate, the language that was used in the question changed their estimate.

Additional questions revealed that the memories may have been forever tainted by that initial question. A week later, subjects were asked if they remembered any broken glass. The key thing to remember in this particular study is that there was no broken glass in the actual video. However, subjects who were asked to estimate speed with the term "*smashed*" were significantly more likely to falsely remember broken glass. Of course, Loftus argued that these kinds of memory errors present a problem for eyewitness testimony because questioning can affect the nature of the memory. It is not a stretch at all to imagine that a detective or police officer, even without meaning to, would permanently affect the status of the memory depending on how the eyewitness was questioned. In other words, in this example, language clearly is having an effect on the mental representations that are being used to answer the questions later on.

Analogy and metaphor

Language can also be used effectively via analogy and metaphor to guide understanding. A good analogy relates concepts that may have a similar deep structure even though they may be different on the surface. Generally, the listener or receiver of the analogy has to attend to the deeper structure to realize these similarities. In the simplest form, if you know that Y is good, and you were told that X is analogous to Y, you infer that there is also something good about X. More concretely, consider an often-cited example: "An atom is like the solar system" (Gentner, 1983). At a certain age, early in primary school, most children have some knowledge about the solar system. They are aware that the sun is large and sits at the centre, that planets revolve around the sun, and that possibly some physical force allows this orbit to exist. Presumably, they know less about atomic structure, but knowing that an atom is like the solar system encourages the understanding that each atom has a nucleus and is surrounded by electrons. Also, some physical force allows this structure to be maintained. These two things are very different on the surface, but there are functional and deep similarities that can be explained and understood via metaphor and analogy. In this case, the analogy allows some of the properties of one domain (the solar system) to extend to another domain (the atom). Just as the sun keeps the planets in orbit via the force of gravity, so too does the nucleus keep the electron in check with the Coulomb force.

Conceptual metaphor

The linguist George Lakoff has suggested that conceptual metaphors play a big role in how a society thinks of itself, and in politics (Lakoff, 1987; Lakoff & Johnson, 1980). I gave the example earlier of a war in Iraq versus the war on Iraq, each of which creates a different metaphor. One is an aggressive action against or on a country; the other is an aggressive act taking place in a country. Lakoff argues that these conceptual metaphors constrain and influence the thinking process. He gives the example of an "*argument*". One conceptual metaphor for arguments is that an argument is like a war. If you think of arguments in this way, you might say things like "*I shot down his arguments*", or "*watch this guy totally destroy climate change denial in two minutes*". These statements are likely to arise from a conceptual metaphor of arguments as some kind of analogy for warfare. Lakoff also suggests another metaphor for argument – that it is a game of chance. In this case, people might say things like, "*you win some, you lose some*". Lakoff suggests that there is an interaction between a given conceptual metaphor and produced statements and utterances and that this interaction relates to how we understand the world.

There are other examples as well. We generally think of money as a limited resource and a valuable commodity. By analogy, we often think of time in the same way. As such, many of the statements that we make about time reflect this relationship. We might say "*You're wasting my time*" or "*I need to budget my time better*" or "*this gadget is a real time-saver*". According to Lakoff, we say the things we do because we have these underlying conceptual metaphors, and these metaphors are part of our culture.

Sometimes metaphors can show real measurable differences in terms of behaviour. A great study by Kempton (1986) investigated the real-world consequences of a metaphor period. He used the example of residential thermostats. He reasoned that home heating systems are relatively simple and are familiar to most people. Even if you don't own your own home right now, you probably grew up in a home with a thermostat that could be used to adjust the temperature. If you live in an apartment, or a university residence hall, you may also have a thermostat that allows you to control the temperature of the room. Kempton pointed out that many people must have some understanding of how the thermostat works because they typically have to adjust them several times a day or at least several times a week. (This excludes the current versions of thermostats which are highly programmable or the so-called "smart" thermostats which eventually learn to adjust home temperature automatically.) Kempton argued that there are broadly defined metaphors or **folk theories** for how the thermostat works. He referred to one as the "feedback theory", which suggests that the thermostat senses the temperature and turns the furnace on or off to maintain that set temperature. He referred to the other as the "valve theory", which holds that the thermostat actually controls the amount of heat coming out – like a valve. A higher setting releases higher heat. Only one of these is correct, the feedback theory, but Kempton observed that not only were both of these theories present, sometimes within the same household, but both had an effect on actual thermostat adjustment behaviour. People who seemed to rely on the valve theory tended to make more extreme adjustments than people who relied on the feedback theory. Kempton also found that people who subscribed to this valve theory tended to make more adjustments. More adjustments translate to higher energy use. In other words, a misunderstanding of how the thermostat works, having the wrong metaphor or analogy for how it works, can have measurable differences in terms of behaviour and energy use.

Universal cognitive metaphors

Others have suggested that across many languages and cultures there seem to exist **universal cognitive metaphors**. In many cases, these reflect a conceptual similarity between a physical thing and a psychological concept. For example, there are many metaphors that relate to the idea of happiness being "up". People can be said to be *upbeat* or *feeling down* if they are not happy, music can be *up tempo*, a *smile is up*, a *frown is down*. All of these idioms and statements come from this same metaphor. Other examples reflect the idea that consciousness is "up". You *wake up*, you *go down for nap*, etc. Another common metaphor is that control is like being above something. You can be "*on top of the situation*", you are in charge of people who "*work under you*", the Rolling Stones recorded a popular song called "*Under my thumb*". These cognitive metaphors are common in English, but they are common in many other languages as well. This suggests that there is a universality to these metaphors, and a commonality among cultures between language and thought.

One possible explanation for the universality of these metaphors is that they are all tied to a physical state of being. The notion of consciousness being "up" relates easily to the notion of standing up when you are awake. If you overpower someone in a physical confrontation, you may find yourself literally on top of them. You may have to hold the other person down. This physiological connection between being on top and being in power helps to explain why these kinds of metaphors are universal and not tied to a specific language.

Definitions

The definitions that we choose for common terms and words can have an effect on how we think about these things. In essence, defining the word involves mapping all of the possible cases. This can be incredibly challenging, as many things with the same name might end up having very little in common with all of the possible cases. Still, definitions are important, especially in legal, medical, and political environments. As an extreme example, consider that until 1973 the American Psychiatric Association defined homosexuality as a mental illness. By defining it as a mental illness, the APA implies that homosexuality is a problem that may or may not require treatment. We do not think about homosexuality this way anymore, but this definition's legacy may be with us for a long time.

BOX 5.2

Homosexual behaviour had been considered a crime and mental illness for many years, but by the end of the 1960s perceptions had changed. People in the United States were becoming more liberal with respect to sexual themes. By the 1970s, many gay psychiatrists were becoming dissatisfied with the state of the definition, and during this era the APA held an annual convention in San Francisco where the leadership was confronted with many prominent gay activists. At the time, the chair of the APA's committee on nomenclature, which is the committee that oversees classifications and naming, was charged with revising the initial version of

(Continued)

(Continued)

the *Diagnostic and Statistical Manual for Mental Disorders*, or DSM. The committee demonstrated that there were no data to link homosexuality and mental illness. In a key vote in December 1973, the Board of Trustees voted, in a very closely watched meeting, to endorse the recommendation to remove the definition. The Board's decision to delete homosexuality from the diagnostic manual was supported by 58% of the membership.

In the twenty-first century, when many countries now permit same-sex marriage, the idea of classifying homosexuality as a mental illness might seem outrageous. But the closeness of the vote and the difficulties of changing the definition within the psychiatric community reflect just how hard it is for a culture to change a societal definition.

Context and contrasts

Take a few moments to think about all the different ways in which linguistic context can change how you think about an event or thing. If you scored poorly on an exam and you called your parents to let them know, they might be a little bit disappointed. If you presented that same news in the context of how well you scored on an exam in another class, it might change the way they interpreted the bad news about the poor grade. Similarly, consider the process that many homebuyers go through when they are shopping for their first home or residence. You might go to see three houses, each of which has a market value of $400,000. If you see two that are listed at $480,000 and $460,000 respectively, and a third which is listed at $406,000, that third house will stand out as either a bargain or possibly a risk. Seen by itself, the price might be right. Viewed in the context of two higher-priced but very similar homes, it stands out. Language helps to direct thinking in this case by changing the perception of one of the individual things.

LINGUISTIC RELATIVITY AND LINGUISTIC DETERMINISM

The discussions above illustrate many of the ways in which language influences how you remember things, how you think about things, and how you make decisions. In short, it is clear that language and linguistic context have an effect on thinking. The strongest form of this claim is often referred to as **linguistic relativity**, and is also sometimes referred to as the "**Sapir–Whorf hypothesis**", after Edward Sapir and his student Benjamin Whorf.

In general, the most well-known version is widely attributed to Whorf (1956). A possibly apocryphal story suggests that some of these ideas arose during the time when Whorf was an insurance claims adjuster. He noticed employees smoking near canisters of gasoline, even though they claimed that the canisters were labelled as empty. An empty canister of gasoline can be very dangerous because of the fumes, but the workers conceptualized them as being empty. That is, they were linguistically empty, but not actually empty at all. Whorf began to believe that one's native language determines what you can think about, and even your ability to perceive things. This story may or may not be accurate, but it still makes an interesting point about the difference between how one describes something linguistically and what that thing actually is. In other words, "empty" may not really be empty.

Whorf's bold claim

A famous quote reads:

> We **dissect** nature along lines laid down by our native language. The categories and types that we isolate from the world of phenomena we do not find there because they stare every observer in the face; on the contrary, the world is presented in a kaleidoscope flux of impressions which has to be organized by our minds – and this means largely by the linguistic systems of our minds. **We cut nature up**, organize it into concepts, and ascribe significances as we do, largely because we are parties to an agreement to organize it in this way – an agreement that holds throughout our speech community and is codified in the patterns of our language [...] all observers are not led by the same physical evidence to the same picture of the universe, unless their linguistic backgrounds are similar, or can in some way be calibrated. (Whorf, 1956: 213–214; my emphasis)

Whorf appears to be challenging Plato's notion of cutting nature at the joints (which was discussed in Chapter 4), meaning a natural way to divide the natural world and concepts. Rather, Whorf suggests that concepts and categories are determined almost exclusively by one's native language. This is often thought of as the strongest form of linguistic relativity. In this case, the theory implies that one's native language necessarily determines thinking, cognition, and perception.

Another popular idea attributed to this is the notion that Inuit languages have many more words for "snow" than does the English language. Whorf made a supposition about this, which was later picked up by media outlets and newspapers as a concrete claim, and with each subsequent version the number of hypothesized Inuit words for "snow" grew. It is pretty straightforward that this particular claim is neither true nor relevant. English has modifiers that allow for many descriptions of snow. Whorf himself never tested or examined the claim, and most reporting of this claim made no distinction about the many different dialects spoken by indigenous northern people. Nonetheless, this is one of those persistent myths and is fairly well-known by most people.

Colour cognition

However, this claim that language constrains or determines perception and cognition was a bold one, and in the middle of the twentieth century was very provocative. Anthropologists, psychologists, and linguists began to look for and examine ways to test this idea. One of the earliest was a study by Berlin and Kay (1969). They looked at the distribution of colour terms across many different languages. They reasoned that if language constrains thought, then native languages may constrain the types of colours that can be perceived and used. In order to be considered, they looked at colours that were **monolexemic**, for example, "red" but not "reddish". A basic colour term cannot be included in the description of any other colour terms; for example, indigo is not a basic term as it is a blueish colour. Basic colour terms cannot be restricted to a narrow class of objects; for example, the colour blonde works for hair, wood, and beer, but not for many other things. Basic colour terms must have a domain-general utility in the language. A basic colour term refers to a property that can be extended to objects in many different classes.

What Berlin and Kay (1969) found is shown in Figure 5.2. All languages contain terms for dark and light. Red is also fairly common, and in languages with only three terms, languages always have a word for black, white, and red. Red is a very salient colour for humans as it is the colour of hot things and blood. As languages evolve, more terms may be added but they still keep the terms from earlier stages.

The Evolution of Colour Terms

Stage	Colours
Stage I:	Dark-cool and light-warm
Stage II:	Red
Stage III:	Either green or yellow
Stage IV:	Both green and yellow
Stage V:	Blue
Stage VI:	Brown
Stage VII:	Purple, pink, orange, or grey

Figure 5.2 This is a list of the stages of colour term evolution in world languages as originally conceptualized by Berlin and Kay (1969).

Berlin and Kay's work does not really argue completely against the linguistic determinism hypothesis, and their initial claims have been softened and criticized (Saunders & van Brakel, 1997). But their work provided a very interesting way to test it. If there are languages with only two or three words for colours, and if the linguistic determinism theory is correct, then speakers of that language should have difficulty categorizing colours with the same colour name. Eleanor Rosch (Heider, 1972) carried out a test like this with an indigenous group in Papua New Guinea. The Dani people have only two words to denote colours, and thus to linguistically define colour categories. One category is called *mili* and refers to cool, dark shades, such as the English colours blue, green, and black. The second category is *mola*, which refers to warmer or lighter colours, such as the English colours red, yellow, and white.

In several experiments, Rosch asked her subjects to engage in a **paired associate learning** task with colour chips. A paired associate task is when participants are asked to learn a list of things and each thing is paired with something they already know. So if you are asked to learn a list of new words, each word is paired with a word you already know. The word you already know serves as a memory cue. In Rosch's task, the things to be learned were the colour chips and each colour chip was paired with word. Some of these colour chips were what are referred to as "focal colours". In other words, these colour chips were selected as the best example of a colour category in the prior study with English speakers. When asked to pick the "best example", Rosch found widespread agreement for colours with the highest saturation. Thus, the focal colour for red was the single-chip that would be intensified by most speakers of English as being the best example of red. Other chips might also be called red, but were not identified as the centre of the category as the best example. And still other chips might sometimes be called red, and at other times might appear to be another colour. You can pick out focal colours yourself. If you go to select a new colour for text in your word-processing program, you can see a wide arrangement of colours, but one seems to stick out as the best example of red, the best example of blue, the best example of green, etc. In other words, we would all probably agree which exact shade is the best example of the colour green. This would be the focal colour for green.

In Rosch's experiment, subjects were shown a chip and taught a new name. This was done for 16 colour word pairs. Rosch reasoned that English speakers would have no difficulty learning a paired associate for a focal colour because it would already activate an existing colour category. They should perform less well on paired associate learning for non-focal colours because they would not have a linguistic label to hang on that colour. Speakers of the Dani language should behave similarly, except they should show no advantage for most of the focal colours. That is because, if linguistic determinism is operating, the so-called focal colours would not be special in any way because speakers of the Dani language do not have the same categories. As far as linguistic determinism is concerned, they should not have the same focal colours as English speakers because they have different colour categories. Our focal colours are the centre of our colour categories. Being shown a focal red should not activate an existing linguistic category for speakers of the Dani language, and so they should show little difference between learning the paired associates for focal colours and learning the paired associates for non-focal colours.

This is not what Rosch found, however. Speakers of the Dani language showed the same advantage for focal colours over non-focal colours that English speakers showed. This suggests that even though their language has only two words to denote colour categories, they can perceive the same differences in colours as English speakers can. Thus, this appears to be evidence against linguistic determinism. The Dani language was not constraining the perception of its speakers. In many ways, this should not be surprising because colour vision is carried out computationally at the biological level. Regardless of linguistically defined categories, we all still have the same visual system with a retina filled with photoreceptors that are sensitive to different wavelengths.

Naming common objects

More recent work continued to cast doubt on the linguistic determinism theory. Barbara Malt's (Malt, Sloman, Gennari, Shi, & Wang, 1999) research looked at artifacts and manufactured objects, and the linguistic differences between English and Spanish. Participants in the experiment were shown many different common objects, such as bottles, containers, jugs, and jars. For speakers of North American English, a "jug" is typically used to contain liquid, is about four litres in volume, and has a handle. A bottle is typically smaller, has a longer neck, and no handle. A jar is typically made out of glass and has a wide mouth. A container is usually not made of glass, but of plastic. Containers come in round and square shapes, and are usually used to contain non-liquid products. Speakers of English may vary in terms of the exact category boundaries, but most will agree on what to call a bottle, what to call a jug, etc.

Whereas speakers of North American English refer to jugs separately from jars, speakers of Spanish typically label all of these things with a single term. In other words, a glass bottle, a jug, and a jar might all be labelled with the term "*frasco*". If linguistic determinism held true for manufactured objects, Spanish speakers should show less ability to classify them into different categories based on surface similarity. In other words, if you speak a language that has only one term for all of these objects, you should minimize attention to the individuating features and instead tend to classify them as members of the same group. However, Malt's results did not support this prediction. English-speaking and Spanish-speaking subjects did not differ much from each other when classifying these containers via overall similarity. That is, they might have the same label for all of the different objects, but when asked to sort them into groups based on similarity, they all sorted them in roughly the same way as English-speaking subjects. The linguistic label did not interfere with their ability to perceive and process surface features. In short, these results do not support the strong version of the linguistic determinism theory.

Count versus mass nouns

Despite the failings of the linguistic determinism theory, we have already shown that language can affect memory and cognition. Language also affects perception and interpretation in some cases. For example, consider the distinction between objects and substances. In English, as in many languages, we have nouns to refer to objects and nouns to refer to collections of things or substances. So-called **count nouns** refer to entities, objects, and kinds. We can say "*one horse, two horses, five cats, and 13 cakes*". On the other hand,

mass nouns typically denote entities that are not considered individually. In other words, a substance rather than an object. We might say "*a pile of leaves*", "*a dash of salt*", or "*a lot of mud*". Even though the substance denoted by the mass noun might be made of individual objects, we are not referring to the individual objects with the mass noun; rather, we are referring to the collection of them as a thing.

A study by Soja, Carey, and Spelke (1991) looked at when we acquire the ability to tell the difference between objects and substances. Do children learn to do this through exposure to their native language? The researchers examined English-speaking two-year-olds. The children were shown objects that were given an arbitrary name. They were then asked to pick out similar objects to the one they had just been shown and given a name for. For example, children might be shown a solid object or a non-solid object and told, "*This is my blicket*" or "*Do you see this blicket?*" The children were then asked to extend the concept by being asked "*show me some more*". In extending these words to new displays, two-year-olds showed a distinction between object and substance. When the sample was a hard-edged solid object, they extended the new word to all objects of the same shape, even when made of a different material. When the sample was a non-solid substance, they extended the word to other-shaped puddles of that same substance but not to shape matches made of different materials. This suggests that the distinction may be acquired via language, because both the object and the term were new. Even two-year-old children are able to generalize according to linguistic information.

Linguistic differences in time perception

A final example of how language affects the thinking process is demonstrated in a study by Lera Boroditsky (2001). She noted that across different languages and cultures there are differences in the metaphors that people use to talk about time. This is related to Lakoff's ideas on conceptual metaphors. English speakers often talk about time as if it is horizontal. That is, a horizontal metaphor would result in statements like "*pushing back the deadline*" or "*moving a meeting forward*". Mandarin speakers, on the other hand, often talk about time as if it is on a vertical axis. That is, they may use the Mandarin equivalents of up and down to refer to the order of events, weeks, and months.

It should be noted that this is not entirely uncommon in English, especially when considering time on a vertically oriented calendar. In fact, when I look at the Google calendar on my smartphone, it is arranged in a vertical axis with the beginning of the day at the top and the end of the day at the bottom. Although I still use terms like "*I've been falling behind on this project*", I am also pretty used to thinking about time in the vertical dimension. We also have English vertical time metaphors, such as doing something "at the top of the day". Exceptions aside, these metaphors seem to be linguistically and culturally entrenched in the idioms and statements that are produced.

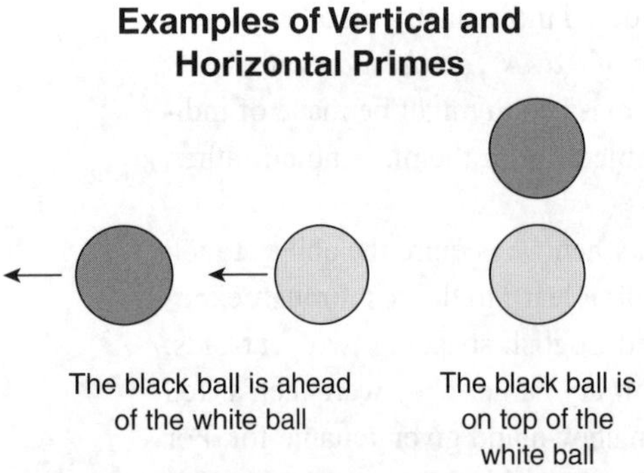

**Examples of Vertical and
Horizontal Primes**

The black ball is ahead
of the white ball

The black ball is
on top of the
white ball

Figure 5.3 This is an example of a horizontal visual prime (on the left) and a vertical visual prime (on the right). If subjects are shown one or the other prime before making a temporal inference, it can facilitate or interfere with the inference depending on how the speaker conceptualizes time.

In order to test if the conceptual metaphor and language affects subjects' ability to understand the scene, subjects were first shown a prime to orient them to the horizontal or vertical dimension. They were then asked to either confirm or disconfirm temporal propositions. Figure 5.3 shows an example of a prime. In the first, an English example of a horizontal prime is shown: "*The black ball is ahead of the white ball*". The second shows an English example of a vertical prime: "*The black ball is on top of the white ball*". Boroditsky reasoned that if a prime activated a vertical metaphor, and you spoke a language that encouraged thinking about time in a vertical dimension, you should see a processing facilitation. That is, you would be faster at judging the temporal proposition. If you saw a prime that activated the vertical metaphor, but you spoke a language that encouraged thinking about time in a horizontal dimension, then you should see some cost and would be slower at judging the temporal proposition.

This is what Boroditsky found. After seeing a vertically oriented prime, Mandarin speakers were faster to confirm or disconfirm temporal propositions compared to when they had seen the horizontal prime. She found the reverse effect for English speakers. This suggests that language differences may predict aspects of temporal reasoning by speakers. This finding supports linguistic determinism. Yet subsequent studies showed that this default orientation can be overridden. For example, Boroditsky trained English-speaking subjects to think about time vertically, giving them examples of vertical metaphors. In this case, after the training, the English speakers exhibited the vertical rather than the former horizontal priming effect. In short, about 15 minutes of training and instruction with a vertical time metaphor could override 20 years of speaking English and relying on a horizontal time dimension.

Although this study shows a clear impact of language on thought, it is not strong evidence for linguistic determinism because the native language does not seem to determine how time is perceived. Instead, local effects of linguistic context seem to be doing most of the work.

SUMMARY

Although many different species communicate with each other, only humans have developed an expansive, productive, and flexible natural language. And because language provides the primary point of access to our own thoughts, language and thinking seem completely intertwined.

In Chapter 3, it was argued that memory is flexible and malleable. This flexibility can occasionally be a liability as memories are not always accurate. Memories are a direct reflection of the linguistic processes used during the encoding process and the retrieval process. This point was demonstrated in the discussion of eyewitness testimony and how the language used during questioning can change the content of the memory itself. In other words, memory for events is created by and affected by the language we use when describing the event to ourselves and to others.

In Chapter 4 on concepts and categories, we suggested that concepts might be represented by definitions, lists of features, or centralized prototypes. Although each of these theories makes different claims about what is represented, all of them assume that a category and a concept can have a label. The label is linguistic. Although the present chapter makes it clear that our concepts are not exclusively defined by a language, categories' verbal labels still provide an important access point. We access categorical information in many ways by using the linguistic label.

In Section 2, we will examine the role of language in reasoning. In deductive logic, language use must be precise in order to determine a valid argument from an invalid argument. We will also look at the role of language in mediating between the faster, instinct-based behaviours produced by System 1 thinking and the behavioural outcomes produced by the slower, more deliberative System 2 thinking. Linguistic ability helps to mediate between these two systems. Furthermore, System 2 is generally thought to be language-based. In Chapter 9 in Section 3, language use can influence how decisions are made by providing a context or frame. The same decision can be framed as beneficial or as a potential loss. In other words, linguistic content and semantics can have a sizeable impact on the behavioural outcome of decisions.

SECTION 2
THINKING AND REASONING

6 INFERENCE AND INDUCTION

At a fundamental level, when we think about "thinking", we are often considering cognitive actions like figuring out a problem, or trying to predict how someone will react, or relying on our knowledge and existing conceptual representations to make sense of and interpret new events. Another way of describing this particular behaviour is that we rely on our past experiences to predict what might happen in the future in similar circumstances. In previous chapters I have given the example of shopping at a farmer's market, so let's consider that example again. When I go to the farmer's market, I rely on my past experiences to help me predict what to expect the next time I go. I expect there to be vendors, produce, other shoppers, and prepared food. If I pick up a butternut squash, I can predict what it looks like on the inside based on my prior knowledge of similar butternut squashes that I have purchased and processed in the past. The entire experience is one that relies heavily on prior knowledge to make predictions.

This all seems straightforward, and happens so quickly that we don't realize the power inherent in what we are doing. We are using the past to make predictions about the future. And usually these predictions come true so often that we don't even notice. This is the power of inductive reasoning: induction is about predicting the future.

THE ROLE OF INDUCTION IN THINKING

Inferences and conclusions

Induction and inductive reasoning is a process that we use for many common activities and behaviours. Obviously, we use induction to make inferences. **Inferences** are conclusions based on available evidence. For example, I often get telephone calls from telemarketers between the hours of 4:00pm and 7:00pm (when I am making and/or eating supper). When the phone rings at that time, I usually make an inference that the caller is just trying to sell something, so I rarely pick up. Because this has happened in the past, I have made enough observations to draw a reasonable conclusion about who will be on the phone. On the other side, the telemarketing company relies on their evidence to make an inductive inference that I will be at my home phone between 4:00pm and 7:00pm. We are both making inductive inferences.

Generalization

Induction is also used when we make generalizations. A **generalization** is also an inductive conclusion, but rather than describing a specific prediction, as in many of the previous examples, generalization is a broad conclusion about a whole class or group of things. For example, let's consider the thinking behind football rivalries. In the UK, there are many fierce rivalries between football clubs in the premier league. Imagine a person who supports Arsenal FC, and suppose that they have had less than positive experiences with some Chelsea FC fans (or the other way around: I'm not picking sides). Based on a few of those negative interactions, the Arsenal fan might form a negative generalization about Chelsea fans. This is the basis of many stereotypes and prejudices.

In both of the examples above, whether or not the conclusion was made about a specific telemarketing call or a general conclusion about Arsenal or Chelsea fans, the evidence was specific. Inductive reasoning usually involves making specific observations and then drawing conclusions from that available evidence.

It seems that we make inferences all the time. If you call a restaurant to place an order for pick up/delivery/take away, you make a basic inference that the food you order will be ready for you to pick up. When the driver in front of you puts on his turn signal, you make an inference that he will turn left or right. We rely on induction to make inferences about how people will behave and react to what we say. We rely on induction to make inferences about how to use new ingredients when cooking dinner. Young children rely on induction when they pick up an object and learn about how size predicts the weight of objects. Parents make inductions when they predict how their young children might behave after a short nap or a long nap.

The list is extensive because induction is such a critical aspect to the psychology of thinking. In summary, we rely on inductive reasoning **to discover something new by thinking**.

HOW INDUCTION WORKS

Hume's problem of induction

In the era of the Scottish Enlightenment, the philosopher David Hume considered induction to be one of the greatest problems for philosophers to solve. Unlike deductive logic, which many believed could be explained by formal operations, induction seemed to defy this. Hume gave a description of what he called the "**problem of induction**". As we discussed, induction is essentially the act of relying on past experience to make inferences and conclusions about the future. Hume was concerned that this is a circular argument. The reason is as follows: induction works if we assume that the future will resemble the past. We must have confidence in our judgements about the future to the degree to which the future resembles the past. Hume claimed that this only works because the future has always resembled the past… in the past. To say that the future has always resembled the past in the past might strike you as unnecessarily confusing. But what this means is that your inductions and conclusions were probably correct in the past. You might be able to recall inductions and conclusions that you made yesterday, two weeks ago, or two months ago that turned out to be true. As a concrete example, if you were at a farmer's market yesterday, and you made an inference about what the inside of a hubbard squash would look like, and your prediction was later confirmed, you could say that *yesterday, the future resembled the past*.

The problem with this, according to Hume, is that we cannot use these past inductive successes to predict future inductive successes. We simply cannot know if the future will resemble the past. In other words, it is impossible to know if your inductions will work in the future as well as they worked in the past without resorting to the circular argument of using induction. Just because your inductive inferences worked yesterday, two weeks ago, two months ago, does not guarantee that they will work now, tomorrow, or two weeks from now. Induction is based on the understanding that the future will resemble the past, but we only have information about how well this has worked in the past. To make this assumption requires the acceptance of a circular premise. In essence, we are relying on induction to explain induction.

By now, your head might hurt from considering all the past futures and future pasts, and you would be right. Hume concluded that from a strictly formal standpoint, induction cannot work. But it *does* work and humans rely on induction. We rely on induction because we need to. Hume suggested that the reason we rely on induction is that we have a "habit" of assuming that the future will resemble the past. In a modern context, we might not use the term "habit", but instead would argue that our cognitive system is designed to track regularities in the world, and make conclusions and predictions on the basis of those regularities. Let's consider some the fundamental mechanisms that allow induction to work.

Basic learning mechanisms

All cognitive systems, intelligent systems, and non-human animals rely on the fundamental processes of associative learning. There is nothing controversial about this claim. The basic process of classical conditioning provides a simple mechanism for how inductions might work. In classical conditioning, the organism learns an association between two stimuli that frequently co-occur. In Chapter 2 on similarity, we discussed the example of a cat that learns the association between the sound of the can of food opening and the subsequent presentation of her favourite food. The cat has learned that the sound of the can being opened always occurs right before the food. Although we tend to talk about it as a conditioned response, it is also fair to discuss this as a simple inductive inference. The cat doesn't have to consider whether or not it is reasonable that the future will resemble the past; the cat simply makes the inference and acts on the conditioned response. In other words, the cat makes a prediction and generates an expectation.

Stimulus generalization

Another conceptual advantage of relating induction to basic learning theory is that we can also talk about the role of similarity and stimulus generalization. Consider a straight-forward example of operant conditioning. Operant conditioning, somewhat different from classical conditioning, is characterized by the organism learning the connection between a stimulus and a response. We can imagine the stereotypical rat in a Skinner box learning to press a lever in response to the presentation of a colour. If a red light goes on and the rat presses the lever, it receives reinforcement in the form of rat food. If the blue light goes on and the rat presses the lever, it receives no reinforcement. Not surprisingly, the rat learns pretty quickly that it needs to press the lever only when the red light comes on. We can argue that the rat has learned to make inductive inferences about the presentation of food following various lights.

However, the rat can do more than just make a simple inference. The rat can also generalize. If you were to present this rat with a red light that was slightly different from the original red light that it was trained on, it might still press the lever. Its rate of pressing might decrease, however. You would also find that the rate would decrease as a function of this similarity. The more similar the new light is to the training light, the higher the rate of lever pressing (Figure 6.1). This decrease is known as a generalization gradient. So pervasive is this generalization gradient that Roger Shepard referred to it as **the universal law of stimulus generalization** (Shepard, 1987). Not only is the rat making what amounts to an

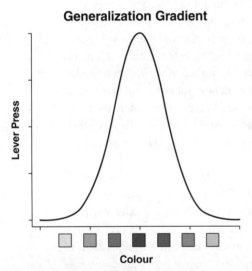

Generalization Gradient

Lever Press

Colour

Figure 6.1 An example of a typical generalization gradient. The animal (a rat, for example) will press the lever vigorously for the red light. The maximum lever press rate corresponds to the peak. The rat also presses the lever when colours that are similar to red are presented, but the rate of lever pressing drops off considerably as a function of decreasing similarity.

inductive inference about the relationship between lights and food, but the rat is also making these inductive generalizations in accordance with the similarity between the current state of affairs and previously encountered instances.

What we see is that there is something fundamental and universal about generalizing to new stimuli as a function of how similar they are to previously experienced stimuli. This has implications for understanding induction. Our tendency to base predictions about the future on similarity to past events should also obey this universal law of stimulus generalization. If one's past experiences are very similar to the present situation, then inferences have a high likelihood of being accurate. As the similarity between the present situation and past experiences decreases, we might expect these predictions have a lower probability of being accurate.

Goodman's problem of induction

Although stimulus association and generalization seem to explain how induction might work at the most basic level, there are still some conceptual problems with induction. According to Hume, induction may be a habit, but it is difficult to explain in logical terms without resorting to some kind of circular argument. Hume's concern was not so much with how induction worked, but rather that it seemed to be difficult to describe philosophically. Nelson Goodman, the twentieth-century philosopher, raised a very similar concern, but the example is somewhat more compelling and possibly more difficult to resolve (Goodman, 1983).

Goodman's example is as follows. Imagine that you are an emerald examiner (I know it is not really a thing, but just pretend that it is). Every emerald you have seen so far has been green. So we can say that "All emeralds are green". By ascribing to emeralds the property of *green* what we are really saying is that all emeralds that have been seen are green and all emeralds that have not yet been seen are also green. Thus, "emeralds are green" predicts that the very next emerald you will pick up will be green. This inductive inference is made with confidence.

But there is a problem with this. Consider an alternative property called *grue*. If you say that "All emeralds are *grue*", it means that all the emeralds that you have seen so far are green and all emeralds that have not yet been seen are blue: green emeralds in the past, but blue emeralds from this moment forward. Yes, this sounds a little ridiculous, but Goodman's point is that at any given time this property of *grue* is true. Both properties are true given the evidence of green emeralds. I've illustrated this in Figure 6.2. Notice that the past experience (green emeralds) is identical for both properties. Goodman's suggestion is that both of these properties, *green* and *grue*, can be simultaneously true, given the available evidence. It is possible that all the emeralds are green, and it is also possible that some are blue, but you have not seen them yet. But these properties also make opposite

An Example of "Green" and "Grue"

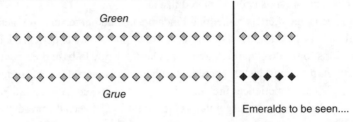

All the emeralds that have so far been seen....

Figure 6.2 This is a schematic of Nelson Goodman's example of *green* and *grue* emeralds. As can be seen, all the emerald set up and seen so far are simultaneously *green* and *grue*, and so both properties are true. Emeralds that have not yet been seen are to the right of the black line. Each property makes a different prediction about the subsequent emeralds to be examined.

predictions about what colour the next emerald you pick up will be. If *green* is true, then the next emerald will be green. If *grue* is true, then the next emerald will be blue. And since both are true, a clear prediction cannot really be made. And yet, of course we all predict that the next emerald will be green. Why? This is the problem of induction.

Entrenchment and natural kinds

With the earlier problem of induction defined by David Hume, the solution was straightforward. Hume stated that we have a habit to make inductions. And our current understanding of learning theory suggests that we naturally generalize. Goodman's problem of induction is more subtle. If we have a habit to make inductions, how do we choose which one of the two possible inductions to make in the emerald example? A possible solution is that some ideas, descriptors, and concepts are entrenched. **Entrenchment** means that a term or a property has a history of usage within a culture or language. In the emerald example, *green* is an entrenched term. *Green* is a term that we can use to describe many things. And so it is the useful property to make predictions from, and about. By saying that a collection of things (emeralds) is green, we can describe all the things. *Grue* is not entrenched. There is no history of usage and no general property of *grue* outside the emeralds that were *grue* yesterday and blue tomorrow. Goodman argued that we can only make reliable inductions from entrenched terms.

The philosopher W. V. O Quine, in his essay "Natural kinds" (Quine, 1969), argued that natural kinds are natural groupings of entities that possess similar properties, much like what we have referred to earlier as a family resemblance concept (Rosch & Mervis, 1975). Quine suggested that objects form a kind only if they have properties that can be projected to all the members. For example, an *apple* is a natural kind. This is a natural grouping, and what we know about apples can be projected to other apples. "Not apple" is not a natural kind because the category is simply too broad to be projectable. This grouping consists of everything in the universe that is not an apple. Quine argued that all humans make use of natural kinds. Reliable inductions come from natural kinds.

Granny Smith apples and Gala apples are pretty similar to each other and belong to the same natural kind concept. Anything you know about Granny Smith apples can be projected to Gala apples with some confidence, and vice versa. The same would not be true of Gala apples and a red ball. True, they may be similar to each other on the surface, but they do not form a natural kind. Whatever you learn about the Gala apple, can't be projected to the red ball.

Quine's notion of a natural kind suggests a solution for Nelson Goodman's problem of induction. Quine pointed out that *green* is a natural property. Green emeralds are a natural kind, and the property of green can be projected to all possible emeralds. *Grue*, being arbitrary in nature, is not a natural kind and cannot be extended to all possible members. In other words, green emeralds form a kind via similarity; *grue* emeralds do not.

CATEGORICAL INDUCTION

If we consider the research discussed above, we can first conclude that most organisms have a tendency to display stimulus generalization. This can be as simple as basic conditioning or generalizing about a group of people. Second, basic stimulus generalization is sensitive to the similarity between the current stimulus and mental representations of previously experienced stimuli. Third, we have shown in other chapters that concepts and categories are often held together by similarity. As a result, a productive way to investigate inductive reasoning is to consider that inductions are often based on concepts and categories. This is known in the literature as **categorical induction**.

The structure of an induction task

For the present purposes, we can define categorical induction as the process by which people arrive at a conclusion or a statement of confidence about whether a conclusion category has some given feature or predicate after being told that one or more premise categories possess that feature or predicate. In many of the examples we discuss below, the induction is made in the form of an argument. The argument contains one or more premises. A **premise** is a statement of fact about something, someone, or a whole class. The premise contains **predicates**, which can be things and properties. In most of the examples, the predicates are properties or features of category members. The inductive argument also contains a conclusion statement. The **conclusion** is the actual inductive inference, and it usually concerns possible projection of a predicate to some conclusion object or category. In an inductive argument, participants would be asked to decide whether or not they agreed with the conclusion. They might be asked to consider two arguments and decide which of the two is stronger. For example, consider the inductive argument below, which first appeared in Sloman and Lagnado (2005).

Argument

Premise: Boys use GABA as a neurotransmitter

Conclusion: Therefore girls use GABA as a neurotransmitter.

The first statement about boys using GABA as a neurotransmitter is a premise. Boys are a category and the phrase "use GABA as a neurotransmitter" is a predicate. How strongly do you feel about this conclusion? Part of how you assess the strength has to do with whether or not you think girls are sufficiently similar to boys. In this instance, you probably agree that they are pretty similar with respect to neurobiology, and therefore you would endorse the conclusion.

When you were answering this question, you may wonder what GABA is beyond being a neurotransmitter. You may not have actually known what it is, and may not have known whether or not it is present in boys and girls. But this is the way the statement is designed. The categorical induction statement works because it asks you to infer a property based on category similarity, rather than on retrieving the property from semantic memory. Thus, in the example above, GABA is a **blank predicate** (Rips, 1975). It is a predicate because it is the property we wish to project. But it is blank because we do not assume to know the answer. It is plausible, but not immediately known. And because you cannot rely on your factual knowledge about GABA as a neurotransmitter, you have to make an inductive inference. Thus, the blank predicate is crucial in inductive inference research because it forces the participant to rely on categorical knowledge and induction, rather than on the retrieval of a fact from semantic memory.

Research using this paradigm has described several strong phenomena regarding how people make categorical inductions. These include inductions and conclusions about specific cases and inductions and conclusions about whole categories. In most cases, the strength of the argument is dependent upon how similar the premise (or premises) is (or are) to the conclusion. And categorical structure plays a role as well. When we have evidence that a feature is associated with a member of a category that is highly typical, we tend to trust other inductions as well.

Using this basic paradigm, we can investigate some general phenomena about categorical induction.

Premise similarity

For example, if things in the premise and the conclusion are similar to each other, are from similar categories, or are from the same category, inductions can be made confidently. This is referred to as **premise-conclusion similarity**. According to Osherson et al. (1990), arguments are strong to the extent that the categories in the premises are similar to the categories in the conclusion. We are more likely to make inductive inferences between similar premise and conclusion categories. For example, consider the following two arguments:

Argument 1

Premise: Robins have a high concentration of potassium in their bones.

Conclusion: Sparrows have a high concentration of potassium in their bones.

Argument 2

Premise: Ostriches have a high concentration of potassium in their bones.

Conclusion: Sparrows have a high concentration of potassium in their bones.

In this example, the *high concentration of potassium in their bones* is the blank predicate. This is the new property we are making an inductive inference about. Argument 1 should seem stronger, and in empirical studies research participants find this to be a stronger argument (Osherson et al., 1990). The reason is that robins and sparrows are fairly similar to each other; ostriches and sparrows are not very similar. The low similarity between the ostrich and the sparrow is evident on the surface, as is the high similarity between the robin and the sparrow. We assume that if the robin and the sparrow share observable features, they may also share non-observable features like the concentration of potassium in the bones.

Premise typicality

The example above emphasized the role of similarity between the premise and the conclusion, but in the strong similarity case you may have also noticed that the robin is a very typical category exemplar. For all intents and purposes, the robin is one of the most typical of all birds. And remember that typical exemplars share many features with other category members. Typical category members have a strong family resemblance with other category members. And they can also be said to cover a wide area of the category space. What is true about robins is true of many exemplars in the bird category.

Premise typicality can affect inductions about the whole category. For example, consider the following set of arguments:

Argument 1

Premise: Robins have a high concentration of potassium in their bones.

Conclusion: All birds have a high concentration of potassium in their bones.

Argument 2

Premise: Penguins have a high concentration of potassium in their bones.

Conclusion: All birds have a high concentration of potassium in their bones.

In this case, you might agree that the first argument seems stronger. It is easier to draw a conclusion about *all birds* when you are reasoning from a typical bird like a *robin*, which covers much of the bird category, than from a very atypical bird like *penguin*, which does not cover very much of this category. If we know that a penguin is not very typical – it possesses many unique features and does not cover very much of the bird category – we are not likely to project additional penguin features onto the rest of the category. We know that many penguin features do not transfer to the rest of the category.

Premise diversity

The preceding example suggests a strong role for typicality, because typical exemplars cover a broad range of category exemplars. But there are other things that can affect the coverage as well. For example, the **premise diversity** effect comes about when several premises are dissimilar to each other. Not completely unrelated, of course, but dissimilar and still in the same category. When being presented with two dissimilar premises from the same category, it can enhance the coverage within that category. For example, consider the two arguments below:

Argument 1

Premise: Lions and hamsters have a high concentration of potassium in their bones.

Conclusion: Therefore all mammals have a high concentration of potassium in their bones.

Argument 2

Premise: Lions and tigers have a high concentration of potassium in their bones.

Conclusion: Therefore all mammals have a high concentration of potassium in their bones.

Looking at both of these arguments, it should seem that Argument 1 is a stronger argument. Indeed, subjects tend to choose arguments like this as being stronger (Heit & Hahn, 2001;

Lopez, 1995). The reason is that lions and hamsters are very different from each other, but they are still members of the same superordinate category of mammals. If something as different and distinct as the lion and a hamster have something in common, then we are likely to infer that all members of the superordinate category of mammals have the same property. On the other hand, lions and tigers are quite similar in that both are big cats, both appear in the zoo in similar environments, and they co-occur in speech and printed text very often. In short, they are not very different from each other. And because of that we are less likely to project the property of potassium in the bones to all mammals and are more likely to think that this is a property of big cats, or cats in general, but not all mammals. The diversity affect comes about because the diverse premises cover a significant portion of the superordinate category.

The inclusion fallacy

Sometimes, the tendency to rely on similarity when making inductions even produces fallacious conclusions. One example is known as the **inclusion fallacy** (Shafir, Smith, & Osherson, 1990). In general, we tend to prefer conclusions in which there is a strong similarity relation between the premise and the conclusion category. We tend to discount conclusions for which there is not a strong similarity relation between the premise and the conclusion. Usually, this tendency leads to correct inductions, but occasionally it can lead to false inductions. Take a look at the statements below and think about which one seems like a stronger argument.

Argument 1

Premise: Robins have sesamoid bones.

Conclusion: Therefore all birds have sesamoid bones.

Argument 2

Premise: Robins have sesamoid bones.

Conclusion: Therefore ostriches have sesamoid bones.

It is very easy to agree that the first argument seems stronger. Robins are very typical members of the bird category and we know they share many properties with other members of the bird category. And so it seems reasonable to conclude that if robins possess sesamoid bones, so too do all other birds. Most people find the second statement to be less compelling. Yes robins are typical, but ostriches are not. We know that robins and ostriches differ in many ways, so we are less willing to project the property of sesamoid bones from robins to ostriches. The reason why this is a fallacy is that all ostriches are included in the "all birds" statement. In other words, if we are willing to accept Argument 1 that a property present in robins is present in all birds, then that includes ostriches already. It cannot be the case that a single member of the "all birds" category is less compelling than all birds. If we are willing to project the property to an entire category, it is not correct to assume that specific members of that entire category do not have that property. Otherwise, we should not be willing to accept the first argument.

But most subjects find the first argument to be more compelling because of the similarity of robins to other birds. The atypicality of the ostrich undermines the argument. People are likely to use similarity relations rather than category inclusion when making these kinds of arguments. So similarity seems to be the stronger predictor of inferences. Category membership is important, but featural overlap may be even more important (Osherson et al., 1990; Shafir et al., 1990; Sloman, 1993; Sloman & Lagnado, 2005).

Casual factors

Sometimes, we make inferences based on our understanding of how the world works. These might not be based on category inclusiveness or even similarity and feature overlap. Instead, causal relationships may play a role. Consider the following two arguments (Lo, Sides, Rozelle, & Osherson, 2002):

Argument 1

Premise 1: House cats can carry the floxum parasite.

Premise 2: Field mice can carry the floxum parasite.

Conclusion: Therefore all mammals can carry the floxum parasite.

Argument 2

Premise 1: House cats can carry the floxum parasite.

Premise 2: Tigers can carry the floxum parasite.

Conclusion: Therefore all mammals can carry the floxum parasite.

Both of these arguments are fairly strong. And the first statement might seem to be an example of the diversity effect, because the two premises mention category members that are fairly diverse – house cats and field mice cover a fair amount of the mammal category. House cats and tigers are also diverse, but are members of the same near superordinate category of cats. So the coverage effect should predict that the first argument is stronger. However, subjects (children specifically) tend to find the first argument to be weaker (Lo et al., 2002). The reason is that most of us recognize why house cats and field mice might carry the same parasite. If the mice carry the parasite, and the cats catch the parasite from the mice while hunting, it suggests a causal link. This causal link is very specific and idiosyncratic to this house cat/field mice relationship. As a result, it may not conform to

Quine's notion of a natural kind. We are less likely to project the property of the parasite to all mammals on the basis of this evidence. Thus, the alternative argument concerning house cats and tigers seems stronger because there is no causal link between house cats and tigers. There is only a biological link between the two.

Sometimes, this causal effect arises even when the same terms are used. A study by Doug Medin and colleagues asked subjects to consider a variety of premises (Medin, Coley, Storms, & Hayes, 2003). They found that when the order of presentation highlighted a causal relationship, people preferred that argument over the same terms when the order did not highlight the causal relationship.

Statement 1

Premise: Gazelles contain the protein retinum.

Conclusion: Therefore lions contain the protein retinum.

Statement 2

Premise: Lions contain the protein retinum.

Conclusion: Therefore gazelles contain the protein retinum.

Subjects generally preferred statements like the first one. In that statement, the order of terms highlights a plausible causal link. Gazelles have this protein, and so lions may also have this protein because they often hunt and eat gazelles. They ingest the protein from the gazelle. Mentioning gazelles first and lions second highlights this causal link. The second statement still mentions the same terms, but in a different order. When you read that lions contain this protein, and you are asked to infer that gazelles may also contain it, the causal explanation is downplayed and you are likely to reason from category membership. It is not a bad argument, but without the additional causal information, it is not as strong as the first one. Unlike the previous example, in this case the causal link strengthens the argument because we are not making conclusions about all members of a category.

THEORETICAL ACCOUNTS OF CATEGORICAL INTRODUCTION

The similarity coverage model

Several theoretical accounts have been developed to deal with the kinds of facts shown above. The first is the similarity coverage model of Osherson and colleagues (Osherson et al., 1990; Shafir et al., 1990). This theory assumes that inductive inferences are made on the basis of similarity between premise and conclusion, and the degree of coverage that premises have over the lowest-level category that includes all of the premises and the conclusion. This theory accounts for the natural tendency to project an object's attributes to other similar objects and to similar categories. It also is a natural tendency to activate the superordinate category when a premise is stated. That is, when given information about apples and pears, the fruit category can be assumed to be automatically activated.

The similarity coverage model accounts for things like the premise and conclusion similarity effect, the typicality effects, and the diversity effects. However, the similarity coverage model in its basic form may have difficulties accounting for effects like the inclusion fallacy. In the inclusion fallacy, people tend to prefer similarity relations over category membership.

The feature coverage theory

The feature coverage theory (Sloman, 1993; Sloman & Lagnado, 2005; Sloman, Love, & Ahn, 1998) is similar to the similarity coverage model in that it emphasizes premise and conclusion similarity. It differs from the similarity coverage model in that it downplays the role of category inclusion. In other words, it reduces the role of similarity and category coverage and replaces it with the notion of **feature coverage**. When a premise and a conclusion are similar to each other, they share many features and thus there is a high degree of feature coverage. When two dissimilar premises are used, as in the diversity affect, they do not tend to share many features with each other, and thus there are more features activated overall, which strengthens the conclusion. Formally, this is equivalent to claiming category coverage, but the feature coverage theory explains how and why the category coverage effect works. It works by activating more features, and those features are eligible to be projected onto the conclusion category.

The feature coverage theory handles the inclusion fallacy fairly well. Because it doesn't make the assumption that subjects will rely on category membership, it tends to predict that inductions will be strong on the basis of shared features. In the inclusion fallacy, "robin" activates several common bird features. We know that robin is typical, and so we are willing to agree with the conclusion that if robins have some new feature, it is probable that all birds have this feature. The feature coverage model predicts that we will not prefer the second argument when we are projecting features from robins to ostriches. Although technically still a logical fallacy, the feature coverage model explains why we prefer the first statement. There is very little feature overlap between ostriches and robins as birds.

INDUCTION IN THE WILD

Given how important induction is to thinking, it is worth looking at some examples of inductive reasoning in cases outside the laboratory. The specific examples we gave above demonstrate some of the key effects related to categorical induction and inductive reasoning in general. But they are also somewhat circumscribed and designed to illustrate and elicit these specific effects. It is also worth examining some cases of categorical induction in more naturalistic settings.

As a starting point, let's consider a study by Medin and colleagues (1997). This paper will also be discussed in greater detail in Chapter 11 in the context of expertise. Although this study was conducted in the laboratory, the materials used were more naturalistic. In this case, the researchers were interested in reasoning and categorization in a very specific expert population: tree experts. They defined three kinds of expert: expert botanical taxonomists, who were all university faculty members with expertise in the classification of trees; landscape designers and architects, who were all experts in how trees should be planted and cared for; and city arborists and park maintenance personnel, who were all experts in the care of trees. Although all of these groups were experts, they all have specific goals in mind with respect to their expertise. The researchers predicted that these groups would classify trees with respect to these expert level goals, and might also display systematic differences in inductive reasoning.

Subjects were asked to examine cards that had the name of a specific tree on it. They were asked to sort these cards into as many groups or as few groups as they thought reasonable based on how the trees "go together". One of the key findings, which will be discussed in Chapter 11 on expertise, is that subjects tended to sort the trees into categories as a function of what kind of expert they were. Botanists sorted the trees primarily according to scientific taxonomy. Landscape architects and arborists chose more idiosyncratic sorting strategies, sometimes based on the specific goals they might have when planting trees. In other words, if you work with trees from a practical standpoint, your natural tendency might be to group them into categories like "weed tree" and "trees needing space". These are understandable functional groupings, but may not reflect the best grouping for categorical induction. Certainly, a category of trees that may be treated as weeds is not the same kind of natural kind, according to Quine (1969), that "Japanese Maple" would be.

Interestingly, when the same subjects were asked to make inductions about specific trees, Medin et al. (1997) created a series of forced-choice triads that pitted functional grouping against taxonomy. Subjects were then asked an induction question along the lines of "Suppose a new disease was discovered that affected the [target tree]. Would you be likely to see this disease in [choice A] or [choice B]?" In some trials, one of the choices might reflect the thematic or goal-oriented choice and the other would reflect a taxonomic choice.

Not surprisingly, expert taxonomists tended to make inductions in accordance with the taxonomic category and maintenance workers tended to reason in accordance with the genus level and folk taxonomy. For those cases when there might be a conflict between folk taxonomy and scientific taxonomy, maintenance workers often relied on their own goal-oriented classifications. In contrast, landscape architects relied on reasoning strategy that did not reflect their initial goal-oriented strategy. Landscape architects tended to be quite flexible in their understanding of trees, and tended to make inductions on the basis of scientific taxonomy. In other words, although the landscapers sorted trees into goal-oriented categories, it did not seem to undermine their understanding of natural-kind-based induction.

Representativeness heuristic

Categorical induction is commonplace in social interactions. For example, the well-known **representativeness heuristic** occurs when people base their predictions about things, on the prototype of the category for which that thing is a member. The idea is that if valuable knowledge exists in our understanding of basic categories, then we tend to project the category's properties to individual members of the category. This is entirely within the scope of our current understanding of categorical induction. If we assume something is true of a category, we assume it can be true of individual members.

We also know that sometimes individual category members may not resemble the prototype or the overall family resemblance. Even in a category with strong family resemblance structure, the very definition of family resemblance assumes that there may be category members that differ on a number of features from other category members and the prototype. The most well-known examples are those described by Kahneman and Tversky (Kahneman & Tversky, 1973; Shafir et al., 1990; Tversky & Kahneman, 1983). One particularly famous example is the case of "Linda the bank teller". It illustrates not only the effect of representativeness, but also an effect known as the **conjunction fallacy**. In this task, subjects are given a description and are asked to choose one of two options that reflect a conclusion about the person. For example:

> "Linda is 31 years old, single, outspoken, and very bright. She majored in philosophy. As a student, she was deeply concerned with issues of discrimination and social justice, and also participated in anti-nuclear demonstrations."
>
> Which is more probable?
>
> Linda is a bank teller.
>
> Linda is a bank teller and is active in the feminist movement.

Not surprisingly, in the original study subjects chose option 2 (Tversky & Kahneman, 1983). The reason they chose option 2 was that she is representative of what many people considered to be the "feminist movement". Yes, it is possible she is a bank teller as well, but we probably don't have a strong, coherent representation of that category. Think about this problem in reverse and you will see its connection to some of the earlier premise and conclusion statements we studied. To say that Linda is a bank teller suggests she is a member of a large and maybe not very distinct category. To say that she is a member of a bank teller category and the feminist movement suggests she is a member of a smaller, more distinct category. We tend to prefer that relationship, and project the properties consistent with feminist movement on to Linda. The reason this is a fallacy is that both options include membership in the bank teller category. Formally, it cannot be the case that she is more likely to be a member of two categories (the conjunction) than either one of those single categories. In other words, the probability of being a member of one is greater and the probability of being in the conjunction. And yet, because of our understanding of representativeness and a tendency to rely on that heuristic, we all prefer the second option. We tend to rely on feature coverage and similarity.

Consider another well-known example, again from Kahneman and Tversky – the "engineer lawyer problem". The original version appeared in 1973, and has appeared in other studies in other forms many times since then (Kahneman & Tversky, 1973). In the original and fundamental version, subjects were given some base rate information about how many people in a group of 100 were engineers and how many were lawyers. In one case, subjects were told to assume that of the 100, 30 were engineers and 70 were lawyers. In other words, there is a 70% base rate of lawyers in this group. They were then given the description of a person who was sampled at random from the group of 100:

"Jack is a 45-year-old man. He is married and has four children. He is generally conservative, careful, and ambitious. He shows no interest in political and social issues and spends most of his free time on his many hobbies, which include home carpentry, sailing, and mathematical puzzles."

Subjects were then asked to estimate the probability that Jack was a lawyer or an engineer. If subjects were paying attention to base rates and category membership exclusively, they should estimate the likelihood of Jack being an engineer at 30%. After all, most of the people in this group were lawyers, and any one randomly sampled person should have a 70% probability of being a lawyer. Clearly, Jack does not conform to the representativeness of lawyers, and this description reads to us like a stereotypical engineer. Bear in mind that this study was carried out in the early 1970s; our understanding of engineers and lawyers has probably changed somewhat.

But the main point is that subjects seemed to ignore the given base rate of information and focused instead on features. Jack possesses features that are representative of engineers and thus we overestimate the likelihood of him being an engineer.

When I present this study in a lecture, nearly everyone who has not seen the study before is incredulous. I typically get comments like "but he is obviously an engineer", or "yes, we realize the base rate is 70% lawyer, but for any individual it's the features that matter!"

And these students are right. A common criticism of this paradigm is that people rely on many sources of information to make judgements and inferences about things. We predict or project features on the basis of category membership, typicality, representativeness, shared features, causal relations, etc. Furthermore, other researchers have suggested that our reliance on representativeness versus base rates can be affected by the way the problem is framed. In cases where the features are stereotypical, subjects tend to rely on representativeness. But in other cases where the features might be less extreme or stereotypical, or where sampling is explicitly random, people may rely on base rates more often (Gigerenzer, Hell, & Blank, 1988).

Even Daniel Kahneman more recently has suggested both pros and cons for representativeness. He points out that representativeness has many virtues. The intuitive impressions that one makes via rapid access to category level information are more accurate than chance alone. As an example, Kahneman suggests that, on most occasions, people who act friendly actually *are* friendly. And that people with a PhD are more likely to subscribe to the *New York Times* than people with a high school diploma only. These are facts and they also conform to representativeness (Kahneman, 2011).

Still, Kahneman also argues that representativeness can lead people to make erroneous inferences. One of the biggest problems is that because the influence of category level information is so strong, we may overlook other, more rational sources of information. Consider again Kahneman's example of the *New York Times* and education level. If you see someone on a subway in New York City reading the *New York Times*, which alternative is more probable? She has a PhD or she does not have a college degree? Although we might agree that having a PhD is representative of readers of the *New York Times*, it would not be a rational inference given the general base rate of *New York Times* readership in New York City. So although the representativeness is based in fact and may often be a helpful and unavoidable inductive heuristic, it still can result in biases and errors.

If we examine our own behaviour, we might see examples of representativeness all around. For example, we may know that close to 50% of all initial marriages end in divorce. But we certainly would not assume that half of our friends will get divorced, especially if they seem happy. Furthermore, if one's own marriage is happy and enjoyable, one would not predict a 50% failure rate. For example, my wife and I have been married for 15 years, and we have an enjoyable, happy relationship. As a result, I do not assume that our marriage has a 50% chance of ending in a divorce. My personal knowledge overrides this base rate statistic. In other words, I believe my own marriage is representative of a happy marriage that won't end in an unhappy way.

Representativeness affects many of our choices and decisions. We often choose things based on what they remind us of, or on what category they are representative of. I might go to the wine shop and pick out a new wine based on its attractive packaging. The attractive bottle is representative of a quality product. And I would do this even if I knew that there was a low base rate of wines that I would enjoy.

Of course, we apply representativeness heuristics in ways far less benign than the lawyer and engineer example. Representativeness is also at the heart of many destructive and negative racial and ethnic stereotypes. The base rate of people who follow the Muslim religion and that also engage in terrorist activity is unbelievably low (almost no one is a terrorist, regardless of religion or ethnicity). Nevertheless, many people, and even many elected government officials, tend to overestimate the connection between Muslims and terrorism. This is clearly an example of the representativeness heuristic in action, and suggests a reasoning error.

BOX 6.1

A particularly fascinating and salient example of racial and ethnic stereotyping was a feature piece written for the *New Yorker* magazine in 1992 (Graham, 1992). The report was written by Lawrence Graham, who at the time was a 30-year-old corporate lawyer at a midtown Manhattan firm, earning $105,000 a year (Manhattan-based corporate lawyers make much more than that now; this was in the early 1990s). Graham noticed that although he was doing well in his law firm, and although he had graduated from Harvard, he was not excelling to the degree that his white colleagues were. One possible reason, he suspected, was that his white colleagues would often be invited to tennis or golf at exclusive country clubs that did not have any black members.

Graham wanted to find out how these clubs operated, and why they excluded black members who clearly had the same income level and credentials as their white counterparts. So he crafted a fictitious resumé that cast him as a middle-class, black man with a reasonable education: someone who went to Tufts University for two years; not a slacker, but clearly not a Harvard law graduate either. And he applied for a job as a bus boy.

When he got the job, what surprised him most was the casual racism that he observed. Although he was black, he was also a bus boy, and therefore patrons treated him as representative of the bus boy category. In other words, he needed the job. He was part of the structure, not an individual. In the same way that you can talk in front of a coffee machine, you can also talk in front of a bus boy. Patrons would use racial slurs without even noticing they were doing so in front of a black person. On one particular occasion, when he fulfilled a request and said "you're quite welcome", the patron remarked to her friend that the bus boy had very good diction – almost as good as a white person.

(Continued)

(Continued)

Of course it did not occur to anyone that the bus boy would have been well educated or would even have individual characteristics. Most patrons, relying on a representativeness heuristic, treated him as nameless staff. Because he possessed the outward features of a bus boy, they projected and inferred these other characteristics. They did not infer intelligence, legal training, and an Ivy League degree.

SUMMARY

Inductive logic and inference are cornerstones of human thinking. As was discussed early in this chapter, the tendency to make inferences is rooted in fairly primitive associative mechanisms. Inferential behaviour can be observed in non-human species – rats, birds, primates, etc. It would be safe to argue that all living organisms make inferences. An inference allows an organism to generate expectations, make predictions, and to learn from past experience. This is not only a central aspect of human thought; it is also a central aspect of thought in general. Induction is in many ways what keeps us from living in an absolute present.

The topic covered in this chapter connects with topics covered earlier. The idea of categorical induction relies not only on the formation of concepts and categories, which was covered in Chapter 4, but also on the general principle of similarity, covered in Chapter 2. As a general rule, the more similar the current situation or event is to some previously experienced situation or event, the easier it is to make inferences, and the more likely we are to trust those inferences and inductions. In Chapter 5, one aspect of language processing we discussed was the tendency to need to generate expectations when hearing or reading a sentence. For the most part, our linguistic inferences help to reduce the inherent ambiguity in language, even though it occasionally produces a false inference, such as the "garden path sentence".

The psychology of inferential reasoning suggests that many of our internal representations are structured and designed in order to facilitate inductive inference. In many ways, this is the main function of a concept.

As with other aspects of human thinking, the design features of our conceptual representation system, similarity, and inferential prediction system allows us to behave adaptively and to make predictions with a minimal amount of computation and to maximize benefits. In many cases, we rely on cognitive shortcuts like the representativeness heuristic. This heuristic is adaptive but occasionally produces errors in reasoning. Subsequent chapters, specifically Chapter 9 on decision-making and Chapter 10 on problem-solving, will explore these kinds of heuristics in greater detail.

7 DEDUCTIVE REASONING

My children (who were 10 and 13 when I was writing this book) have occasionally left something at school, such as a jacket, a book, or even a phone. Later, when they are home, one of them might say "I can't find my jacket". The conversation that usually proceeds is one of retracing steps and trying to remember where the object was last seen. I might offer a suggestion, such as "Well, if it's not in your backpack then it must be at school". By saying that, I'm essentially inviting a logical deduction. We start with the fact that it must be at one location or another and then look to verify the conclusion. My kids might not realize it, but they are working through a basic deduction problem. And sometimes this deductive process results in finding the missing item.

DEDUCTION AND INDUCTION

The previous chapter discussed inductive reasoning. Induction involves making predictive inferences from observations. Induction moves from specific to general (based on evidence) and the conclusions are probabilistic. For that reason, many of the examples in the literature were framed as statements of confidence in a prediction or a generalization. Induction can also be described as going beyond the given evidence to discover something new via thinking. With deductive logic, on the other hand, we are attempting to explain how people make very specific conclusions. Deduction often starts with a general statement ("My jacket is either in my backpack or at school"), and then proceeds to more specific statements ("It's not in my backpack"). Rather than going beyond the given evidence to discover something new via thinking, deduction often involves verifying that which is already known.

The two kinds of reasoning are related in terms of how we use them in everyday thinking, even though the psychology of induction and deduction differ, so much so that it can be difficult to tell if you are using inductive reasoning or deductive reasoning. For example, if I buy a coffee from McDonald's, take a sip, and discover that it is very hot, I conclude that *McDonald's coffee is very hot*. That is a generalization, and I can infer that other McDonald's will serve hot coffee. Categorical induction might even allow me to project the property of "hot" to coffee purchased at other, similar restaurants. In both cases, I am relying on inductive reasoning and past experience to make some conclusions about the future.

Suppose, then, that I form a general premise about McDonald's coffee. This premise can be stated as:

Premise: McDonald's coffee is hot.

A premise like this can be used to make precise conclusions. For example, combined with additional premises and a conclusion, we can create an entire **categorical syllogism**.

Premise: All McDonald's coffee is hot.

Premise: This coffee is from McDonald's.

Conclusion: Therefore this coffee is hot.

In a deductive statement, it is assumed that the premises are true. Given these two premises, the deduction is considered to be valid if the conclusion follows directly from the premises. A valid deduction is one where the conclusion is the only possible conclusion given the premises. In other words, there can be no other possible conclusion from these premises. If these true premises allow for alternative conclusions, then the deduction is not valid.

In the following sections, I consider some basic examples that show how deduction is used in a simple, everyday context. I then consider more complex examples, and show how people often fail to consider the parameters of logical reasoning. Finally, the chapter discusses classical reasoning and conditional reasoning in greater detail, and how these are occasionally challenging for people in reasoning tasks.

THE STRUCTURE OF A LOGICAL TASK

The previous example with McDonald's coffee shows that deduction can be used to arrive at a conclusion about a member of a category. People can also rely on deduction to make predictions about options and outcomes. For example, imagine that you are planning to go shopping at the shopping centre with your friend. She texts you to say that she will meet you by the Starbucks or by the shoe store. You have two options that cannot both be true, but one that must be true. This can be stated more formally as:

Premise: Your friend is waiting at Starbucks or by the shoe store.

Premise: Your friend is not at Starbucks.

Conclusion: Therefore your friend is by the shoe store.

A deductive statement (a **syllogism**) has several components. As with the examples in the preceding chapter on induction, the statement has one or more **premises** and a **conclusion**. The premise gives basic factual information that we can reason from and reason about. In a deductive task, we assume that the premises are true. That is a crucial aspect of deductive logic, because, in many ways, the challenge of deductive logic is evaluating the validity structure of the task (we will discuss some problems with this idea later in the chapter).

Each premise can contain facts and operators. **Facts** are just what you would expect them to be: facts are things that can be true or things that can be false, descriptions, statements about properties, and predicates. The **operators** are crucial to the deduction task, and they are part of what make this different from inductive reasoning. In the example above, the operator "OR" adds meaning to the understanding of the task. This is what allows us to think conditionally about the two alternatives. She is either here OR there. One must be true, but both of these cannot be simultaneously true. If you are given information that one of these is false, then you can conclude that the other must be true. Other common operators are AND, NOT, IF, ALL, SOME, NONE, etc. Each of these defines the nature of the deduction and can modify the complexity of the argument.

The deductive task also has a conclusion, which is usually marked off with expressions like THEREFORE, THEN, etc. In most deductive logic tasks, subjects are usually asked to assume that the premises are true and then determine whether or not the conclusion logically follows. A valid conclusion is one in which the given conclusion is the only possible conclusion given the truth of the premises. An invalid conclusion in one where the same set of premises can give rise to more than one possible opposing conclusion.

Deduction can seem counterintuitive

Although people are constantly making inferences, drawing conclusions, and making predictions about things, deductive logic can often seem counterintuitive. One of the reasons for this is that we may agree with a stated conclusion even if it is not logically valid. Alternatively, we may reject conclusions that are valid. And in other cases, we may agree with a valid conclusion, but for idiosyncratic reasons. Consider an example that comes from a paper by Mary Henle (1962). This was one of the earliest attempts to understand the psychology of deductive logic and thinking. Subjects were given syllogisms in the form of a basic narrative and were then asked about their conclusions.

Syllogism: A group of women were discussing their household problems. Mrs Shivers broke the ice by saying: "I'm so glad we're talking about these problems. It's so important to talk about things that are in our minds. We spend so much of our time in the kitchen that of course household problems are in our minds. So it is important to talk about them."

This is a fairly straightforward syllogism, and Henle asked her subjects to verify if the conclusion (*that it is important to talk about household problems*) was valid. She also asked her subjects to explain why or how they arrived at that conclusion.

She found that many of her subjects failed to reason logically. That is, they failed to distinguish between a conclusion that was logically valid and one that was factually correct or one that they agreed with. These two things are not the same. Henle referred to this as the **failure to accept the logical task**. That is, subjects seemed to place a heavy premium on the content of the syllogism and did not reason logically. For example, one subject in her study suggested that this was not a valid conclusion, and said:

> "The conclusion does not follow. The women must talk about household problems because it is important to talk about their problems not because the problem is in their minds."

In this case, the subject was incorrect to suggest that the conclusion was not valid, and the subject also provided a reason that was based on her own understanding of why we should talk about problems. This is a failure to accept a logical task.

Other subjects suggested correctly that this was a valid conclusion, but gave reasons that suggested a failure to reason logically. For example, another subject said:

> "Yes. It could be very important to the individual doing the talking and possibly to some of those listening, because it is important for people to get a load off their chest. But not for any other reason unless in the process one of the others learned something new of value."

This subject suggested that the conclusion was valid, but again provided an answer that was idiosyncratic and rooted in personal belief. Although the conclusion was correct, this is still a failure to reason logically.

One way in which we can evaluate the validity of this statement is to simplify it somewhat, and then replace some of the facts with variables. Using variables can help because it allows us to examine the structure of the argument separately from the semantics. Henle's syllogism can be simplified as follows:

Premise 1: It is important to talk about the things that are on our mind.

Premise 2: Household problems are on our mind.

Conclusion: It is important to talk about household problems.

We can replace the facts with variables as follows: the phrase "It is important to talk about the things that are on our mind" can be rewritten as "It is important to do A".

The second premise tells us that something else is equivalent to the first fact and we can say B is equal to A.

Premise 1: It is important to do A.

Premise 2: B is equal to A.

Conclusion: It is important to do B.

So the logical task is valid, and it is a fairly straightforward task as a substitution. Henle's point was that people often misunderstand what it means to be logical. People place a heavy premium on the content of the task.

Henle noted other, related problems with deductive thought. For example, subjects often restated specific premises as being universal (Henle, 1962). Consider this syllogism:

> **Syllogism**: Mrs Cooke had studied home economics in college. "Youth is a time of rapid growth and great demands on energy," she said. "Many youngsters don't get enough vitamins in their daily diet. And since some vitamin deficiencies are dangerous to health, it follows that the health of many of our youngsters is being endangered by inadequate diet."

Subjects were asked to indicate if they thought that it was a valid conclusion to say that the "health of many youngsters is being endangered by inadequate diet". Many subjects extended the first premise to be universal by ignoring the word "many" and restating it as "Youngsters do not get enough vitamins". In doing so they endorsed this conclusion.

In short, Henle (1962) noted that people seem not to accept logical tasks as being deducto-logical. They misstate premises, omit premises, and generally fall prey to the kinds of cognitive biases that Kahneman and Tversky would later describe with respect to judgement, inductive reasoning, and decision-making (Kahneman & Tversky, 1973; Tversky & Kahneman, 1973, 1974). It is important to note that these results do not indicate that subjects were unable to reason logically, but only that they did not treat this as a logical task, even when directed to. Henle (1962) suggested that the problem was that people focused on the semantics and the content rather than on the form of the argument itself. And later work confirmed many of these biases and shortcomings. Johnson-Laird suggests that naïve reasoners with no training in formal thought may make many cognitive errors in reasoning and yet still manage to achieve their goals and make good decisions (Johnson-Laird, 1999). He refers to this as a **fundamental paradox of rationality**. This is a paradox because rationality should be a necessary condition for correct decision-making and should be a hallmark of formal, mature thinking, and yet in many ways it does not seem to be necessary at all.

Deductive logic is challenging for most people. The fact that we fail can be attributed to both the complexity and abstractness of the tasks (Johnson-Laird, 1999) as well as the general effectiveness of many cognitive heuristics (Anderson, 1990; Gigerenzer et al., 2011; Sloman, 1996). It may be that for many basic decisions and conclusions, logical deduction is not needed and the additional resources needed to reason correctly may be suboptimal.

BOX 7.1

When I lecture about the psychology of deduction, I have occasionally referred to a movie from 1985 called *Labyrinth* (despite being from the 1980s, I am surprised how many students have seen it). It is principally a children's movie, but several parts are interesting for adults as well. I will summarize the plot briefly.

At the beginning of the movie a young girl, Sarah, expresses some frustration about having to take care of her baby brother. It is a fantasy movie. At some point she wishes that a goblin king will take the baby away. Of course, her wish comes true and the goblin king steals the infant and hides him in a castle. Sarah can retrieve the baby only if she makes it through a labyrinth.

Early in the movie, she is faced with a single passage that ends with two doors. One of the doors is red and one of the doors is blue, and each of these doors has a guard that relates the rules of the "game" that she must play in order to figure out which door to open. The game is a version of a classical logical problem known as the "Knights and Knaves" problem. The guards tell her that one of the doors leads to the castle and the other leads to certain death. They also tell her that one of them always lies and the other always tells the truth. Sarah has to figure out which door to open. In other words, we can state the problems as follows:

Premise: Either the red door leads to the castle or the blue door leads to the castle.

Premise: Either the red guard tells the truth or the blue guard tells the truth.

If you haven't seen this movie before, you may want to take a moment to find this clip on YouTube: it is easily available. And whether or not you have seen the clip, try to solve the problem. There is a correct answer, and I will give the solution at the end of the chapter.

CATEGORICAL REASONING

Categorical reasoning occurs when we make conclusions on the basis of category membership. This is also referred to as **classical reasoning**, because we are reasoning about a class of things. In the previous chapter on inductive reasoning, we also emphasized the importance of categories. In that case, the emphasis was on the similarity between the premise and the conclusion. Stronger similarity results in stronger inductions. With respect to deduction, the emphasis is on category membership rather than similarity. An often-repeated classical syllogism is the following:

Major premise: All men are mortal.

Minor premise: Socrates is a man.

Conclusion: Therefore Socrates is mortal.

In the classical syllogism, the standard format is a major premise, which refers to a statement about the category. In this case, we are suggesting that the category "men" is predicated by the category "mortal". In other words, there is an overlap between the category of men in the category of mortal. In the minor premise, the statement offers specific information. In this syllogism, the major premise tells us about the relationship between the two so that we can transfer the properties of one category to the other. Since all men are mortal and we know that Socrates is a member of the men category, we can conclude that he is also a member of the mortal category, because of the relationship between the two categories stated in the major premise. Notice that there is little role for similarity or featural overlap in these statements. It does not matter how similar (or not) Socrates is to the category of men.

There are many different varieties of formal classical syllogisms. For our purposes, we can focus on four basic versions.

Universal affirmative

The **universal affirmative** is a statement in which the relationship between the two categories is universal for all members, as stated. For example, if we say that "all cats are animals", we are using the universal **affirmative** form. Substituting with variables, we have "All A are B", as shown in Figure 7.1. One aspect of this universal **affirmative** form is that it is

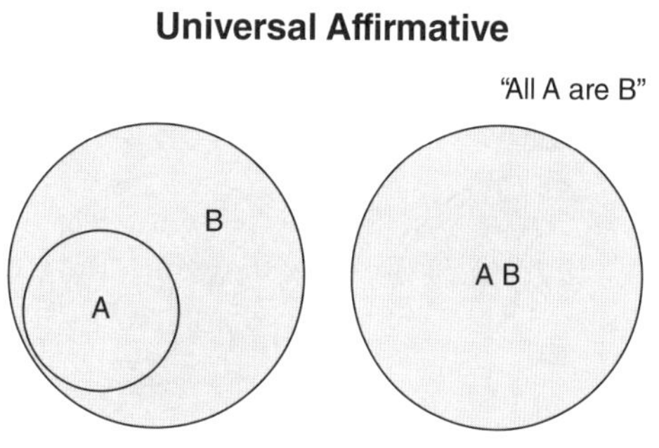

Universal Affirmative

"All A are B"

Figure 7.1 Two possible circle diagrams that illustrate the universal affirmative.

not reflexive, and thus has two possible forms. The first, shown on the left suggests that all members of category A are contained within a larger category B. This suggests a hierarchical relationship such that B is the larger category and A is a subcategory. In this case, it is true to say that all A are B, but the reverse is not true. It is not true to say that all B are A. On the right is the other form of "All A are B". In this case, there is a reflexive relationship and everything in category A is the same as members in category B.

Particular affirmative

If we say "some cats are friendly", we are using an expression known as a particular affirmative. The **particular affirmative** suggests that some members of one category can also be members of another category. As shown in Figure 7.2, there are four possible versions of this statement. Considering the abstract version "Some B are A", the diagram on the top left shows a large category B and a small subordinate category A. In this universe, the statement "Some B are A" is true, because all of the members of category A are also members of the category B, but there are many other members of the category B which are not also members of category A. At the top right, the diagram shows two partially overlapping categories. And so in this universe, the statement "Some B are A" is also true, because whatever is contained in the overlap between the A category and the B category confirms this premise.

The two diagrams on the bottom are more difficult conceptually. When we hear that "Some B are A", it is important to realize that the word "some" can mean *at least one, and possibly all*. The reason is that as long as one member of category B is also a member of category A, the statement is true. And even if all the Bs are members of category A, the statement "Some B are A" is still true. Or think about it this way, if it turned out that all cats were friendly, and I said to you "some cats are friendly", I would not be telling a lie. This would be a true statement. "Some" does not preclude "all".

So in the bottom left, the diagram shows that all members of category B are equivalent to the members of category A. Although this is an example of a universal affirmative, it can also be an example of a particular affirmative. The statement "Some B are A" is still true. Admittedly, it is an incomplete statement but in a universe in which all members of category A are equivalent to all members of category B, it does not render the

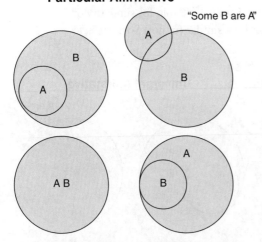

Particular Affirmative

"Some B are A"

Figure 7.2 Four possible circle diagrams that illustrate the particular affirmative.

statement "Some B are A" to be untrue. This is also the case for the figure on the bottom right. Here we see that category A is the superordinate category, and that all members of category B are subordinate. In this case, we can still say "Some B are A", and that is a true statement within this arrangement of categories.

What this means is that the particular affirmative is a very difficult statement to evaluate. It gives reliable information about the status of at least one and possibly all members of category B. It tells you very little about the status of category A and it tells you very little about the entire relationship between categories A and B. When evaluating a series of statements for which one of them is a particular affirmative, considerable care must be taken to avoid an invalid conclusion.

Universal negative

If we say that "no cats are dogs", we are using a statement referred to as a universal negative. The **universal negative** expresses a relationship between two concepts for which there is absolutely no overlap. In contrast to the universal affirmative and the particular affirmative, the universal negative has only one representation. It is also reflexive. The statement does not tell us much about other relationships with respect to category A and category B, except to tell us that these two categories do not overlap at all (see Figure 7.3).

Particular negative

If I say that "some cats are not friendly", I'm using the **particular negative**. In this case, I want to get across the point that some members of one category are not members of another category. As with many of the other examples, there are several ways for this statement to be true. In Figure 7.4, we see three different ways in which the statement "Some A are not B" can be true. On the top left is shown the case where the superordinate category A contains a subordinate category B. This allows for the statement to be true, because there are many members of category A which are not contained within the

Universal Negative

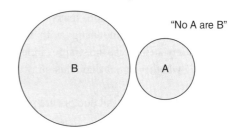

Figure 7.3 One circle diagram that illustrates the universal negative.

Particular Negative

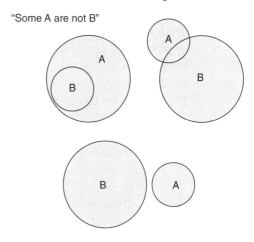

Figure 7.4 Three possible circle diagrams that illustrate the particular negative.

subordinate category B. On the top right, we see the example with a partially overlapping category A and category B. In this example, the statement is still true because there are many members of category A which do not overlap with category B. At the bottom of the figure, a diagram shows a case where the two categories do not overlap at all. Although this diagram also represents a universal negative relationship, the statement "Some A are not B" is still technically true in this case. Yes, the diagram suggests that no As are B, but that does not mean that the "Some A are not B" statement is untrue.

Context errors in classical reasoning

Reasoning about categories and concepts is a fairly common behaviour, but because of the occasional ambiguity and complexity of these classical relationships people often make errors. In addition, many of the errors that we make are a result of conflating personal beliefs and knowledge with the notion of logical validity. One way to avoid making these errors is to use the simple circle diagrams like those shown in Figures 7.1–7.4 to determine whether or not a conclusion is valid. Consider the following syllogism:

Premise: All doctors are professional people.

Premise: Some professional people are rich.

Conclusion: Therefore some doctors are rich.

The first premise tells us something about the relationship between doctors (for the present example let's assume medical doctors) and the category of professional people. It tells us that everyone who is a doctor is also a member of this category. It leaves open the possibility that the two categories are entirely overlapping, or that there is a larger category of professional people which also includes teachers, engineers, lawyers, etc. The second premise tells us something about some of the professional people. It tells us that some of them (meaning at least one and possibly all) are rich. Both premises express a fact, and in both cases the facts conforms to our beliefs. We know the doctors are professional, and we also know that at least some people in the category of professional people can be rich.

The conclusion that we are asked to accept is that some doctors are also rich. The problem with this deduction is that it conforms to our beliefs and those beliefs can interfere with our ability to reason logically. We might know a rich doctor, or have friends or family who are rich doctors. That is not an unreasonable thing to believe because although not all doctors are rich, certainly we are all aware that some of them can be. We know this to be true from personal experience, but that knowledge does not guarantee a valid deduction. A conclusion is valid only if it is the only one that we can draw from the stated premises.

Figure 7.5 shows two of several possible arrangements of the categories. On the left, it shows one possible arrangement of the categories such that the premises are true and the conclusion is true. It shows doctors as a subcategory of professional people, and it shows

An Invalid Deduction

Premise: All doctors are professional people
Premise: Some professional people are rich
Conclusion: Therefore, some doctors are rich

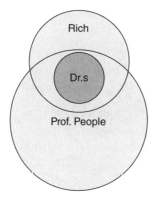 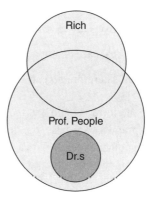

Figure 7.5 This is an example of an invalid categorical statement. Both sets of circles allow for the premises to be true and yet they support contradictory conclusions.

a category of rich people that overlaps with professional people and includes the doctors. And so in this universe, the first premise is true because all of the doctors are professional people. The category of rich people overlaps partially with the category of professional people, allowing the second premise to be true. Finally, because the category of rich people overlaps with the category of professional people and includes the doctors, it allows for the conclusion to be true as well. This state of affairs conforms to our understanding of doctors as generally being financially well-off.

The problem is that this is only one of many possible arrangements of the classes that allows for the premises to be true. On the right is an alternative arrangement. In this case, the category of doctors is still completely subsumed within the category of professional people, thus allowing for the first premise to be true. This also shows that the category of rich people partially overlaps with the category of professional people, thus allowing for the second premise to be true. However, the overlap between the rich people and the professional people excludes all of the doctors. In this arrangement, both premises are still true but the conclusion is not. In this arrangement, no doctors are rich. The existence of both of these arrangements, which allow for the premises to be true but make different predictions with respect to the conclusion, indicates that this is not a valid syllogism. Of course, one might protest the conclusion of invalidity because it is not true that no doctors are rich. You surely know one or two rich doctors or at least have heard of one or two rich doctors. That is one of the things that is challenging about deductive logic. This is not a valid argument and yet the conclusion can still be true. In logical deduction, it is often difficult to separate truth from validity.

A related problem can occur for valid deductions. It is possible to have a valid argument that is unsound. An unsound but valid deduction is one for which the conclusion directly follows from the premises but is still unacceptable. This can arise when one of the premises is false. Consider the following example (Evans, 2005):

Premise: All frogs are mammals.

Premise: No cats are mammals.

Conclusion: Therefore no cats are frogs.

In this case, the form is valid and the conclusion is both true and validly drawn. And yet, because the premises are false, the deduction is not sound.

Consider another example with a valid structure but a false conclusion rather than a true conclusion, as in the preceding example:

Premise: All students are lazy.

Premise: No lazy people pass examinations.

Conclusion: Therefore no students pass examinations.

In this case, although one could imagine the second premise being true, the first premise is not true. However, the structure of the task is valid. And so it does follow from these two premises that no students pass examinations. This is demonstrably false, and so this argument is considered to be valid but not sound. A **sound argument** is a valid argument based on true premises. An argument that is sound guarantees a true valid conclusion.

All of these examples suggest a clear limitation for deductive reasoning within the scope of human thinking abilities. Johnson-Laird (1999) suggests that the main limitation of deduction is that it really does not allow one to learn new information because logical arguments depend on assumptions or suppositions. He suggests that deduction may enable you to arrive at conclusions that were drawn about evidence that is present, but it may not add new information in the way that induction can. Deduction allows a person to test the strength of their conclusions and beliefs. Induction allows a person to acquire new information by thinking.

CONDITIONAL REASONING

In the previous section I considered reasoning about classes of things, but people also reason about conditionality and causality. These kinds of deductions are usually framed within the context of if/then statements. For example, "if you study for an exam, then you will do well". This statement reflects a relationship between a behaviour (studying) and an outcome (doing well). It reflects only one direction; there may be other things that affect your doing well. And as with categorical reasoning, there are several forms of conditional reasoning. The combination of these forms allows for a variety of valid and not valid statements to be expressed and evaluated.

Before describing the different versions of conditional reasoning, consider the components of a conditional reasoning statement:

Premise: If A, then B.

Premise: A is true.

Conclusion: Therefore B is true.

In the first premise, "A" is referred to as the **antecedent**. It is the thing or fact that occurs first. "B" is referred to as the **consequent**. The consequent is the thing that happens as a consequence of A being true. The second premise gives information about the antecedent within the premise. In this example, it gives information about the antecedent being true.

Affirming the antecedent

A common conditional syllogism is one in which a relationship is expressed between an antecedent and a consequent and with the given information that the antecedent is true. Consider the example below:

Premise: If the cat is hungry, then she will eat her food.

Premise: The cat is hungry.

Conclusion: Therefore she will eat her food.

In this case, we are informed that if the cat is hungry (the antecedent), then she will eat her food (the consequent). The second premise indicates that she is hungry and thus affirms the antecedent. Thus, it can be concluded that she will eat her food. If you accept these premises, you know that if the cat is hungry she will eat. This is a straightforward relationship that is often referred to as **modus ponens**, which in Latin means "the mode of affirming that which is true". This deduction is valid. It is also easy for most of us to understand because it is consistent with our bias to look for confirmatory evidence. This chapter will discuss confirmation bias later.

Denying the consequent

In the previous example, the statement affirmed the antecedent to allow for a valid deduction. However, imagine the same initial premise and now the second premise denies the consequent:

Premise: If the cat is hungry, then she will eat her food.

Premise: She will not eat her food.

Conclusion: Therefore the cat is not hungry.

In this example, the consequent is that she will eat her food. If that consequent is denied by saying "She will not eat her food", then you can deduce that the antecedent did not happen. The first premise tells you the relationship between the antecedent and the consequent. If the antecedent occurs, then the consequent must happen. If the consequent did not happen, then it is valid to deduce that the antecedent did not happen either. This relationship is more difficult for most people to grasp. It runs counter to the bias to look for confirmatory evidence, even though it is still valid. This form is also known by a Latin name, **modus tollens**, which is a statement that means "the mode of denying".

Denying the antecedent

When you affirm the antecedent or deny a consequent, you are carrying out a logically valid form of conditional reasoning. Both of these actions allow for a unique conclusion to be drawn from the premises. However, other premises produce invalid conclusions. For example, the statements below show an example of denying the antecedent:

Premise: If the cat is hungry, then she will eat her food.

Premise: The cat is not hungry.

Conclusion: Therefore she will not eat her food.

In this example, the first premise is the same as the previous cases, but the second premise denies the antecedent by telling us that the cat is not hungry. With this information, you may be tempted to assume that the consequent will not happen either. After all, you are told that if she is hungry, she will eat. You then find out she is not hungry, so it is natural to assume that she will not eat as a result. You cannot conclude this, however. The reason is that the first premise only gives us information about what happens with a true antecedent and a consequent. It does not tell you information about the false antecedent. In other words, it does not rule out the possibility that the cat could eat her food for other reasons. She can eat even if she is not hungry. And so, finding out that she is not hungry does not allow you to conclude that she will not eat. You can suspect this. You can possibly infer that it might happen. But you cannot arrive at that conclusion exclusively.

Affirming the consequent

The final example is one where you receive information that the consequent is true. Just like the preceding example, this one might seem intuitive but is not logically valid. An example is below:

Premise: If the cat is hungry, then she will eat her food.

Premise: The cat will eat her food.

Conclusion: Therefore the cat is hungry.

The first premise is the same as the preceding examples and expresses the relationship between the hungry cat and the cat eating her food. The second premise affirms the consequent, that is, you are told that she does in fact eat her food. You may be tempted to infer backwards that the cat must have been hungry. But just like the preceding example, the first premise tells you a directional relationship between the hungry cat and eating, but does not tell you anything at all about other possible antecedents for the cat eating her food. As a result, knowing that she eats her food (affirming the consequent) does not allow for an exclusive conclusion that the cat's hunger (the antecedent) was true. And so this is also an invalid deduction.

CARD SELECTION TASKS

Some of the most well-known reasoning tasks in the psychological literature are the various card selection tasks. These tasks are able to assess the ability of a person to evaluate evidence and arrive at deductions. Unlike the categorical and conditional examples given above, in which we might be asked to say whether or not a given conclusion is valid, the card selection tasks ask the subject to arrive at the deduction and make a choice on the basis of that deduction. In these tasks, subjects are typically given one or more rules to evaluate. The rules refer to the relationship of symbols, letters, numbers, or facts that are presented on two-sided cards. In order to determine whether or not the rule is valid, subjects indicate which cards should be investigated. In this respect, the card selection tasks might have some degree of ecological validity with respect to how deduction is used in everyday thinking. The card task tries to answer the following question: If you are given a series of facts, how do you go about verifying whether or not those facts are true?

Because these tasks have been so well studied, they have also helped to uncover several biases in human reasoning. The first and most extensive is what I have referred to as the **confirmation bias**. This bias shows up in card selection tasks but also in other kinds of thinking behaviour. A confirmation bias reflects that bias in humans to search for evidence that confirms our belief. This bias is pervasive and ubiquitous (Nickerson, 1998). Earlier in this chapter I discussed an invalid categorical syllogism concerning some doctors being rich. If you believed that doctors were rich, you might show a confirmation bias if you only searched for evidence of rich doctors. The confirmation bias would also show up if you tended to downplay or discount information that was inconsistent with your belief, or that would disconfirm your belief. In other words, even if you did meet a doctor who was not rich, you might downplay that evidence as an anomaly, or someone who just wasn't rich yet.

We often see evidence of confirmation bias in popular media. In the 1990s, dietary advice strongly suggested that the best way to eat healthily and reduce weight was to reduce the amount of fat in the food you ate. There was a heavy emphasis on "low-fat" foods. At the same time, there was a heavy emphasis on eating high carbohydrate foods. Plain pasta was good, butter and oil were bad. Although we know now that this advice was not very sound, it had a long-lasting effect on personal health. One of the possible reasons is that when people were avoiding fat, they were avoiding higher calorie and richer foods. This may have given the impression that it was the fat that was causing dietary problems when in fact it may have been a simple issue of overall consumption. People notice many positive factors when switching to a restricted diet of any kind, such as vegan diets or so-called "paleo" diets. If you switch to a diet like this, and you notice some weight loss, you tend to attribute the weight loss to the specifics of the diet rather than the general tendency to be more selective. This is a confirmation bias. You believe that eating a high protein diet will result in weight loss, and you may miss the alternative explanation that a restricted diet of any kind can also result in weight loss. The low-fat diet craze of the 1990s was even more difficult because of the strong but incorrect belief of the equivalency between dietary fat and body fat. It is possible that the surface-level correspondence between these two kinds of fats encouraged people to see a confirmatory match where one was not present.

Wason card selection task

The confirmation bias has often been studied with a card selection task. The most well-known example of a card selection task is the one developed by Wason in the 1960s (Evans, 2005; Wason, 1960, 1966; Wason & Evans, 1975). The most elemental version is shown in Figure 7.6. Subjects are shown four cards laid out on a table. Each card can have a number or a letter on each side. Subjects are then given a rule to evaluate and are told to indicate the minimum number of cards to turn over in order to verify whether or not this rule is true. For example, considering the cards shown in Figure 7.6, the rule might be:

Premise: If a card has a vowel on one side then it has an even number on the other side.

Looking at these cards, which ones would you turn over in order to evaluate this rule? Most people agree that the first card to turn over would be the one with the A on it. If you turn this card over and there is no even number, then the rule is false. This is straightforward because it is an example of affirming the antecedent. The antecedent in this case is "If a card has a vowel on one side", so you can see if that is true with the A card. You turn it over to see if the rule is being followed. In the original studies, Wason also found that people almost always suggested turning over the "4" card in addition to the A card. By turning over the 4 card, subjects were looking to see if there was a vowel on the other side. But this is an example of a confirmation bias where you look for evidence to confirm the statement. This is also an example of affirming the consequent, which is known to be an invalid form of conditional reasoning. The rule does not specify the entire range of possibilities with respect to even number cards. The even number can occur on the other side of a vowel card, as suggested by the rule, but the rule does not exclude the possibility of an even number occurring on the back of other cards. In fact, the rule would be true even if even numbers occurred on the back of all cards. If every single card shown in this array had an even number on the other side, the rule would be true.

Wason argued that the correct solution to this problem is to turn over the A card, and also the 7 card. The 7 card looks to disconfirm the rule. This is an example of denying the consequent. If the 7 card has a vowel on the other side, then the rule is false. Wason and others have argued that this confirmation bias can also be described as a matching bias (Wason, 1966; Wason & Evans, 1975). In other words, subjects tend to match their behaviour to the stated hypothesis.

How does this matching behaviour come about? One possibility is limitations in attention and working memory capacity. Given the statements, it may simply be a less demanding task to pick two cards that conform most closely to the hypothesis that was stated. Choosing to turn over a card that tests for denying the consequent requires the consideration of a premise that is not explicitly stated. In order to arrive at this implicitly stated premise, the subject must have sufficient working memory resources to hold the stated premise in mind along with the unstated premise. This is not impossible, but it may not be straightforward. As a result, people tend to choose confirmatory evidence.

Wason Card Selection Task

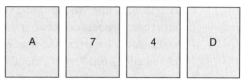

"If a card has a vowel on one side then it has an even number on the other side."

| A | 7 | 4 | D |

Figure 7.6 This is the standard version of the card selection task.

In some ways, the pervasiveness of confirmation bias may be related to the notion of entrenchment. It is culturally and linguistically entrenched to think in terms of describing something *that is*. So when a person confirms a hypothesis, they look for evidence that something is true. The resulting search space is smaller and is constrained, and there is a direct correspondence between the hypothesis and the evidence. When searching for disconfirmatory evidence, the search space is much larger because people will be searching for something that "*is not*". Goodman and others have argued that "what something is not" is not a projectable predicate (Goodman, 1983).

Deontic selection tasks

The standard confirmation bias shown in the Wason card selection task does not always play out. Alternative versions of the card selection task can be arranged that are formally equivalent on the surface but ask the subject to adopt a different perspective. In many cases, a **permission schema** is easier for subjects to consider. That is, when thinking about categories, it makes sense to think about what something *is* but not so much to think about what it is not. An animal can be described as a member of the DOG category, but it is not very informative to describe the same animal as not being a member of the FORK category, or the BEVERAGE category. The list of categories for which the animal is not a member is essentially infinite. So, with respect to category membership and reasoning, it is understandable that humans display a confirmation bias. Confirmatory evidence is manageable whereas disconfirmatory evidence is potentially unmanageable.

But when thinking about permission, it is common to think about what you can do and what you cannot do. In fact, this is essentially how we think about permission. Technically permission is something you are permitted or allowed to do, but we often conceive permission to be freedom from restriction. Speed limits tell us how fast we are permitted to travel, but we tend to consider the ramifications of exceeding the speed limit. The green light at a traffic intersection permits you to drive, but the bigger deal is what happens when the red light comes on and you have to stop.

Wason's card selection task can be reconstructed as one requiring permission. This is referred to as a deontic selection task (Griggs & Cox, 1983). Figure 7.7 shows an example. In this case, the cards have

Deontic Selection Task

"If a person is drinking alcohol they must be over 19."

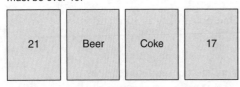

| 21 | Beer | Coke | 17 |

Figure 7.7 This is the deontic version of the card selection task that invokes a permission schema.

ages and beverages on either side. Just as in the standard version, subjects are given a rule to evaluate and asked to indicate the minimum number of cards they need to turn over in order to evaluate this rule. In this case the rule might be:

Premise: If a person is drinking alcohol they must be over 19.

I am using 19 here because that's the legal drinking age in Ontario where I live. Different countries have different minimum drinking ages, so just replace that with the age where you live when you consider this example. Subjects rarely fail this task. It is straightforward to realize that you need to check the age of the beer drinker, and you need to check with the 17-year-old who is drinking. Even if you have never been in a scenario where you need to ensure that an establishment or club is following the law, most people know what it means to have permission to legally consume alcohol. Very few subjects show a confirmation bias here.

The explanation is that this task appeals to the permission schema. The permission schema limits the number of hypotheses that need to be considered. It is important to note that this task succeeds in eliciting logical behaviour not because it makes it more concrete or realistic, but rather because the permission schema reduces the number of options and makes it easier to consider what violates the rule. Other research has shown the same effects even with fairly abstract material (Cheng & Holyoak, 1985).

Context effects

The deontic selection task shows that perspective and context can affect reasoning behaviour as well. For example, in the task shown in Figure 7.7, if you are trying to enforce drinking laws, you check the beer drinker and the 17-year-old. But if you are trying to make sure that people who can drink legally are in fact consuming the alcohol (suppose you want to really increase sales), you can imagine checking the 21-year-old to make sure that they are actually drinking beer. After all, in that scenario, you may want them to drink beer.

Several studies have looked at the effect of context more systematically. Figure 7.8 shows an example of four cards that have facts about how much a person has spent in the store and whether or not they took a free gift. Subjects are told to evaluate the following rule:

The Role of Schema

"If a customer spends more than $ 100 then they may take a free gift."

Figure 7.8 A modified version of the selection task that can show effects of local schema and context.

Premise: If a customer spends more than $100 then they may take a free gift.

In addition to just being shown the cards and given the premise, subjects are then given one of two perspectives. If subjects are given the perspective of a store detective looking for customers who might be cheating the free gift policy, they tend to choose cards 2 and 3. In this case, you work for the store and you want to make sure that the person who has the free gift spent enough to deserve it, and you also want to make sure that the person who did not spend enough to take a free gift did not in fact take one. You don't care about the person who did not take the gift, even if they spent enough, because you are looking out for cheaters.

Other subjects are told to assume the perspective of a consumer or customer advocate. In this case, you want to make sure that the store is keeping its promise. These subjects turned over cards 1 and 4. In this case, you are on the side of the customer. You want to make sure that the person who spent $120 was indeed offered a free gift. And you want to make sure that the person who did not take the free gift was not offered one because he or she did not spend enough. You are less concerned about the person who received the free gift.

SUMMARY

Deductive reasoning is fairly straightforward to describe in many ways. Deductive tasks generally follow a strict logical form. There are clear cases for deductions that are valid and not valid. And there is a fairly straightforward definition for sound and unsound deductions. And yet, most people have difficulty with deductive reasoning. Deductive reasoning seems to be outside the ability of many people. And as discussed in this chapter, many people reason, make decisions, and solve problems in ways that define a logical deduction and yet still succeed in allowing people to accomplish goals. This raises important questions about the role of deductive logic within the psychology of thinking.

Several of the upcoming chapters in Section 3 will discuss the psychology of decision-making, probability estimation, and problem solving. Many of the cognitive biases that undermine deductive reasoning will also undermine sound decision-making. But, as with deductive reasoning, evidence suggests that many people still make adaptive and smart decisions despite these biases.

Solution to the two doors problem

In Box 7.1, I presented a logical problem based on a movie. If you watched the movie, Sarah solves the riddle. She says to the guard of the red door, "Would he tell me that this door leads to the castle?" In other words, she asks RED, "Would he (BLUE) tell me that this door (RED) leads to the castle?" RED says "yes". From this, she is able to determine BLUE is the right door and RED is the wrong door. She is able to arrive at this conclusion without knowing who is lying and who is telling the truth. Her reasoning is as follows:

If RED is telling the truth then BLUE is a liar.

If BLUE would say RED leads to the castle, it would be a lie.

Therefore RED does not lead to the castle.

BLUE = castle, RED = Death

If RED is telling the lie then BLUE is telling the truth.

It is a lie that BLUE would say that RED leads to the castle.

Therefore BLUE would say that BLUE leads to the castle.

Therefore BLUE = castle, RED = Death

8 CONTEXT, MOTIVATION, AND MOOD

One of the most exciting areas in the field of the psychology of thinking is the study of how situational contexts, motivational factors, and mood state influence people's thinking. For example, nearly everyone has some experience of a frustrating or demanding commute to work in the morning, or a very busy morning routine. Think about how those events might affect your ability to solve a problem or make an important decision. If you have had a stressful drive to work and are immediately faced with needing to make an important decision, it is not unreasonable to think that your ability to make that decision may be compromised. In fact, some research suggests that when you have experienced some cognitive fatigue, you are more likely to use decision-making heuristics (Vohs et al., 2008). Furthermore, you are more likely to use those heuristics unwisely and to fall prey to decision-making biases.

Or consider another example. You have received a really nice message from a good friend right as you sit down to your laptop to work. This puts you in a very good mood. Your good mood has energized you and you are able to work on a work-related problem that has been bothering you for a while. The good mood gives you stamina to keep going and you solve the problem. Contrast this with a feeling of frustration that might come from trying to do too many things at once. Thinking about competing deadlines and the short timeframe in which you need to solve the work-related problem may interfere with your ability to solve it properly.

In both of the preceding examples, the context around the problem-solving or decision-making event may be having an effect on your ability to behave optimally. Consider the role of context on thinking as it has been covered so far in this book. Most of the chapters in this text have discussed different kinds of thinking in controlled environments, such as research laboratories. In Chapter 3 on memory, we discussed the role of context in the activation of schemas. Chapter 4 on concepts and categories was about how information is structured in memory so that it can influence thinking behaviours. Chapter 6 discussed the role of knowledge in many of the inductive inferences that people make and how this can sometimes lead to biases like the representativeness heuristic. We saw in Chapter 7 the role of knowledge and context in human reasoning. In this chapter, I will discuss how physiological, contextual, and social factors affect many of the core thinking processes that have already been covered, and also the core processes that will be covered in subsequent chapters. I have placed this chapter before those discussing decision-making and problem-solving because I think it will be helpful to provide this context.

THE DUAL PROCESS ACCOUNT

The dual process account was covered briefly in Chapter 1. This theoretical account of human cognition is sometimes called the "dual systems" account, and both terms are in common parlance. I use the term "**dual process**" because it is the more common of the two. The two components of the dual process account are usually referred to as "systems". Thus the dual process account is comprised of two systems. I will also sometimes use the term "process" to refer to the individual, basic cognitive processes (like working memory, or attention) that make up one or the other system in the dual process account. I realize this terminology can be confusing, but I've tried my best to be consistent. The dual process account has been one of the more influential theories about the thinking process in the last 20 years (Sloman, 1996). Much of the research on how mood affects thinking or on how cognitive fatigue affects thinking can be understood within the framework of this dual process account.

System 1

System 1 has been described as an evolutionary primitive form of cognition (Evans, 2003). This means that the structures and processes associated with System 1 are likely to be shared across many animal species. At the lowest level, all animal species are able to make quick responses to threatening stimuli. All animals are able to generalize responses to stimuli that are similar to threatening stimuli. The same can be said for stimuli that fulfil a basic drive. An animal can respond quickly to a potential food source, a potential mate, etc. For cognitively primitive species, we do not consider this kind of behaviour to be thinking. A mouse that moves towards a food source and away from an open space that could expose it to predators is not thinking about its behaviours. Rather, it is behaving. This is a combination of innate responding and instinct and learned associations. The larger cat that is watching the mouse and seemingly waiting for the ideal time to pounce is also not thinking about its behaviours. The cat is also behaving in accordance with instinct and learned associations. Neither the cat nor the mouse possesses sufficient cortical volume to be able to carry out what we consider to be thinking. They cannot contemplate various outcomes, they cannot consider the pros and cons of when to run and when to pounce. The cat and the mouse don't think. They just behave.

The same mechanisms that allow the mouse and the cat to make fast decisions influence fast decision-making in cognitively more sophisticated animals like non-human primates and humans. Humans, of course, possess many of the same instincts that other animals do. We remove our hand from a painful stimulus without thinking about it. The neural structures that subserve this instinct do not engage higher-level cognitive processes. Subcortical structures, such as the amygdala and the limbic system in general, regulate emotional responses to stimuli. This is how we are able to react to hunger, and to proceed cautiously when we detect the state of potential threat. This is also how we can experience anxiety in a state of uncertainty.

Properly described, System 1 is not a single system but rather a cluster of cognitive and behavioural subsystems and processes that operate somewhat independently, and with some autonomy. For example, the aforementioned instinctive behaviours which exist in all animals are part of this system. The general **associative learning system** that is responsible for operant and classical conditioning is also part of the system. This includes a dopaminergic reward system, whereby a positive outcome strengthens connections between neural responses and a non-positive outcome does not strengthen the associations. Most dual process theorists assume that the information processing carried out by the collection of cognitive processes that make up System 1 are largely automatic, take place outside conscious access, and are not amenable to cognitive appraisal. Only the final output of these processes is available to consciousness (Evans & Stanovich, 2013). System 1 cognition is also generally conducted in parallel. That is, many of the subprocesses can operate simultaneously without cost.

System 2

System 2 is generally thought to have evolved in humans much later than System 1. Most theorists assume that System 2 is uniquely human. System 2 thought is characterized by slower processing. System 2 is also assumed to be mediated by linguistic processes. In other words, the contents of our thoughts are able to be described via language. We use language productively to arrive at a decision using System 2.

System 2 thought is also generally carried out in serial or sequential fashion, rather than in parallel fashion, as in System 1. System 2 makes use of humans' working memory and attentional systems. In other words, relative to System 1, cognition and information-processing carried out by System 2 is slower, more deliberative, and limited in capacity. However, despite these limitations, System 2 is able to carry out abstract thinking that is not possible in System 1. As an example, consider the two most common ways of arriving at a simple decision. When faced with the opportunity to make a purchase, you can make an impulsive decision, based on what "feels right", or you can deliberate and consider the costs and benefits of buying versus not buying the item. The impulsive decision is likely driven by the processes in System 1, whereas the deliberation is made possible by the ability to hold two alternatives in working memory at the same time, to assess attributes and to think proactively and retroactively to consider the costs and benefits. This takes time. This takes cognitive effort. And this cannot be carried out in the fast, intuitive, and associative System 1. This kind of thinking can be carried out only in the slower, deliberative System 2.

BOX 8.1

The **marshmallow test** is the common name for an effect first discovered by Walter Mischel and Ebbe B. Ebbesen in 1970 (Mischel & Ebbesen, 1970). The original study was designed to investigate the phenomenon of delayed gratification in children. Children aged 4–6 were seated at the table and a tempting treat was placed before them (it is often a marshmallow, but is just as likely to be a cookie or something similar). The children were told that they could eat the treat now or, if they could wait 15 minutes without eating it, they could get two treats. The researchers then left the room. Typically, younger children were unable to wait the 15 minutes; they ate the treat. Other children, in order to try to make themselves last the 15 minutes, covered their eyes or turned away. In some cases, children became agitated and were unable to sit still while they waited. In general, the results showed that many children could wait, but other children could not. Age was one of the primary predictors. But the researchers speculated that personality characteristics or temperament might also be playing the role. Later research discovered that the children who were most able to resist temptation of instant gratification were likely to have higher test scores.

The children who took part in the original study were followed up 10 years later. Many of the children who were able to delay gratification were more likely to be described by their peers as competent. Later research found that subjects who were able to delay gratification were more likely to have greater density in the prefrontal cortex whereas subjects who were less likely to delay, or who had shorter delay times, had higher activation in the ventral striatum. This area is linked to addictive behaviours. The suggestion is that the "marshmallow test" taps into a self-regulatory trait or resource that reliably predicts other measures of success later in life.

One possibility is that the struggle between eating the marshmallow right away or sooner versus delaying for a larger reward represents the conflict between System 1 thought and System 2 thought. System 2 thought is highly associated with the prefrontal cortex areas that showed greater activation in those participants who were able to delay gratification longer. The implication is that they may have earlier access to the substructures that make up System 2. These children were able to consider the costs and benefits. These children were able to delay the gratification because they could reason whereas other participants could not delay the gratification. Relatively less well developed processes of inhibitory control would mean that the faster System 1 would initiate and carry out the behaviour and the System 2 would be unable to override it.

The marshmallow test is not typically interpreted within the context of dual systems theory; however the notion of conflict between an instinctive response and a measured response is perfectly in line with the theory.

Experimental evidence for the dual process account

The previous section described the general characteristics of the two thought systems. In this section I want to describe some of the key empirical research that supports this distinction. One of the strongest paradigms to show a role for two different systems in reasoning ability is what is known as a **belief bias task**. Evans (2003, 2008; Evans & Stanovich, 2013) carried out several studies that were designed to create a conflict between the output of System 1 and the output of System 2. In this case, System 1 output is the result of memory retrieval and beliefs, whereas the output from System 2 is the result of a logical deduction. Memory retrieval is fast and automatic, and represents a quick way to make a heuristically based response. System 2 typically handles logical reasoning.

In the belief bias task, participants were presented with different kinds of syllogisms that display different degrees of conflict between the output of the two systems. The first kind of syllogism was a **no conflict syllogism** in which the argument was both valid and believable. For example:

Premise: No police dogs are vicious.

Premise: Some highly trained dogs are vicious.

Conclusion: Therefore some highly trained dogs are not police dogs.

The conclusion is the only one that can be drawn from the premises. Furthermore, it is quite believable that there are some highly trained dogs which are not police dogs. And so there is no conflict between the participants' memory and belief, and their ability to comprehend the logical task.

Other syllogisms were valid but the conclusion was not believable. These were **conflict syllogisms**. For example:

Premise: No nutritional things are inexpensive.

Premise: Some vitamin tablets are inexpensive.

Conclusion: Therefore some vitamin tablets are not nutritional.

In this case, the structure is logically valid such that the conclusion is able to be drawn unambiguously from the stated premises. However, most people regard vitamins as being nutritionally beneficial. Leave aside any recent medical evidence that many vitamin supplements are less than what they purport to be, this is only an example, and the experiment was carried out in an era when vitamin supplements were regarded positively by both the scientific and non-scientific communities. In this case, the conclusion that some vitamins are not nutritional is less believable.

An alternative kind of conflict argument is one in which the argument is invalid and yet the conclusion is believable. For example:

Premise: No addictive things are inexpensive.

Premise: Some cigarettes are inexpensive.

Conclusion: Therefore some addictive things are not cigarettes.

This can be a challenging syllogism. It is not logically valid (refer back to Chapter 7 on deductive reasoning to see other examples for why this syllogism is not valid but believable).

Finally, participants were also shown a syllogism in which there was no conflict because it was neither valid nor believable. For example:

Premise: No millionaires are hard workers.

Premise: Some rich people are hard workers.

Conclusion: Therefore some millionaires are not rich people.

There is no conflict here because whether you try to solve this from believability and memory or from logical reasoning, the syllogism is still false.

In the experiments, participants were explicitly told to engage in a logical reasoning task and to indicate as acceptable *only* the syllogisms that were logically valid. That is, they should endorse the first two examples because they are both valid. It shouldn't matter whether they are believable or not. Not surprisingly, however, the participants in Evans' experiments were influenced by the believability. That is, when there was no conflict, the valid argument was accepted more often, and when there was no conflict, the invalid argument was accepted less often. For conflict cases, there was much less clarity. According to the dual process account, these participants were unable to negotiate the conflict between the memory-based solution provided by System 1 and the logical solution provided by System 2. When there is no conflict, and the systems generate the same answer, the endorsements are correct. When there is conflict, the endorsements are incorrect.

The dual process account is compelling and relevant to the psychology of thinking because many of the topics discussed below deal with situational or state variables that interfere with the operation of one system or the other. For example, if your cognitive resources are taxed and depleted, it may interfere with the operation of System 2 and thus allow System 1 to provide the behavioural output. Alternatively, if subjects are in a good mood, it may facilitate the operation of System 2, which makes it easier to override System 1. Both of these topics are discussed below. Finally, as we will see in Chapter 11 on expertise, if the information provided by System 1 is driven by a considerable experience and a rich knowledge base, it may be preferable to the output provided by System 2. This is a debate that is ongoing in the literature and will be explored in greater detail later.

MOTIVATION AND THINKING

Personal motivation and contextual motivation can affect the thinking process. As a very straightforward example, think about the difference between doing something because you want to do it versus doing something because you have to do it. That is the difference between **intrinsic motivation** and **extrinsic motivation**. When I was a student in primary school, I spent a fair amount of time avoiding the assigned work. Like many students, I brought my own reading material to school and spent time reading books like *Lord of the Rings* rather than texts that were assigned by the teacher. In the same vein, I spent time designing characters and campaigns for the *Dungeons & Dragons* game, which in early 1980s was very popular among some non-athletic kids (e.g., me). Other students would do the same things, although perhaps their interests were sports or popular culture. The point is that all of us spent a lot of time and energy thinking about these things, designing things, drawing things, writing short stories. None of this was related to the actual instruction time. We did these things because we liked them. Because we wanted to do them. And so we put more effort into them.

Contrast this with what typically happens to students on classroom assignments. You might wait until the last minute to get started. You procrastinate. You avoid. You may try to get by with minimal effort. Schoolwork is often accomplished through extrinsic motivation, such as the desire for good grades, or often the fear of screwing up in front of other kids. This kind of behaviour is by no means unique to my situation; it is probably common in most school-age children.

Adults may do the same thing. Many of us have a job or a career but also spend considerable time on hobbies. I have friends who are engaged in performing music as a hobby, reading poetry, organizing community events, participating in fantasy sports leagues. During the summer, I put in a fair amount of time coaching my daughters' competitive softball teams. We do these things because we want to, not because we have to.

Regulatory focus

These are general examples, but the psychological literature has addressed the role of motivation as well. For instance, one well-studied phenomenon deals with a person's motivational state and distinguishes between approach and avoidance. **Approach goals** are desirable states that one wants to more towards and achieve, while **avoidance goals** are undesirable states that one wants to avoid. These goals often interact with a cognitive style known as regulatory focus. Tory Higgins' (Förster & Higgins, 2005; Higgins, 1997, 2000) **regulatory focus** theory suggests that the motivational system can be focused either on potential gains (approaching) or potential losses (avoiding) in the environment. People can have either a **promotion focus**, which is characterized by a focus on the achievement of desired outcomes and possible gains or non-gains in the environment, or a **prevention focus**, which is characterized by a focus on the avoidance of undesirable outcomes and possible losses or non-losses in the environment.

As a simple example of the differences between promotion focus and prevention focus and how this relates to gains and losses, consider the situation a job applicant faces when applying for a new job. You are being interviewed by a personnel manager or hiring manager and are adopting a promotion focus. You are trying to impress that person. If you succeed, you will gain something in terms of getting a job. What often happens is that you strive to present yourself in the best way possible by drawing attention to all of the things that you can do. This works for a job interview, but it might not work for keeping your job in every situation. If you already have a job, and it's one in which there is a lot of competition (a sales job, for example), you may find yourself in a prevention focus. You need to do everything you can to avoid losing your job. Drawing attention to all of the things that you *can* do may not help in this case. Rather, preventing yourself from losing things and not making mistakes might be a better way to keep your job. Applying for a job requires a promotion focus, but keeping a job requires a prevention focus.

According to Higgins' theory, people have an internal promotion focus or a prevention focus that is constant and unchanging through time. This can be described as **trait focus**. A second type of regulatory focus can be temporarily induced by certain situations and is called **situational** or **state regulatory focus**. The situations necessary to induce a promotion or prevention regulatory focus can consist of feedback or task instructions emphasizing either gains/non-gains or losses/non-losses, respectively. Regulatory focus theory also distinguishes between strategies of goal pursuit. People can either pursue goals with eagerness means (ensure hits, ensure against misses) or vigilance means (ensure correct rejections, ensure against false alarms).

Regulatory fit

Higgins (2000) expanded this theory of regulatory focus with the idea that the way people attempt to reach a goal can either match or not match with their regulatory focus. When one's method of goal pursuit and regulatory focus match, **regulatory fit** is said to be present and this fit is said to increase the value and feeling of fluency of one's actions. This feeling of fluency might play a role in encouraging more systematic thinking and a greater reliance on System 2 thought. A promotion focus and a strategy focused on gains and a prevention focus and a strategy focused on non-losses are examples of regulatory fit. Conversely, a promotion focus and a strategy focused on non-losses and a prevention focus and a strategy focused on gains are examples of not matching. The regulatory mismatch may interfere with the functionality of System 2 thinking. So, generally speaking, it is desirable to be in a state of regulatory fit, and not desirable to be in a state of regulatory mismatch. Both can have an effect on cognition.

The effects of regulatory fit and focus on thinking

Several studies have examined the effects of regulatory focus and regulatory fit on thinking. For example, Roney, Higgins, and Shah (1995) showed that a promotion or a prevention focus can be temporarily induced through feedback in an anagram-solving task. In a task like this, participants were presented with solvable and unsolvable anagrams and had 45 seconds to solve each one, although subjects were given the option of quitting the task before the time was up. Subjects in the prevention condition were more likely to quit before they ran out of time than promotion condition subjects. In another task, subjects were told that they could perform either a fun or boring sounding task once they had completed an anagram-solving task. Subjects with a promotion focus spent more time than prevention focus subjects on the unsolvable anagrams. These two experiments show how regulatory focus can be temporarily induced experimentally to influence motivation.

A promotion focus engenders an eagerness to attain goals, while a prevention focus engenders vigilance against losses.

As a more direct example of how regulatory focus can influence thinking, Markman, Maddox, Worthy, and Baldwin (2007) administered the Remote Associates Test (RAT) to subjects. In this task, subjects are shown three seemingly random words and are asked to generate a fourth word that is related to all three words. For instance, the words "coin", "quick", and "spoon" are unrelated but the word "silver" is related to each word (this task is described in greater detail in Chapter 10 in the subsection on creativity). It was assumed that finding the missing word was inherently rewarding, which gives the task a gain reward structure. Subjects were put in either promotion or prevention conditions. Markman et al. predicted that **regulatory fit** (promotion–gain) subjects would solve more items and would solve more difficult items than subjects in the **regulatory mismatch** (prevention–gain) condition.

Subjects were given either a promotion or a prevention focus upon entering the experiment: **promotion** subjects were told that if they performed well on an unrelated task they would be entered into a draw for $50; **prevention** subjects were told that if they performed well they wouldn't lose their entry into the draw for $50. Items were divided into easy, moderate and difficult groups. It was found that subjects in both conditions solved the same amount of items. However, subjects in the regulatory fit condition (promotion–gain) solved a greater proportion of hard items than regulatory mismatch subjects (prevention–gain). Subjects in the prevention condition solved more easy items than promotion focus subjects. While this only shows the influence of regulatory fit in a gains situation, it shows that regulatory fit can be manipulated to affect learning in cognitive research.

Other work has examined the effects of regulatory focus on classification learning tasks that measure hypothesis testing and rule acquisitions. These are behaviours associated with System 2 thinking. Maddox, Baldwin, and Markman (2006) argued that in addition to the feeling of fluency that Higgins (2000) argues comes from regulatory fit, regulatory fit also increases **cognitive flexibility**. Flexibility is defined as an increase in ability or willingness to try different strategies for the purpose of achieving a goal. This increase in flexibility is relative to subjects in a regulatory mismatch condition and is in contrast to the strategy of making gradual, incremental changes to achieve a goal. When regulatory fit is advantageous to category learning, it is expected that subjects in a regulatory fit condition will perform better than subjects in a regulatory mismatch condition, but when cognitive flexibility is disadvantageous to category learning, people in a regulatory mismatch condition are expected to perform better than people in a regulatory fit condition. To test this fit-flexibility hypothesis, Maddox et al. (2006) used three classification learning task structures where cognitive flexibility was either advantageous or disadvantageous for category learning.

Across all three experiments, a promotion focus was induced by telling subjects they would be entered into a draw for $50 if they achieved a criterion of performance. A prevention focus was induced by telling subjects they would lose an entry into a draw for $50 if they failed to reach a criterion of performance. Gains and losses reward structures were implemented by having a points meter shown on the side of the computer screen where subjects performed the experiment and the bonus pointed out. The gains point meter started out empty, and for each correct response the point meter increased, filling up with points as subjects approached the bonus. The losses point meter started out full of points, but for each incorrect response the point meter decreased by three points and for each correct response the point meter decreased by one point. A cash register sound was heard by subjects for each correct response and a buzzing sound for each incorrect response.

In the experiments, subjects learned a category structure where cognitive flexibility was advantageous for performance. Subjects learned a category set in which they had to switch from a simple, suboptimal rule to a more complex, optimal rule to reach a criterion of performance. Maddox et al. reasoned that subjects in the regulatory fit conditions would perform better than subjects in the regulatory mismatch condition. This is a novel design because the regulatory fit can come about from a promotion focus or a prevention focus, as long as the focus matched the rewards structure of the task. In general, subjects in the regulatory fit condition were more accurate in their responding for most blocks, exceeded the criterion sooner, and were more likely to exceed the criterion in the final block of trials than the regulatory mismatch subjects.

In subsequent experiments, subjects learned a classification task in which cognitive flexibility was disadvantageous for category learning. This might seem counterintuitive, but cognitive flexibility is not necessarily helpful in achieving certain goals; there are some goals that would be reached more easily by making gradual changes in strategy as opposed to widely varying strategies. In these tasks, subjects in the regulatory fit condition performed worse than subjects in the regulatory mismatch condition early in learning. Overall, these experiments show that regulatory fit in classification learning leads to an increase in cognitive flexibility and better performance when cognitive flexibility is advantageous for category learning, but not when cognitive flexibility was not advantageous. Classification learning is a task that can make use of System 1 and/or System 2 thinking, depending on the nature of the task. Those categories that were helped by cognitive flexibility were more likely to benefit from regulatory fit than those that relied on System 2 thinking. Thus, regulatory fit may enhance System 2 thought.

THE EFFECTS OF MOOD ON THINKING

Separate from motivation, mood state has been shown to affect thinking and cognition as well. Like motivation, an emotion or mood has core links with physiological states. For present purposes, I will only distinguish between positive mood and negative mood in general. A finer-grained distinction would be with the kind of positive mood (e.g., happy, excited, etc.) and the kind of negative mood (e.g., angry, despondent, etc.). This is a distinction of intensity versus valence.

The effects of negative mood

Some studies have reported findings in line with the hypothesis that negative mood narrows attentional focus. This means that you are less likely to be distracted by irrelevant stimuli. For example, Gasper and Clore (2002) asked subjects to make judgements about stimuli like those shown in Figure 8.1. The target shape is a triangle made of smaller triangles. One of the stimuli matched the local features (the small triangles) and the other stimulus matched the global features (the configuration). If negative mood narrows attentional focus, then subjects in a negative mood would be more likely to make local feature matches.

This is essentially what Gasper and Clore found. Subjects were put into a happy mood or a negative mood by asking them to write a story about a correspondingly happy or sad event. The negative mood subjects were more likely to choose matches based on the local features. Other research has uncovered similar patterns. Baumann and Kuhl (2005) reported that people primed with negatively valenced words before each trial of a global–local response task were slower to respond to global trials than people primed with neutral words. Oaksford, Morris, Grainger, and Williams (1996) reported that negative mood participants performed less well on a variant of the Wason card selection task than neutral mood participants. The card selection task was covered in greater detail in Chapter 7.

Not all research with a negative mood has found that it narrows attention. The specific effects may depend on the intensity of the negative mood. In other words, being angry may narrow your attention focus but being sad or depressed might actually broaden it. This seems intuitive. When people are feeling particularly sad they might have trouble focusing on any one thing and feel unfocused in general. The psychological research has tended to support this intuition. Gable and Harmon-Jones (2010) manipulated **sadness** and found that it led to broadened attention relative to a neutral mood condition on a global–local

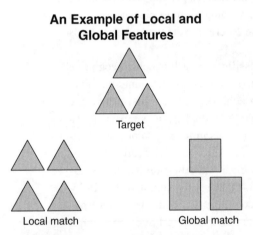

An Example of Local and Global Features

Target

Local match

Global match

Figure 8.1 This is an example of stimuli which can assess local or global attention. The target stimulus at the top is similar to both of the possible matches on the bottom. The possible match on the left is a local match because, although the shape is a different configuration, it is made of the same small triangles. The possible match on the right is a global match because, although it is made of squares, the overall shape and configuration matches.

reaction time task, with participants in the sad mood condition exhibiting longer response times to local response trials. The authors suggested that depression might also broaden attention and be related to enhanced creativity. In line with this hypothesis, von Hecker and Meiser (2005) found that university students who reported higher levels of current depressive symptoms performed the same as students with lower levels of self-reported depressive symptoms on a word recognition task, but students with high self-reported depressive symptom were more likely to correctly remember the colour of the frames around the words, indicating that they noticed non-essential elements of the task better than students with lower levels of self-reported depressive symptoms. Although these results do not show that depression enhances creativity, it is possible that a less inhibited, defocused state of attention (which was displayed by the students with higher levels of self-reported depressive symptoms) could result in enhanced cognitive flexibility.

Other researchers have failed to find support for this claim. An extensive meta-analysis failed to find a relationship between negative mood and creativity (Baas, De Dreu, & Nijstad, 2008). Furthermore, impairment on tasks that benefit from cognitive flexibility has also been reported in depressed patients. For instance, major depression has been linked with poor performance on the Wisconsin card sorting task (Merriam, Thase, Haas, Keshavan, & Sweeney, 1999). In line with the idea that flexible processing is impaired in depression, Smith, Tracy, and Murray (1993) reported that university students and adult patients with higher than average self-reported depressive symptoms were impaired on a category learning task that benefited from a flexible, rule-based strategy, but were unimpaired on a task that could be learned via similarity.

In summary, it seems that being in a negative mood can affect thinking in more than one way. General negative mood and/or an angry negative mood may narrow attentional focus. It is tempting to imagine an evolutionary reason for this. Perhaps when people are in an angry mood they want to focus on the thing that is causing that unpleasant state. But when people are in a depressive negative mode, research has tended to find the opposite. A depressive mode seems to broaden the attentional focus, interfere with the ability to selectively attend to a single stimulus, and inhibit attention to competing stimuli. This too has an intuitive connection to general depressive thoughts. One possibility is that people who suffer from depression have difficulty inhibiting negative cognition. This may be an overall cognitive style.

Positive mood

When you are smiling, the whole world smiles at you. Or so the song goes. It's clear that when people are in a positive or happy mood, things seem different. A task that might seem challenging under normal circumstances might seem fairly easy when you are in a good mood. It is a common cliché to say that "time flies when you're having fun".

Rule Defined and Non-rule-Defined Category Structures

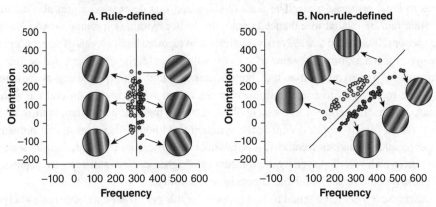

Figure 8.2 An example of two different kinds of category sets. The large circles with light and dark bands represent examples of the actual stimuli. The distribution of stimuli in psychological space is represented by the open circles or filled circles on the graph. On the left is an example of a rule-defined category set in which the participant must learn the rule that corresponds to spatial frequency of the light and dark bands in order to classify all of the stimuli into categories. On the right is an example of a non-rule-defined category set in which the participant must learn to classify all of the stimuli.

Metaphorically, this relates to the notion that when we are in a happy mood, we are able to be engaged in what we are doing. We don't tend to watch the clock distractedly. Given these colloquial and popular benefits to positive mood, it is worth examining research on positive mood and thinking.

Positive mood has been associated with the enhancement of an array of cognitive skills, including creative problem-solving (Isen, Daubman, & Nowicki, 1987), recall of information (Isen, Shalker, Clark, & Karp, 1978), verbal fluency (Isen, Johnson, Mertz, & Robinson, 1985), and novel task switching (Dreisbach & Goschke, 2004). Positive mood has also been associated with cognitive flexibility (Ashby, Isen, & Turken, 1999). In general, these are tasks that tap into System 2 thinking.

In my lab, my students and I investigated the effects of mood on a category learning task like the one shown in Figure 8.2 (Nadler, Rabi, & Minda, 2010). In our classification learning task, our subjects were asked to learn one of the two category sets shown in Figure 8.2.

On each trial, subjects were shown a single pattern (one of the disks with the alternating light and dark bands), and they were instructed to assign a classification to it: category 1, or category 2. After each trial, subjects received feedback. After several hundred trials, subjects were able to extract and learn something about the category set. The category set in the left panel is an example of a rule-defined category set. In this case, the rule corresponds to the spatial frequency of the light and dark bands in the stimuli. But notice that the orientation of the light and dark bands also varies. In order to learn this classification subjects need to test both hypotheses, and they must also learn to ignore or inhibit attention to the irrelevant orientation dimension. The right panel of the graph shows a category set that is not defined by rule. In this case, both orientation and spatial frequency contribute equally to the classification and there is no easily verbalized rule that subjects can learn. In this case, there is no advantage for hypothesis testing or inhibition. In other words, subjects need to rely on some degree of System 2 thinking in order to successfully learn the rule-defined categories. On the other hand, associative learning (System 1) works better for the non-rule-defined categories on the right.

In our study, we induced a positive, neutral, or negative mood in our subjects, and then asked them to learn either the rule-defined or the non-rule-defined category set. To put our subjects in a positive mood, we asked them to listen to some happy music and watch a video with a very happy laughing baby (you can probably still find this video on YouTube). We used a similar technique for the negative mood and the neutral mode except we used corresponding music and videos. We found that the subjects in the positive mood condition performed significantly better on the rule-defined task relative to both the neutral mood subjects and the negative mood subjects. But positive mood did not seem to have an effect on performance in the non-rule-defined category set. In other words, being in a good mood seemed to enhance the cognitive flexibility of our participants, enhance their System 2 thinking, and improve their performance.

COGNITIVE RESOURCES

At the beginning of this chapter, I gave the example of driving in difficult conditions and then trying to carry out sophisticated thinking. I suggested that it might be difficult because cognitive resources might be taxed or depleted after a difficult drive. In other words, when your mind is tired and when your cognitive resources are depleted, performance on other tasks might suffer. There is some support in the research literature for this idea.

Ego depletion

The idea of ego depletion comes from work by Roy Baumeister and colleagues (Baumeister, Vohs, & Tice, 2007). This theory argues that self-regulation is an essentially finite resource. Baumeister argues that cognitive resources and self-regulation are analogous to physical stamina. After a hard workout, or a long walk, your muscles are tired. According to the ego depletion theory, your self-regulatory resources work in the same way. That is, they get tired. And if these resources get tired, your performance suffers.

Maintaining performance in a demanding cognitive task can deplete resources, and these depleted resources are known to have a detrimental effect on subsequent tasks that depend on them. Baumeister and colleagues originally used the term "ego-depletion" as an homage to Freud (Baumeister, 2014) because Freudian theory emphasized the idea of self-regulatory resources. However, they stress that their theory does not bear a theoretical resemblance to Freud's theories.

In an early study on ego depletion, Baumeister, Bratslavsky, Muraven, and Tice (1998) found that being asked to perform a challenging act of self-regulation can affect performance on a subsequent executive function task, suggesting that the two types of task share resources. For example, they found that when participants forced themselves to eat radishes instead of chocolates, they displayed reduced persistence on a subsequent puzzle-solving task compared to participants who did not exert self-control over eating. In other tasks, subjects were asked to watch movies that would normally elicit a strong emotional reaction. In the ego depletion manipulation, these subjects were asked to suppress any emotional reaction or distress. These subjects displayed impaired subsequent performance at solving anagrams.

A more recent study by Schmeichel (2007) showed that participants who were asked to engage in a task that depleted their cognitive regulation resources, such as regulating their emotions, controlling their attention, or taking a working memory test, performed more poorly on subsequent tests of working memory span and inhibitory control. This suggests a correspondence between ego depletion and System 2 thinking because both of these executive functions fall under the System 2 heading. In fact, ego depletion also influences decision-making abilities. Depleted participants tend to make poorer decisions and fail to take into account decision alternatives as well as control individuals. Depleted individuals also tend to depend more heavily on heuristics and often fail to weigh all of their options carefully (Masicampo & Baumeister, 2008).

The ego depletion theory stresses the connection between self-regulatory resources and physiology. As a result, some researchers have examined the physiological toll of ego depletion. For example, Gailliot and colleagues (2007) asked participants to engage in a variety of self-regulatory behaviours, such as ignoring text on a visual display, suppressing stereotypes, or engaging in a demanding Stroop task. Gailliot et al. found that across these tasks, exerting self-control used up a relatively large amount of measurable glucose (as measured via blood glucose levels pre- and post-test). Interestingly, replenishing blood glucose with a sugary drink counteracted ego depletion effects. In other words, the ego depletion task depleted resources, but drinking the energy drink restored them. Just as engaging in self-regulatory behaviour depletes resources, rest or refuelling counteracts those effects.

It should be noted that the ego depletion phenomenon is not the same as general fatigue. In other words, ego depletion corresponds to the condition of having one's self-regulatory resources in a state of depletion. This is fatigue limited to cognitive control. This is not the same as overall tiredness or overall fatigue. This distinction was made in a clever task that relied on sleep deprivation as a comparison to ego depletion. If ego depletion is the same as general fatigue, then ego depletion subjects should perform in the same way as sleep-deprived subjects (Vohs, Glass, Maddox, & Markman, 2011). However, the research does not support this conclusion. Sleep-deprived participants suffered from fatigue and did not display the ego depletion effects. These authors argue that, unlike general fatigue, ego depletion is the "exhaustion of the inner energy that modulates unwanted responses" (Vohs et al., 2011: 171).

In my lab, some of my students and I carried out a task that was similar to the mood induction task described earlier. In other words, we relied on a classification task in which some subjects were asked to learn a rule-defined task like the one shown in Figure 8.2 and others were asked to learn a non-rule-defined task (Minda & Rabi, 2015). We also manipulated the ego depletion state of our subjects. Some subjects were asked to write a story with no restrictions (the control condition) or without using two common letters (the ego depletion condition). Resource-depleted participants performed more poorly than controls on the rule-defined task, but did not differ from controls on the non-rule-defined task, suggesting that self-regulatory resources are required for successful rule-defined category learning. Our study was consistent with much of the other research on ego depletion, and suggests a correspondence between ego depletion and System 2 thinking.

SUMMARY

The topics in this chapter covered thinking in different contexts, but, behind the scenes, these contexts reveal the possibility of two different systems being responsible for human thought. System 1 is involved in making fast, instinctive, and intuitive decisions. At the same time, System 2 is involved in making slower, more deliberative decisions. Sometimes a contextual or cognitive factor can interfere with one or the other system and this can have beneficial or deleterious effects on cognition.

For example, negative mood can focus attention and may encourage vigilance in a task, but only certain kinds of negative mood have this effect. Depressive negative mood seems to have the opposite effect where attention is broad and vigilance is challenging. Positive mood, on the other hand, is associated with enhancing cognitive flexibility. Enhanced cognitive flexibility can improve performance on many different tasks, but especially tasks that involve hypothesis-testing and executive function, or, more generally, System 2 thought.

Motivation also has several different effects on thinking. For example, if your motivational focus is one in which you seek to achieve gains, and it matches with the environment, then this match can encourage cognitive flexibility and may enable System 2 to operate more efficiently. If there is a mismatch between the focus in the task, it interferes with thinking.

Finally, research on cognitive capacity and ego depletion suggests that when cognitive resources are taxed or depleted, it has an effect on a wide variety of thinking behaviours, such as tasks that measure creativity and tasks that measure hypothesis-testing. Most of these seem to be associated with System 2.

SECTION 3
THINKING IN ACTION: DECISION-MAKING, PROBLEM-SOLVING, AND EXPERTISE

9 DECISION-MAKING

If you are using this textbook in a course, stop for a minute and consider why you decided to take the course. Is it part of a programme of study? Was this a course that you had been planning to take for a while, or is it one that you decided to take without much advance planning? I suspect there are a range of possibilities, but whatever the reason, it is probably true that many students pick their courses without much serious thought and others plan extensively and think about what courses they need and which courses will help them the most in the future.

Decision-making is about reducing uncertainty, minimizing risk, and maximizing benefit. Of course, many of the decisions we make are trivial. Deciding whether to have toast or a bagel for breakfast is still a decision, but it is one that has little or no uncertainty, very little risk associated with either outcome, and only modest benefit. But other decisions are much more serious. When you are deciding on a university major or plan of study, there is uncertainty associated with the outcome. Choosing between engineering and epidemiology carries with it many unknowns. What will the job market be like for engineers and epidemiologists in five years' time? What are the risks associated with each programme? How difficult are the courses? What is the completion rate of students who enter the programme? How likely is it that you will be able to finish near the top of your class versus the middle? Will that matter?

People do not like uncertainty. Animals do not like uncertainty. Uncertainty often introduces a state of anxiety. Most organisms behave in ways that reduce uncertainty and maintain a status quo. The idea of uncertainty reduction, risk avoidance, and the maintenance of the status quo are central to understanding how humans make decisions. This first half of this chapter covers a fundamental aspect of decision-making – the understanding of probability and base rates. In the second half of the chapter, several theories of decision-making are introduced and these explain human decision-making in terms of reducing uncertainty and maximizing outcome.

MAKING A DECISION

We make many decisions every day. We decide what to have for breakfast, we decide which route to travel to work. We decide how to allocate time, money, and recourses. We might decide to stay with a romantic partner, or to leave. These decisions can be trivial or life-altering. They can be made quickly or with extensive deliberation. They can be right, wrong, or neither.

Decisions that are made with some degree of explicit awareness often involve several steps. The first step can be called the **identification** phase, in which the person identifies the need to make a decision. This might be something as simple as being confronted with an overt decision (ordering food at a restaurant) or something more complicated, like deciding how to invest some of your money in the stock market. At some point prior, there is no need to make a decision, but at this identification phase, the need for a decision is realized. More importantly, the decision is framed. **Framing** a decision involves stating the decision in terms of known costs and benefits, or perceived gains and losses. The way in which a decision is framed can drastically alter the way the decision is made. For example, if you are deciding to enrol in a course, it may change the decision if you frame it as a requirement versus framing it as an option. One alternative is framed as something that you *have to do*; the other is framed as something that you *want to do*. Framing effects will be discussed in greater detail later in this chapter.

A second stage is the **generation** stage. In this stage, the decision-maker begins to generate alternatives. For example, if the decision involved is where to take a romantic partner on a date, you might start to think of the options: movie, club, dinner, golfing, the beach. The generation phase is affected by several factors. Individual factors, such as personal knowledge and experience, play a role by limiting or enhancing the number and kinds of alternatives that can be generated. Cognitive factors, such as working memory limitations, can have an effect by reducing the number of alternatives that can be generated. Environmental factors, such as the amount of time available, can also affect the number of alternatives that can be generated; time pressure reduces the number of alternatives.

These alternatives can be evaluated in a **judgement** phase. Judgements are made about probabilities, costs, benefits, and the value of alternatives. Judgements can be made about real or perceived risk. In many cases, judgements are susceptible to many of the biases that have been discussed in other sections of this book. Both **availability** and **representativeness** can affect how alternatives are assessed and evaluated. For example, alternatives that come to mind very quickly might be judged as favourable, but this can be an artifact of the availability effect. In some cases, alternatives that are highly salient, and thus available in memory, are likely to be brought to mind quickly. This can lead to a bias, and occasionally errors if these alternatives are not optimal (Tversky & Kahneman, 1974).

Difficulties and challenges

In general, humans tend to make fairly good decisions. Not exclusively, of course, but many decisions simply do not involve much risk or uncertainty. But there are occasional conflicts. Sometimes, there are simply too many choices. For example, sometimes when I am eating at a restaurant with my family, one of my kids will express frustration because of all the choices on the menu. The problem is that she likes nearly everything. As a result, she can't decide what she will enjoy the most. Sometimes she will resolve this conflict by relying on a heuristic and resorting to a standard order: A chicken-caesar wrap (pretty standard pub fare in Canada).

Other challenges arise when costs and benefits are comparable across many alternatives, or when the alternatives are orthogonal or not directly comparable. Recall from Chapter 2 that similarity comparisons and evaluations can sometimes only be made among items that possess allignable attributes (Gentner, 1983). A comparable process can interfere with decision-making as well. For example, it might be fairly straightforward to consider the differences between several types of automobiles on the metric of price, or of fuel efficiency, or of power. Considering these together is more complex. How should one reasonably balance these attributes? Is a more expensive car with better fuel economy a better choice? This depends on the price of fuel, the future price of fuel, and the relative importance that one places on personal savings (money) versus the environmental savings of a vehicle that uses less fuel. This is not a clear-cut decision by any means, and the optimal decision changes as a function of which attributes are weighted in the generation and judgement phases.

UNDERSTANDING PROBABILITY

In order to fully understand the decision-making process, it is useful to have an understanding of how probability works, and how people usually assess probability. Many decisions are made with a reference to the likelihood of a given outcome or in the face of uncertainty, and in order to fully explain the errors that come about when making these kinds of decisions, an understanding of probability is helpful. Probability is normative. That is, the likelihoods of different outcomes exist in the world and are affected by other events.

Probability theories

As observers, humans have a number of ways to track and interpret these probabilities. Jonathan Baron describes three ways in which people make sense of probabilities (Baron, 2007).

Frequency theories suggest that humans make probability judgements on the basis of their knowledge of prior frequency events. In Bayesian terms, this is known as information about the **priors**. For example, if you are reasoning about the likelihood that you will catch influenza (seasonal flu) this year, you might base your judgement of the probability on your knowledge of the frequency of catching influenza in the past. If you have never had the flu, you are likely to underestimate that probability. If you get the flu every year, you may overestimate the probability. The true probability may be somewhere in between those extremes. The important thing about frequency theories is that it requires attention in order to encode the event and memory in order to make the judgement. As discussed earlier in this book, memory can be quite susceptible to bias. Evidence suggests that people remember highly salient events and base their judgements on these memories, which gives rise to the availability heuristic (Tversky & Kahneman, 1974). The availability heuristic was described in detail in Chapter 3 on memory. An availability heuristic occurs when people make judgements about the probability and likelihood of things on the basis of the information that is available in their memories. This can lead to a bias if low frequency information has a strong memory representation because of its salience or recency. A commonly cited example is that people often overestimate the risk of an airline disaster or a shark attack because even though those events are low frequency and have a very low probability of occurring, they are reported widely in the media and are thus strongly represented in memory.

People can use **logical theories** as well. Use of a logical theory requires knowledge of the actual probability of a given event and knowledge of the actual likelihood. In practice, this is very difficult because probabilities are affected by many factors. However, people can make use of logical theories for what are known as **exchangeable events**. An exchangeable event is one for which the probability is known and not affected by surface variation. Standard playing cards are an example of exchangeable events. The probability of drawing an ace of clubs from a standard deck of cards is the same for all standard decks. And it is the same for all people. The probability is thus completely exchangeable because it is not affected by these environmental factors. Furthermore, it is not affected by frequency and availability. The likelihood of drawing an ace from a standard deck is the same whether or not you have drawn aces in the past. Even if you have never drawn an ace of clubs from a deck of cards, the probability does not change as a function of your personal memory for the frequency.

Baron (2007) points out that purely exchangeable events are difficult and nearly impossible to find. And even on those occasions when truly exchangeable events are being considered, they may be subject to personal and cognitive biases. For example, if you draw many aces in a row (or no aces) you may experience a shift in expectations as a result of the conflict between your logical probability knowledge and the knowledge gleaned from your own frequency theory.

Baron also suggests that people make use of **personal theories** as well. Personal theories can contain information about event frequency and information about logical probability, but can also contain additional information. Specifically, personal theories contain information about context, expert knowledge, what should happen, and what you want to happen. The personal view is very flexible because it takes into account the personal beliefs and understandings of the decision-maker. These beliefs can differ among and between people as a function of personal knowledge, and so two people can reasonably be expected to differ in their assessments of probability. Experts and novices would be expected to differ as well. For example, a naïve medical diagnosis made via consultation with a medical website can differ significantly from a diagnosis made by an experienced physician because the physician has specialized knowledge and diagnostic experience. On the other hand, one of the shortcomings of the personal view is that it assumes that people make use of idiosyncratic and irrational information as well. Beliefs about luck, fate, and divine intervention can affect our personal theories of probability. These can be difficult to evaluate objectively, but still affect people's decisions.

How to calculate probability

At its most basic, probability is described as the likelihood of some event occurring in the long run. If something can never happen, the probability is 0.0. If something always happens, the probability of occurrence is 1.0. Most probabilities are therefore somewhere in between 0.0 and 1.0. An event with a .25 probability of occurrence suggests that on 25% of possible occurrences that event will occur, and on 75% of possible occurrences that event will not occur. Probability can also be described as the odds of occurrence, such as 1 out of 4. In this chapter, I will use values between zero and one for simplicity.

To calculate the probability of occurrence according to the simplest logical theories, the number of desired outcomes is divided by the number of possible outcomes. For a simple coin toss, the number of possible outcomes is two: heads or tails. So the probability of getting a heads on one coin toss is 1 divided by 2, which equals .5. This corresponds with our intuition that a fair coin has a .5 probability of heads and a .5 probability of tails on any toss. Practically, that means that if you toss the coin several times in a row, you tend to expect some heads and some tails. You don't expect it always to be an even distribution of heads and tails, but you expect that over many tosses (or an infinite number of tosses) the frequency of heads and tails should balance.

Other exchangeable events are calculated in much the same way. The probability of rolling a 6 on a regular die is calculated by taking 1/6. That is one desired outcome divided by six possible outcomes. In this case the probability of rolling a 6 is .167. The probability of rolling a number less than 4 on the same regular die is calculated by taking the three desired outcomes (1, 2, 3) and dividing it by the six possible outcomes. Thus, the probability is 3/6, which equals .5. Just as in the case with the coin toss, we assume that this is a fair die. We also assume that these probabilities hold up over the long run, but allow for variation in small numbers of samples.

BOX 9.1

Calculating the probability of occurrence in coin tosses and other exchangeable events assumes that those events are random. For most practical purposes, they are random. But true randomness is exceedingly difficult to achieve. Even most computer algorithms that generate random numbers can be shown to have a bias. An interesting website is www.random.org. The algorithms at random.org listen to atmospheric noise to generate random sequences. This can be used to generate sequences of random numbers, random card draws, coin flips in a variety of things. It is worth investigating just to find out about true randomness, and it can be a useful resource for anyone who needs random data.

Independent probabilities

When calculating the probability of multiple events, the individual probabilities can either be multiplied or added. Figure 9.1 illustrates this.

For example, to calculate the probability in a coin toss of obtaining two heads in a row, one would take the probability of one head (.5) and multiply it by the probability of another head (.5). So the probability of two heads in a row is .25, and three heads in a row is .125. This means that the probability of several heads in a row is even lower by multiplicative factors. This is referred to as the "**and rule**". It means that the probability of one event *and* another event is calculated by multiplying. When calculating the probability of getting two heads or two tails, one can use what is known as the "**or rule**" and add the probabilities. So the probability of two heads is .25 and the probability of two tails is .25, which results in .5. That means that there is a .5 probability of obtaining two heads or two tales. These rules both assume independence. That means that the result of the first coin toss has no effect on the result of the second coin toss. Although the probability of two heads in a row is .25, the probability of each head alone is still .5. This means that even if you tossed a coin 20 times in a row and obtained 20 heads in a row, the independent probability of the twenty-first toss is still .5 for heads. These events are entirely independent.

Figure 9.2 shows two possible five-card hands from a single deck of 52 cards. The hand on the top is a royal flush with hearts as the suit. This is a very good hand in a game of five-card poker. The hand on the bottom shows three 2s, which is a workable hand but

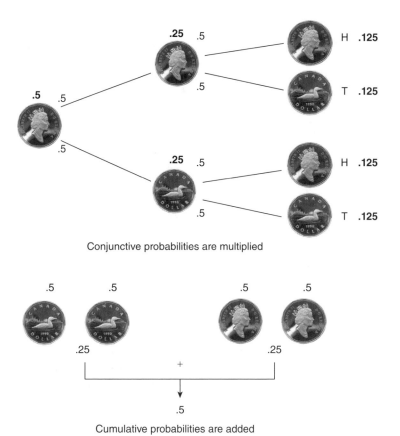

Conjunctive probabilities are multiplied

Cumulative probabilities are added

Figure 9.1 The top panel shows the probabilities of successive coin flips. Each coin flip has a .5 probability of heads and a .5 probability of tails. The successive probabilities are calculated by multiplying. The successive probability of three heads in a row is .125. The bottom panel shows cumulative probabilities. The probability of two tails or two heads (.5) is calculated by taking the probability of obtaining two tails (.25) and adding it to the probability of obtaining two heads (.25).

not a particularly strong one. Although the hand on the top is often thought to be lower frequency, that is only because the value of the bottom hand comes from the fact that there are three 2s of any suit, and two additional cards of any value in the suit. But in reality, the probability of obtaining that exact hand with the two of hearts, seven of clubs, etc. is the same as the probability of obtaining the royal flush shown at the top. To calculate the probability of five specific and unique cards being drawn from a deck of 52 one would calculate the probability of the first card as 1/52, the second card as 1/51, the third card

Two Hands from a Standard Deck

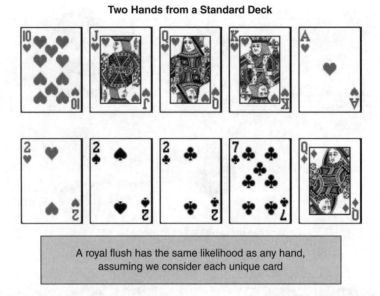

A royal flush has the same likelihood as any hand,
assuming we consider each unique card

Figure 9.2 Shown are two hypothetical hands from a standard deck. The top hand is a royal flush. The bottom hand is three twos. Although the top hand is more valuable in poker, both hands have the same probability of occurring, if one takes into account the exact unique cards shown. Differential probabilities of poker hands arise because a hearts royal flush has only one way of occurring whereas three twos has several ways of occurring.

as 1/50, the fourth card as 1/49, and the final card as 1/48. This is because as one card is drawn the possible cards left are reduced in number. The individual probabilities are multiplied such that the actual probability of obtaining each of these hands is 1/311875200.

Effects of independence

Confusing independence with what we believe to be representative of randomness is known as the **gambler's fallacy**. The gambler's fallacy will be discussed in greater detail later in the chapter. But in this case, an example of the gambler's fallacy would be an overestimation of the probability of tails on the twenty-first coin toss after a sequence of 20 heads. Because the coin toss is known to have a normative probability of .5 heads and .5 tails, a sequence of 20 heads seems unnatural and non-random, even though it is a random occurrence. If people estimate the probability of obtaining details on the twenty-first toss as greater than .5, they are falling prey to this gambler's fallacy. It is a difficult fallacy to overcome. Even if you know that the coin toss is independent and always has a .5 probability of coming up heads and a .5 probability of coming up tails, most of us would feel very strongly that the tails toss is due after 20 heads in a row (Tversky & Kahneman, 1974).

It is fairly easy to see how independence and the multiplication rule work for simple events like coin tosses, but these effects become stronger in more complicated and semantically rich examples. In many cases, subjects are shown to ignore conjunctions and judge probabilities incorrectly. A frequently cited example comes from Tversky and Kahneman (1983). Subjects were shown a description of a person and were then asked to indicate the probability that that person belonged to one or more groups. The most well-known example is the "Linda" example.

> Linda is 31 years old, outspoken and bright. She majored in Philosophy, and as a student she was concerned with issues of social justice and discrimination. She also participated in many demonstrations.

After reading the description, subjects were then asked to rate the likelihood that Linda was a member of several groups. Crucially, they were asked to rate the likelihood that she was a member of the feminist movement, a bank teller, or a bank teller *and* feminist. Subjects rated the likelihood that she was a feminist as being high because the description fits a stereotype or category of feminist. They also rated the likelihood that she was a bank teller as relatively low. There is no reason that Linda cannot be a bank teller, but there is nothing in her description that is strongly indicative. Furthermore, bank teller is a broad category with less clear attributes. The key result is that subjects rated the likelihood that she was a bank teller *and* feminist as being greater than the likelihood that she was a bank teller alone. Logically, it is not possible for the likelihood of a conjunction of two categories to be higher than the likelihood of any one of the single categories. In this case, the strong semantic connection between this description and a stereotype of the feminist movement causes this error to occur. Subjects ignore the conjunction and hone in on the fact that Linda is representative of being a feminist. In other words, the **representativeness heuristic** trumps logical probability.

This example has been criticized for being unrealistic; it has been questioned whether or not this effect was truly a bias and a cognitive error. Gigerenzer and others (Gigerenzer, 1996; Hertwig & Gigerenzer, 1999) have argued that the framing of this example prompts a salience for the feminist category. In other words, people do indeed rely on representativeness, but this might be more appropriately construed as a functional heuristic, rather than a source of error.

Cumulative risks

People often make errors in how they apply the adding rule to cumulative risks. As an example, imagine the likelihood of having a car accident while driving to work. On any given day, the probability is quite low. But over several years of driving daily, the cumulative risks increase. This is because the cumulative risks in this case are calculated via the "or rule". To calculate cumulative risks of being in a car accident on any day out of several years' worth of driving, you would essentially be adding the probability of the accident today with the probability of an accident tomorrow with the probability of an accident the day after that. A very small risk of an accident on any one given day adds up to a larger cumulative risk over the long run.

Calculating probability over the long run, whether it is a normative value or a cumulative risk, is often difficult for people. In many ways, it is counterintuitive to make judgements about things that happen in the long run. In the long run, a coin may have a .5 probability of coming up heads. But this assumes an infinite number of coin tosses. A large number of tosses will tend to balance out, but a small number may not. The problem arises when we make decisions to maximize short-term gains rather than long-term probabilities. From an evolutionary standpoint, this makes sense. Short-term probabilities have some advantages. An organism needs to eat today. It may not be able to consider what is going to happen two months in the future, two years in the future, or two decades in the future.

As another example, consider the decision that many people make to send or receive a text message from their smartphone while driving. Clearly, most people know that this is a distraction. It is well established that using a smartphone while driving can increase the risk of having an accident. In addition, many jurisdictions encourage steep fines for drivers who are caught sending or receiving a text message while driving. Given that the risk is known and the fines are steep, many people wonder why people still engage their smartphones while driving. One possibility is that people do not truly understand the cumulative risk. This is especially true if drivers are basing their decisions on a frequency theory. Unless you have had an accident or a fine, your own perspective and interpretation of the probability is that every time you use your smartphone you do not have an accident. Even drivers who have been using a smartphone while driving for years may have never had an accident. This does not mean that the smartphone is not interfering; it just means that the interference did not result in an accident. And so it is not unreasonable to imagine that a short-term decision based on frequency knowledge of the risk associated with using a smartphone would cause the driver to believe that the smartphone is not a danger, even if that belief conflicts with what the driver knows about the real risks. With no prior personal connection between smartphone use in accidents, most people downplay the risk. While this is sensible in the short term, it is clearly dangerous in the long term.

Chance events and the law of large numbers

The general tendency to focus on short-term probabilities rather than long-term probabilities implies that we sometimes attach special meaning to low probability events. For example, in meteorological phenomena, it is not unusual to hear of a "100-year flood". It is also not unusual for this kind of flood to happen in a span of two or three years. While it is tempting to treat this as a dangerous precedent, it may only be a chance event. Consider some other examples, how likely is it that a mother shares the same birthday with her child? It's not that unusual, but it still seems worth remarking upon. How likely is it that three brothers will marry women with the same first name? Again, it is not that unusual but it is still an event that may be commented on. How likely is it that three sisters will give birth on the same day? This sounds like a very low probability event, but in reality the odds are about 1 to 6,000. All of these events are low likelihood and low-frequency events, but it is physically possible for them to happen. Given enough observations, a very low probability event will eventually occur. This is referred to as the **law of large numbers**. An event with a very low likelihood may eventually be observed, given enough time. This is analogous to the long-term probability of the event.

Base rates

The rate of occurrence for an event (i.e., the long-run probability) is known as its **base rate**. For many exchangeable events, like cards, the base rates may be known. For most events, though, the base rates may not be known explicitly, or they may be estimated via knowledge about the frequency of occurrence. For example, it is nearly impossible to know the base rate of occurrence for the likelihood that the bus you take will not be on time. Furthermore, even if you do have some knowledge about base rates (e.g., the likelihood that the bus you take to work will break down), it is probably a very low probability. A very low base rate means that the event does not happen very often, and so you are likely to ignore this base rate.

Given the inherent difficulties in understanding and using base rates, it should not be surprising that people often ignore them even when they are known and even when using them would be useful. The clearest and most well-known example was provided by Kahneman and Tversky (1973). It was discussed in detail in Chapter 6. Subjects were given information about the base rates of occurrence for engineers and lawyers in a room: 70 lawyers and 30 engineers. They were told that one person was sampled and they were asked to read the description of a person who seemed to be a stereotypical engineer. Subjects typically rated this person as more likely to be an engineer, despite the higher base rate of occurrence for lawyers. Kahneman and Tversky claimed that people often ignore base rates and rely on category typicality to make their judgements and decisions.

Base rate neglect is a phenomenon that occurs in many settings. A very striking example is seen in medical tests and diagnosis. A series of studies by Gerd Gigerenzer investigated how physicians, nurses, and even non-medical subjects arrived at decisions about the efficacy of the medical test (Gigerenzer, Gaissmaier, Kurz-Milcke, Schwartz, & Woloshin, 2008). Most of the experiments presented subjects with scenarios in which

Conditional Probabilities

Test Results	Disease Present	Disease Absent
Positive	a	b
Negative	c	d
Total		

P(disease|positive result)=a/(a+b)

Figure 9.3 This table shows the four cells needed in order to calculate the probability of a disease given the positive result on a test. This probability is calculated by taking the total number in the cell A and dividing it by the total number of cells A and B.

Assuming 100 in 10,000 people

Test Results	Disease Present	Disease Absent
Positive	98	99
Negative	2	9801
Total	100	9900

base rate: 1%   P(d|p)=98/(98+99)=49%
100 out of 10,000

Figure 9.4 Assuming a base rate of 1%, which works out to be 100 in every 10,000, the probability of a person having the disease given a positive test result is .49. Even a diagnostic test can result in a low conditional probability if the base rate is low.

a given disease has some established base rate. Subjects were then given information about tests. For example, consider a serious disease for which early detection can be very beneficial. This disease has a base rate of 1%. This means that 100 in every 10,000 may contract the disease. Early detection requires the administration of a diagnostic exam. The test has a very good hit rate. If the disease is present, 98% of the time the test will also indicate a positive result. This is a great hit rate. If the disease is not present, only 1% of the time will the test indicate a positive result. In other words, the test has a very low false positive rate. Given this information, and given a positive test result, how would you rate the likelihood of a patient actually having the disease?

In order to understand how to arrive at this decision, it is necessary to explain first how to calculate this probability. Figure 9.3 shows a table with four probability cells. The top row shows the values A and B for when the test result is positive. The second row shows the values C and D for when the test result is nega-tive. In order to calculate the probability of the disease actually being present given a positive result, we need to take the value in cell A and divide it by the value of cell A plus cell B.

Figure 9.4 shows the same table with values inserted according to the parameters of the problem. The 1% base rate, remember, assumes that 100 in every 10,000 people will have this disease. In the disease present column, 98 of those 100 people with the disease will show up as a positive test result. Two of those people will show up as a negative test result, despite having the disease. In the disease absent column, the 1% false alarm rate means that 99 people out of the 9,900 that do not have the disease will still show a positive test result, whereas 9,801 will show a negative test result when no disease is present.

The critical information that is often ignored is the number of people with false positives. Although the false positive rate is low, the base rate is low as well. That means that most people actually don't have the disease. And even if a small percentage of those people without the disease show a false positive, the absolute number of false positive cases is higher than desirable. Using the formula described earlier (as shown on the figure), we calculate the probability of the disease given a positive test result as .49. In other words, despite a test with a very high hit rate and a very low false alarm rate, a low base rate results in a low probability of the person with a positive test actually having the disease. In many of Gigerenzer's studies, even experienced physicians overestimated the probability of a positive test result indicating the actual presence of a disease.

RATIONAL APPROACHES TO DECISION-MAKING

Decision-making involves a combination of knowledge about outcomes, costs, benefits, and probabilities. The previous section covered understanding probability, and the errors that may result. This section covers several theoretical approaches that attempt to explain and understand how people make decisions.

Expected values

A rational approach to decision-making sets a normative standard from which we can investigate deviations. In other words, many of the characteristics and aspects of this model are rooted in economic theory, and may not describe the cognitive processes behind decision-making as well as some of the other theoretical approaches we will take. On the other hand, this rational approach describes how one might arrive at an optimal decision. The degree to which people deviate from this optimal decision can be understood in the context of other theoretical approaches, memory, knowledge, and cognitive limitations.

A fundamental aspect to the rational approach is the assumption that people can make optimal decisions. In order to make an optimal decision, it is assumed that people weigh the alternatives, they set an **expected value** for all of the alternatives, and then they proceed to choose the most valuable alternative in the long run. That is, the optimal decision is the one that maximizes the expected value.

The expected value can be thought of as a physical, monetary, or psychological value that is attached to a given outcome. An expected value is calculated by combining what is known about the costs and benefits with the probability of achieving a desired outcome. The formula below shows a straightforward way to calculate an expected value:

$$EV = (Value_{Gain} * P(desired\ outcome)) - (Value_{Loss} * P(non\ desired\ outcome))$$

In this formula, expected value (EV) is a function of the gain and the probability of achieving that gain minus the costs and the probability of incurring those costs. For example, consider a very straightforward set of monetary choices. One option (1) allows you to win $40 with a probability of .2 or else nothing. The other option (2) allows you to win $35 with a probability of .25 or else nothing. The first choice has a higher win but a lower probability. In order to decide which of these is the best option in the long run the values can be inserted into the expected value formula as follows:

Option 1: $EV = (\$40 * .20) - (0 * .80) = \$8.00$

Option 2: $EV = (\$35 * .25) - (0 * .75) = \$8.75$

Despite having the higher payout, Option 1 actually has a lower expected value over the long run. This is because of the way gain and probability combine. This also means that different factors can affect the long-run expected value. In cases where the outcome has some additional utility beyond the actual value, it can affect choice by increasing the value of a win or decreasing the cost for a loss. For example, many people engage in gambling and buying lottery tickets, despite the negative expected value for these events. Most people agree that there is an additional psychological utility that comes from a casino game. Gambling in a casino might be fun, it might be an enjoyable social activity, or it might be part of a vacation. This would essentially minimize the impact of a loss.

Biases and problems with the rational approach

As previously discussed, the rational approach is very effective at describing the optimal decision-making patterns, but very often fails to describe how people actually make decisions. People often make decisions that are in opposition to expected values and optimality. A fairly straightforward example, using the same general framework as the simple gambling option earlier, is known as a **certainty effect**. All things being equal, humans and many other non-human animals resist uncertainty. Uncertainty creates an unwelcome state for any organism. A bias for certainty would occur when people choose an option with a lower expected value that promises certainty instead. In the example below, Option 1 has a higher payout and a higher expected value, but people may also choose Option 2. That is because Option 2 has no probability of a loss. In this case, it is a certain gain of $30.

Option 1: $EV = (\$40*.80) - (0*.20) = \$32.00$

Option 2: $EV = (\$30*1.0) - (0*0.0) = \$30.00$

The effects of certainty are also seen in what is known as the **framing effect**. Originally described by Tversky and Kahneman (1981), the framing effect is an illustration about how the context and semantics of a decision can affect which options seem preferable. The most well-known example consists of a short description of a scenario and two choices. Consider the following statements:

Premise: Imagine that your city is preparing for the outbreak of a disease. If left untreated, the disease will kill 600 people. Two programmes to combat the disease have been proposed.

Programme A. 200 people will be saved.

Programme B. There is a 1/3 chance that 600 people will be saved and a 2/3 chance no people will be saved.

In this scenario, most participants choose Programme A. Although it is implicit in that statement that 200 people will be saved and therefore 400 people will not, the framing is in terms of *lives saved*. Both programmes talk about lives being saved. When framed as a saving or as a gain, people generally display **risk averse behaviour** and prefer a certain outcome (Tversky & Kahneman, 1981).

However, imagine the same scenario but framed as the number of people who will die:

Premise: Imagine that your city is preparing for the outbreak of a disease. If left untreated, the disease will kill 600 people. Two programmes to combat the disease have been proposed.

Programme C. 400 people will die.

Programme D. There is a 1/3 chance that no one will die and a 2/3 chance that 200 people will die.

In this scenario, most participants choose option D. Notice that the numbers are equivalent between Programmes A and C and B and D across both scenarios. This second scenario is framed as a loss (i.e., people dying). When a decision is framed as a loss, people generally display **loss aversion** and are more willing to choose the riskier alternative. This framing example is interesting because it pits loss aversion against risk aversion. Although people generally like to avoid risk and loss, avoiding loss is paramount. Curiously, both may stem from a desire to avoid uncertainty. People tend to avoid risk as a way to reduce uncertainty, but people also tend to avoid loss as a way to avoid uncertainty and protect the status quo.

BOX 9.2

Many retail environments and stores take advantage of our preference for certainty, loss aversion, and risk aversion in the way they advertise. For example, every summer I go with my kids to purchase new sporting equipment for baseball, and in the winter for ice sports. One year we went to a local sporting goods store which had a sign advertising that everything was on sale in the store, up to 50% off. One of my kids said "It is a good thing we decided to come today, they're having a big sale." But the store always has that sign up. What is listed as the "sale price" is the actual price. This is seen in other retail environments where the tag may have a "suggested price" that the object is never sold for. These pricing strategies present a framing effect whereby the advertised price appears to be a bargain.

The work of Richard Thaler (1980, 1985) has examined this idea more systematically. For example, consider the following descriptions of two gas (petrol) stations with different pricing strategies.

Driving down the road, you notice your car is running low on gasoline, and you see two service stations, both advertising gasoline. Station A's price is $1.00 per litre; station B's price is $0.95 per litre. Station A's sign also announces, "5 cents/litre discount for cash!" Station B's sign announces, "5 cents/litre surcharge for credit cards." All other factors being equal (e.g., cleanliness of the stations, whether you like the brand of gasoline carried, number of cars waiting at each), to which station would you choose to go?

With no additional context, subjects will report a preference for Station A. The costs were identical regardless of whether subjects were asked to pay with cash or with credit. However, the first station's policy was framed as a discount for paying cash. This is interpreted as a more favourable pricing strategy and so that station was preferred.

Loss aversion

Several of the preceding examples dealt with the phenomenon of loss aversion. **Loss aversion** occurs because the psychological value assigned to giving up something or losing something is greater than the corresponding psychological value associated with obtaining that same object. We tend to hold on to the things that we already have. We tend to prefer current circumstances. Many people continue to use a favourite pen, to keep old books that they like, or to keep a favourite mug. More consequentially, many people stay in relationships that are not ideal for fear of losing what they have. As humans, our decisions are often ruled by loss aversion.

Loss aversion comes in several forms. In the earlier examples on framing, loss aversion came about when participants were likely to prefer riskier alternatives rather than face loss of life in the disease scenario. On a more personal scale, loss aversion associated with small objects is often referred to as the **endowment effect**. A study by Kahneman, Knetsch, and Thaler (1991) investigated this effect with university undergraduates. Participants were divided into groups. One group, the Sellers, were given university bookstore coffee mugs and were asked whether they would be willing to sell the mugs at each of a series of prices ranging from $0.25 to $9.25. Buyers were asked whether they would be willing to buy a mug at the same set of prices. Choosers were not given a mug and were asked to choose, for each of the prices, between receiving a mug and receiving that amount of money. In other words, Choosers did not have the mug, and their decision was how much they were willing to pay. It is important to note that everyone ended the study with the same amount. But what is interesting is that Sellers priced the mug at a point nearly twice that of the Choosers. The mere act of possessing the mug endowed it with greater value.

Loss aversion also shows up in an effect that is referred to as entrapment, with a sunk cost effect (Thaler, 1980). This can be a very effectively used technique in a sales environment. Essentially, people are unwilling to abandon an undesirable status quo primarily because they have already invested time or money. As an example, imagine that you and your friends go to see a movie. In Canada, where I live, the average movie price is somewhere between $12 and $15. Once you have paid your $12, you expect to see a good movie, but what would you do if the movie was truly awful? Would you stay and watch to the end, or would you get up and leave? When I ask this question in a class, most students indicate that they would stay. The reason that is most commonly given is that they already paid for it. The reasoning is that you have paid money for the movie, it is already bad, but leaving the movie will not make it any less bad. And there is always a chance, however remote, that it might get better. You would miss that chance if you left the movie. In short, once you have sunk some cost into something you desire to see that sunk cost realized.

This effect also arises in other scenarios. If you have ever been on hold with a utility or a telecommunications provider seeking technical or billing support, you will have noticed that it is a common experience to be told something along the lines of "Your call is important to us, please stay on the line and your call will be answered in the order that it was received". This can be very frustrating. There is uncertainty with respect to how soon your call will be taken. When I have been in this situation, I often feel that the longer I wait, the more resistant I am to hanging up. I am unwilling to give up sunk time. This behaviour deviates from the optimal model because the cost has already been paid.

Prospect theory

The biases discussed above suggest that people often make decisions which deviate from rationality. That does not mean that they are bad decisions. And it does not mean that people are making decisions poorly. It just means that there are psychological reasons behind suboptimal decision-making. Kahneman and Tversky proposed an alternative to the standard economic/rational model referred to as **prospect theory** (Kahneman & Tversky, 1979; Tversky & Kahneman, 1983). Prospect theory suggests that people make decisions according to psychological prospects. In addition, this theory takes into account the difficulty that most people have in correctly judging probability and likelihood. Prospect theory assumes that objective probability can be replaced by psychological probability or beliefs. A key aspect of prospect theory is that loss aversion and risk aversion are primary motivators. Loss aversion looms especially large in this theoretical approach.

Prospect theory is best summarized in the graph shown in Figure 9.5. It shows prospect theory's value function. The *x*-axis shows losses and gains in terms of real value. The *y*-axis shows the psychological impact of those losses and gains. There are several things to note about this value function. First, both the loss and the gain curves are concave. That is, there is not a linear relationship between actual gain and the psychological impact of that gain. As shown in the graph, there might be some psychological value placed on

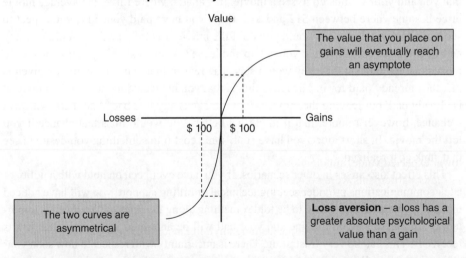

Prospect Theory's Value Function

Value

The value that you place on gains will eventually reach an asymptote

Losses ——————————————— Gains

$ 100 $ 100

The two curves are asymmetrical

Loss aversion – a loss has a greater absolute psychological value than a gain

Figure 9.5 This graph represents the value function for prospect theory. The *y*-axis shows the psychological value associated with losses and gains and the real value of losses and gains is shown on the *x*-axis. In prospect theory, the loss curve is steeper than the gain curve.

gaining $100, but the gain of $200 (twice as much in real dollars) may not be psychologically twice as desirable. According to this theory, the value that you place on gains will eventually reach an asymptote. This is often referred to as "diminishing returns".

A second thing to note about prospect theory's value function is that the curves are asymmetrical. The loss curve is steeper than the gain curve. This reflects the loss aversions and general finding that people sometimes value the status quo more than the prospect of a gain. In terms of *absolute value*, a gain of $100 is not worth the same as a loss of $100. As much as we may appreciate an extra $100, we are likely to take steps to avoid a loss of $100. *Losses loom larger than gains* according to prospect theory.

This general approach accounts for many of the findings that show people's deviations from optimality. Kahneman and Tversky (1979) argue that prospect theory more accurately describes the psychological process behind human decision-making. We behave suboptimally because we value the status quo, we seek to avoid and minimize loss, and we seek to reduce uncertainty. These psychological drives may come in conflict with optimality.

Pseudocertainty

Because prospect theory places a premium on loss aversion and the reduction of uncertainty, it makes predictions about how people might behave in circumstances that *seem* certain, but are not. Tversky and Kahneman (1981) illustrate what can be called **pseudocertainty**. Participants are shown several problems and asked to choose the most desirable option. First, consider this problem:

Problem 1: Which of the following options do you prefer?

A. 25% chance to win $30 and 75% chance to win nothing.

B. 20% chance to win $45 and 80% chance to win nothing.

In this problem, 42% of participants chose option A while 58% chose option B. Note that this is just like the example used earlier in the chapter and option B actually has a slightly lower expected value, although both are fairly close.

Other participants were asked to consider a different problem:

Problem 2: Consider the following two-stage game. In the first stage, there is a 75% chance to end the game without winning anything, and a 25% chance to move into the second stage. If you reach the second stage you have a choice between:

C. A sure win of $30.

D. 80% chance to win $45 and 20% chance to win nothing.

Your choice must be made before the outcome of the first stage is known.

In this scenario, 74% of participants chose option C while only 26% chose option D. The plausible reason is that option C seems to be a certain outcome. However, Tversky and Kahneman (1981) point out that it is not really certain. When considering both stages (which are required in this game) the full probability of winning money is calculated via the multiplicative "and rule" and must take into account the probabilities in the first stage and the second stage. For option C, this is calculated as $(.25 \times 1.00 = .25)$ and for option D this is calculated as $(.25 \times .80 = .20)$, which is the same as the probability of winning money in option A (.25) and option B (.20) respectively. In the second problem, since participants do not have a choice of options in the first stage, participants tend to ignore the first option when evaluating the overall probability, which leads to the pseudocertainty effect.

KNOWLEDGE EFFECTS IN DECISION-MAKING

The rational approach does not rely on personal conceptual knowledge or semantic memory, but rather assumes that decisions are made in accordance with calculated expected values that arise from an understanding of probability and the costs and benefits of each outcome. Prospect theory takes into account personal and cognitive biases by assigning a role for the aversion of risk and the aversion of loss, but there are other, sometimes more idiosyncratic, factors that influence and affect people's ability to make decisions.

Reason-based decision-making

In many cases, one of the influencing factors in decision-making is the ability to provide a reason for the decision. Given several options, it is likely that the most attractive decision is the one that has the best justification, even if it does not have a better possible outcome. For example, selecting a menu item at a restaurant because it conforms with a set of beliefs about what you like (seafood) allows you to give a reason: "I ordered the shrimp risotto because I like shrimp". This is a great reason to order the dish, but does not necessarily reflect a rational analysis. To some degree a prospect analysis accounts for this, if the person wishes to avoid the risks associated with other dishes. But if the diner in question has never eaten risotto before, this decision suggests that risk (risotto) is mitigated by having a good reason to order the dish (I like shrimp).

Shafir, Simonson, and Tversky (1993) examined this effect more systematically. Participants in their study were given one of three scenarios and asked to indicate a decision or choice.

Scenario: Imagine you just finished a particularly difficult final exam and you are walking home. You will not find out whether you passed the exam until tomorrow afternoon. A travel agent has a sign for an inexpensive trip to Acapulco. The offer expires that afternoon, but you can pay $5.00 to hold a reservation until tomorrow. Do you sign up to take the trip or pay the $5.00 fee?

Bear in mind that this study was conducted in an era when most people made their travel plans via a travel agent and not via the web. In this scenario, the majority of the participants indicated that they would pay the extra $5.00, because they wanted a reason to go on the trip (pass or fail). But two other conditions shed additional light on these studies. Another condition asked subjects to make the same decision but under the assumption that they had passed the exam or (another group) that they had failed the exam. In these conditions, subjects generally indicated that they would buy the ticket and forego paying the extra $5.00. Each group now had a good reason (passing or failing). In other words, participants in the uncertain condition were paying for information that will not affect their choice, because either reason (pass or fail) would be a good one. Participants in the uncertain condition did not have a reason yet, and so they elect to pay the $5.00 to defer the decision until a reason is present.

Regret

People often make a decision to avoid experiencing regret for a decision that did not result in a desirable outcome. This is a form of loss aversion. When I teach this topic, I often propose the following example to students. Imagine that everyone in class receives a ticket for a drawing worth $100 (this is a thought experiment, not as an actual drawing). There is no cost. The tickets are free. Because it is a drawing, every ticket has the same probability of winning. No ticket can be considered a winning ticket until the drawing has been made. So when you receive the ticket, your ticket has the same probability of winning as every other ticket in the class. I then ask students if they would consider trading the ticket with the student beside them. Most students indicate that in this scenario, they would be unwilling to trade. The reason is because there is no advantage in trading with someone else because tickets have an equal probability of being winners. However, most students also indicate that if they had traded, and the person next to them won, they would regret having traded. In other words, people avoid the trade in order to avoid a feeling of regret. It would be difficult to avoid feeling regret and to avoid feeling like you had traded away a winning ticket, even though none of the tickets is a winner until the drawing is made.

Satisficing

We tend to assume that it is optimal to be optimal. In other words, there is a psychological and behavioural premium on optimality decision-making. This has an intuitive appeal because if we define optimal as "ensuring the best outcome" it is hard to argue that optimality is the preferred state. But is there any down side to preferring optimality? Consider this scenario. You are in an airport and you have not eaten yet. You have a three-hour flight ahead of you and you need to find something to eat in the next 30 minutes. There are probably hundreds of choices, and you want to get the best meal you can in terms of quality and value. It has to be fast, not too spicy or garlic-laden (you will be on a plane for three or more hours) but also good tasting and healthy. You could stop at each restaurant and vendor and find out what they have to offer and compare this with reviews on social media and review sites. Using this combination of things, you might be able to arrive at the optimal pre-flight meal, but this exhaustive search and evaluation procedure might take a long time, possibly too long given the circumstances.

Instead, you might look at two or three options that are close to you and choose a meal that comes close to satisfying your criteria. The best solution seems to be to set a flexible and modest threshold and choose the first option that seems to meet the basic criteria. The cost of evaluating all of the options to choose the optimal meal is significant, and the benefits are not that great. In addition, there is not much cost to a less than perfect meal in this scenario.

Herbert Simon (1972) referred to this as **satisficing**, which he defined as setting a criterion or aspiration level, and then searching for the first alternative that is satisfactory according to that criterion. Satisficing is sometimes called a "good enough" approach because, in many cases, it is a strategy that is geared towards finding an alternative that is good enough, but maybe not the best. It is a strategy that is explicitly suboptimal. In the airport food example, you might decide to get something for less than $15.00 that is not spicy. This can be met with the first sandwich, hamburger, or sushi platter that you find.

SUMMARY

Decisions underlie many of the important outcomes of cognition. In previous chapters, constructs like similarity, concepts, and induction reflected internal states and behaviour. With decision-making, these internal states interact with external outcomes. Unlike many of the kinds of thinking that were discussed in earlier chapters, there are real consequences to making good and bad decisions.

In Chapter 5, we discussed the interaction between language and thought. One of the points that I tried to make was that the way in which you describe something linguistically can have an effect on how you think about it. In the current chapter, this was made very clear with respect to framing effects. Decisions that are framed as a loss produce different expectations and outcomes compared to decisions that are framed as a gain. In the most striking example, the terms and outcomes were identical; the only thing that differed was the linguistic and semantic content.

Although most decisions that people make are straightforward and are likely to be correct (or close enough), there are many times when bad decisions are made. The research and the ideas discussed in this chapter should make clear that decision-making is at once a fast and seemingly effortless process, and also a process fraught with potential errors and biases. However, cognitive biases and heuristics seem to be at play in so many different scenarios that they may not always be a source of error, but rather of fast and efficient decision-making.

10 PROBLEM-SOLVING

The previous chapter suggested that decision-making is one of the major behavioural outcomes of the thinking process. Humans make many decisions, big and small, throughout the course of a day, a week, or a year. This chapter covers problem-solving, which falls into the same category: that of major behavioural outcomes of the thinking process. When you are faced with some arrangement of physical or cognitive circumstances that do not quite give you what you need, you are being faced with a problem that needs to be solved. Problem-solving is about taking the current state and transforming it into a goal state.

Consider a problem that is faced by many university students: you need to arrive on campus in time for your 8:30 am class, in which there is an exam. This is a pretty straightforward problem. But suppose, on this morning, there is a massive snow storm that began in the early hours of the morning which has affected many of the roads, bus schedules, closed the expressway you usually take, and has generally made things a mess. But the university is not closed. This presents a **problem**. Your goal is to get to the university at 8:30 am, in time for class. The current state is that there is an unusual amount of snow-bound traffic slowing or possibly blocking your route. You might solve the problem in a number of ways. For example, you could consult Google maps for alternative routes. You could rely on general knowledge of the local city to bypass the usual expressway. You might check Twitter to try to pinpoint where the traffic is likely to be heaviest and look for a detour. You might also try to contact your professor to inform her that you are unable to drive in. In this example, the problem is the thing (snow and traffic) that interferes with achieving your goal. Solutions can be generated from memory, consultation, or examining the parameters of the problem in greater detail. And like many problems, there might not be a single best answer.

A GENERAL DESCRIPTION

Parts of a problem

Most problems have several features or aspects that define them as problems. A good working definition of a problem is that of a gap or a barrier between the **current state** and some **goal state** (Newell & Simon, 1972). In the winter storm example, the current state is being at home and the goal state is arriving at the exam on time. The **problem** is the snow and traffic congestion, which is a barrier between the current state and the goal state. In this example, the problem is something that impedes progression from the current state to the goal state. Figure 10.1 shows a schematic diagram of the components of most problems, including the current state and the goal state as the endpoints. Not all problems have these features, and in some cases the degree to which these components are either explicitly or implicitly designated can affect the difficulty and complexity of the problem.

In addition to the goal state and the current state, problems also have **givens**. In problem-solving, a given is an aspect, condition, and/or constraint that the problem-solver must deal with when solving the problem. These may help or hurt the solving of the problem, but are not considered as the gap that is the problem itself. In the winter storm example, suppose that you have a car and to not live near the bus line. In that case, one possible given would be the knowledge that you have to drive to the university, rather than take public transport or an alternative means. This is a given because perhaps you already know that you have to drive because of geographic reasons. As such, it places constraints on the possible solutions and how the problem is solved. Givens can be explicit or implicit in nature. "Needing to drive" is an implicit given. It was not stated explicitly in the original problem, but it is an implicit aspect of the situation.

Parts of a Problem

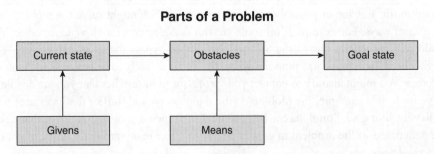

Figure 10.1 Five parts or components of a problem. It is not necessary for all of these parts to be explicitly available to the problem-solver. The degree to which a problem is well defined corresponds to how much of this information is explicitly defined for the problem-solver.

Consider another example. In the USA and Canada (and probably in other parts of the world) many people enjoy watching competitive cooking shows on TV. A popular show during the time when I was writing this chapter was called "*Chopped!*". In this show, contestants must create a dish in 20 or 30 minutes from a set of idiosyncratic ingredients. The ingredients are not revealed until the timer starts. In this case, the givens are the ingredients, the standard cookware, and the set of staple ingredients that each contestant receives. All of these things can either inhibit or facilitate solving the problem of creating a winning dish. Unlike the winter storm example, many of these givens are explicit and known to contestants when they begin.

Figure 10.1 also shows the **obstacles**, which are at the heart of a problem. The obstacles are the things that interfere with a direct path between the current state and the goal state. In the winter storm example, of course, the obstacles are unexpected snow and traffic on the main route. In the *Chopped!* example of being asked to cook a dish from some new ingredients, the obstacles are the short timeframe (in the show it is 20 or 30 minutes) as well as being unfamiliar with how the ingredients should combine. Obstacles may seem more difficult under cognitive limitations like time pressure, multitasking, and evaluation. As we discussed earlier in Chapter 3 on knowledge and working memory, any time a person is required to perform multiple cognitive tasks, performance on any one of those tasks can be negatively affected. This presents an additional problem.

Sometimes the impact of an obstacle can be reduced or almost eliminated when the problem-solver is very familiar with the problem context. Experts, for example, may be able to retrieve a possible solution from memory (Nokes, Schunn, & Chi, 2010; Norman & Brooks, 1997; Posner, 1973; Sweller, 1988). This greatly reduces the cognitive load. In other words, rather than try to solve the problem by working towards a novel or unexpected solution, the expert solves the problem by recalling the solution from memory and prior experience. Consider expertise with respect to the winter storm example. If you are very familiar with traffic patterns, and with your city, you should be able to come up with a detour that may solve the problem with less effort than would be required by someone with no knowledge of the local geography. Or consider expertise with respect to the cooking show example. If a contestant happens to receive ingredients that they are very familiar with, then they can retrieve from memory appropriate ways to combine these ingredients to make an exciting final dish. In general, experts tend to rely heavily on memory retrieval when solving problems, rather than rely on some of the problem-solving heuristics that will be discussed later in this chapter, and this tendency has often been described as one of the cognitive hallmarks of expertise (Chi, Glaser, & Rees, 1982). Expert thinking will be discussed in much greater detail in Chapter 11.

As shown in Figure 10.1, the problem-solving **means** act on the obstacle or obstacles. The means are the operations that are used to change the original state and to move closer to the goal state. Means can be cognitive operations, such as mental imagery, verbalization, or memory retrieval. Other cognitive means are imagining the problem from a different perspective, imagining the solution, or representing the problem in a different way from how it was originally posed. For example, when given a set of ingredients on a competitive cooking show like *"Chopped"*, contestants often proceed in one of two ways. Some contestants start with a final dish in mind and work backwards to decide how to process the ingredients to get to that final dish. Other contestants will occasionally not know what to do with an ingredient. They may begin working on one ingredient without a final dish in mind. Both of these contestants are trying to solve the problem but with different means.

Well-defined and ill-defined problems

It should be evident from the examples given above and from the description of the components of a problem that problems can vary in terms of how well defined they are. A problem with completely specified initial states and goals, well-articulated givens and obstacles, and a specified means of attaining that goal or goals can be considered a **well-defined problem**. An example of a well-defined problem is a multiple-choice problem on an exam. The question is clear, the options are clear, and the goal is to select the one correct answer. There is very little ambiguity in terms of what is required. Another example would be cooking a batch of brownies from a recipe. A well-written recipe instructs the cook on what ingredients are needed, how many and how much is needed, how to combine them, and often includes a picture to show what the final result should look like. Cooking something from a recipe is a well-defined problem.

If one or more of the aspects of the problem is missing or not defined, the problem can be considered an **ill-defined problem**. For examples of ill-defined problems, consider many of the problems that university students and college students are often faced with. If your goal is to obtain a good mark in a given course, it may not be clear what the initial state is, even though the goal state is clear. Furthermore, the givens, constraints, and means may not be very well specified. Additional obstacles may arise during the course that make it more difficult to obtain a good mark in the class. Other examples would include investing money, troubleshooting your computer when it seems to be acting sluggishly but you're not sure, writing an essay for a class without an assigned topic. These are all problems because there is a gap between the initial and the goal state. But in each case there may be some aspects that are defined and other aspects that are not defined. In general, most problems exist between the two endpoints of being well defined and ill defined.

Problem representation

Solving a problem often requires the creation of one or more mental representations to assist in solving the problem. A **problem representation** is a mental representation constructed by the problem-solver to assist in solving the problem. The representation can

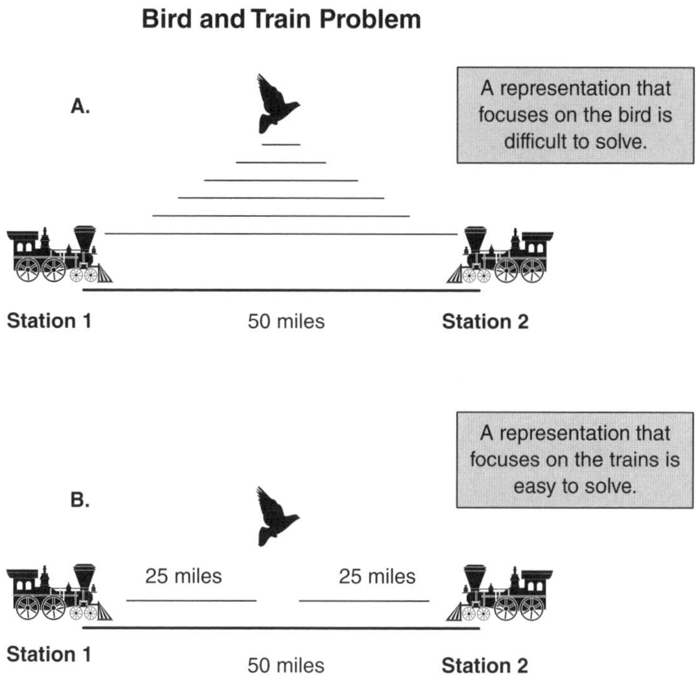

Bird and Train Problem

Figure 10.2 Posner's (1973) "bird and train" problem. This illustrates the importance of proper problem representation. The problem is nearly impossible to solve if the solver focuses on the bird and builds a representation accordingly. A representation that focuses on the train is much easier to solve.

help to clarify the end states as well as the givens and obstacles. In addition, solving a problem often involves changing an ill-defined problem into a well-defined problem by changing the nature of the representations.

For example, we have been discussing the nature of problem-solving in competitive cooking shows. The problem of being given several ingredients and then being asked to create a signature dish can be represented in at least two ways. In one case, the representation focuses on the ingredients and how to transform them. An alternative representation focuses on the final dish and how to incorporate those ingredients into a final dish. Although either of the representations may result in an excellent final dish, it is possible that switching from the ingredient-focused representation to the final dish representation (or the other way around) can assist in solving the problem.

An example by Posner (1973) makes the point more systematically with respect to an ill-defined problem and two possible ways to represent the problem. In the "birds and trains" problem, the initial statement and representation seems very difficult and nearly impossible to solve.

> Two train stations are fifty miles apart. At 2 pm one Saturday afternoon two trains start towards each other, one from each station. Just as the trains pull out of the stations, a bird springs into the air in front of the first train and flies ahead to the front of the second train. When the bird reaches the second train it turns back and flies towards the first train. The bird continues to do this until the trains meet. If both trains travel at the rate of 25 miles per hour and the bird flies at 100 miles per hour, how many miles will the bird have flown before the trains meet?

On the surface, this seems to be a very difficult problem to solve. In the first place, there are some extraneous details like the time and day. Second, the problem itself focuses attention on the bird, as the distance flown by the bird is the unknown that we need to solve for. If the problem is represented in terms of the bird's flight distance, the problem-solver is tempted to try to solve it this way. Solving the problem in this way would mean trying to calculate many simultaneous equations that keep track of the trains moving towards each other, and the cumulative distance of several back and forth flights by the bird, each one shorter than the last. It might not be impossible, but for all practical purposes, it probably is.

On the other hand, it is possible to solve the problem by focusing on the trains and the stations. Figure 10.2 shows two possible representations. At the top is an example of the complexity of solving the problem from the perspective of the bird representation, which is likely to be the initial representation that problem-solvers adopt. At the bottom is a relatively straightforward way of solving the problem from the perspective of a train-focused representation. The train-focused representation takes into account the distance between the two stations (50 miles) and the rate of speed of the trains (25 mph). With that information, you know the two trains are going to meet halfway at 25 miles. The time it takes each train to travel the 25 miles at the rate of 25 mph is 1 hour. Notice that the bird's speed is 100 mph. According to the initial statement of the problem, the bird will have been flying back and forth many times for the entire hour. If the bird is flying back and forth for an hour at a rate of 100 mph, it implies that the bird will have flown exactly 100 miles. This representation ignores the bird until the end. It also ignores the potential pitfalls of figuring out how many back-and-forth trips it takes. It doesn't matter how many trips back and forth the bird has taken; all that matters is that the bird has been flying for 1 hour at a rate of 100 mph.

Posner's bird and train problem underscores the importance of the correct representation. This problem seems difficult at first but when approached in a different way with an alternative representation it can be very simple.

Stages of problem-solving

Problem-solving can be fairly easily divided up into four stages. These stages may not occur in every case, and certainly if the problem is being solved by an explicit memory retrieval of a previously solved problem, then some stages might be skipped.

The first stage can be referred to as the **preparation stage**. In the preparation stage, the problem-solver first understands that the problem exists, evaluates the presence of any givens and the presence of an initial state. At this stage, the problem-solver would also examine any constraints, and try to understand the eventual goal. In this stage, a well-defined problem and an ill-defined problem can be differentiated.

In the **production stage**, the problem-solver begins to generate or produce potential solutions. Many of these could be the result of general-purpose problem-solving heuristics, such as the hill climbing, means end, or working backwards strategies that will be discussed later in this chapter. In addition, if prior knowledge is brought to bear or if previous examples need to be recalled, it is likely to take place in this production stage, which happens right after the problem is realized.

As potential solution paths are generated, the problem-solver engages in the **judgement** or **evaluation stage**. In this stage, tentative solution paths may be explored further, they may be evaluated for the likelihood of success, and if no correct solution is applicable, the problem-solver may give up and stop working on the problem or persist.

In many cases, an additional stage, referred to as the **incubation stage**, may occur even if the problem-solver gives up or moves on to another task. During the incubation stage, spreading activation in semantic memory may continue. In other words, even if the problem-solver is no longer explicitly trying to solve the problem, there may be implicit associations being drawn. Sometimes a problem is only solved by putting it out of mind or by working on something else. Upon returning to the problem, the solution seems evident. This sometimes results in an insight, which may have physiological correlates related to a feeling of satisfaction or relief. Insight problems will be discussed later in the chapter.

THE PSYCHOLOGICAL STUDY OF PROBLEM-SOLVING

The study of problem-solving from a psychological perspective began in earnest in the Gestalt era. I covered some of this in Chapter 1 on historical approaches to the psychology of thinking. For example, Karl Duncker, whose influential work on functional fixedness will be covered later in this chapter, published a book on problem-solving in German in 1935, which was later translated into English (Duncker, 1945). This work covered the general description of what makes a problem, the components of problems, the importance of problem representation, insight, and functional fixedness. Max Wertheimer, another of the major figures in the Gestalt era, was also heavily involved in problem-solving research. His book *Productive Thinking*, covered the topics of problem-solving and representation (Wertheimer, 1959). Although psychology in North America was heavily invested in the behaviourist paradigm, which did not address problem-solving very well, the work of the Gestalt psychologists in Germany helped to lay the foundations for the modern, cognitive approach.

Within the modern era of cognitive psychology and more recently cognitive neuroscience, a key starting point was the publication of *Human Problem-Solving* by Newell and Simon (1972). Newell and Simon approached the study of problem-solving as cognitive scientists. Their goal was to explain, in precise detail, the general problem-solving strategies that humans use. As cognitive scientists and also computer scientists, Newell and Simon were especially interested in how one might instantiate a set of problem-solving heuristics or algorithms via a set of computer instructions. A common way for the computer to carry out tasks and execute instructions is to ask the program to search through stored information and stored bits of instruction. In the same way, Newell and Simon then defined problem-solving as a search through the "problem space". Their problem-solving theory is known as the **problem space approach**. Central to this theory is the metaphor of physical geometry in problem-solving. Conceptual metaphors can be very useful in a complex domain like problem-solving. Recall from Chapter 2 on similarity that we discussed a geometric approach to similarity that made a similar metaphorical link between psychological space and physical space.

The problem space approach assumes that the solving of a problem requires the navigation through the problem space. The problem space is the representation that encompasses all of the possible solution steps. One region of the space represents the initial state and another region of the space represents the goal state. Much like the very simple mazes that you may have done as puzzles when you were a kid, problem-solving requires finding the shortest path from the initial state to the goal state through the problem space. Various operators can be employed to reduce the path, and representing the problem in a different way might reveal a shorter path.

As described earlier, the problem space approach grew out of Newell and Simon's artificial intelligence research. Concurrent with trying to understand how humans solve problems, they were also interested in trying to design a computer algorithm or computer program that would be able to solve general problems. They refer to this as the General Problem Solver. One of the limitations of a computer problem, of course, is that it may not have the extensive background knowledge and subject expertise of human problem-solvers. As a result, their approach emphasized problem-solving algorithms and problem-solving heuristics.

BOX 10.1

Many of the ideas in Newell and Simon's problem-solving approach were first discovered by an analytic technique known as protocol analysis. Newell and Simon conducted several studies in which problem-solvers were asked to think out loud while solving a problem (Ericsson & Simon, 1993; Newell & Simon, 1972). The general idea is that it can be very difficult to figure out all the small steps that take place between the initial state and the goal state. This can be especially problematic if the problems are being solved quickly or if the problem-solver considers several things in parallel before commencing with the solution. By asking subjects to think out loud, it is possible to gain some insight into these intermediate states.

Of course the down side to thinking out loud is that it can interfere with problem-solving strategies. Thinking out loud interferes with general working memory capacity and may also interfere with executive functions. As we discussed in Chapter 3, executive functions mediate many of the complex switching behaviours and goal-oriented behaviours in cognition.

As an example, you know how easy it is to solve basic arithmetic problems, and in many cases you take shortcuts. If you have to stop and think out loud at every step, it is going to slow you down. As another example, I have been using competitive cooking TV shows as a way to illustrate parts of a problem. In these sorts of show, the cooks or contestants are often talking out loud, but most of the commentary comes from interviews that were taken after the actual competition, which are then spliced into the production. It is much more difficult to think out loud when you are doing something stressful than it is to comment about it afterwards.

PROBLEM-SOLVING ALGORITHMS AND HEURISTICS

Newell and Simon's problem space approach (1972) emphasized a reliance on general-purpose problem-solving algorithms and heuristics. For the current purposes, an **algorithm** is a strategy that is guaranteed to find a solution. As an example, using a procedure to do long division in arithmetic is an algorithm. As long as you know the algorithm, and the most basic arithmetic facts, you can generate the solution of any division problem. Other examples might be following a recipe exactly. As long as you follow the steps, you are guaranteed to produce the correct dish. A **heuristic** in problem-solving differs from an algorithm in that it takes advantage of general knowledge to find a solution more quickly. Whereas algorithms, if employed correctly, are guaranteed to find a solution, heuristics may be faster but are not always guaranteed to find a solution. A good heuristic usually results in the correct solution.

Algorithms versus heuristics

As an example of the difference between algorithms and heuristics, imagine the scenario that was discussed in Chapter 1. You and your friends are planning to go out for the evening to a club, restaurant, or pub. You have been assigned to be the designated driver, which means you will not drink, and you have to pick everyone up and drop everyone off at the end of the evening. You wish to drive your car as few kilometres as possible. There are at least two possible ways to determine the shortest possible driving routes. One would be to enter everyone's address into Google maps, enter your address into Google maps, and enter the pub or pubs that you plan to attend into Google maps. You could then construct a map that considers every possible combination until you arrive at the shortest possible one. In order to know which one was the shortest, you would need to calculate all the possible combinations. This is an algorithm, and although it would be computationally intensive, you would be guaranteed to find the shortest possible route.

Alternatively, you could use what you know about the general geography of your neighbourhood, and where your friends live to estimate what you think would be the shortest possible route. Perhaps starting with the closest friend, and ending with a friend that is nearest to the destination. This is a heuristic because it is a cognitive shortcut that relies on general knowledge. It is likely that this would also arrive at the best possible solution, but it is not guaranteed. The trade-off is that it is computationally far less intensive. Given the trade-off, many people use heuristics to solve problems that are likely to result in the correct answer but require relatively less effort.

Exhaustive search

The algorithm described above, which is considering all the possible alternatives, is referred to as an **exhaustive search**. The problem-solver searches all the possible routes to the problem space and chooses the one that is the most efficient. This can be a workable algorithm if the problem space is sufficiently small. For example, children looking for a lost toy in their room might employ a strategy like this where they check everywhere. But this algorithm becomes unwieldy when the problem space is larger. In chess, for example, there are 20 opening moves, then 400 moves from that, 7.5 million moves from that, and 225 million moves from that. Clearly, an exhaustive search is impossible for a human to carry out. Computer chess programs that employ algorithms like this do not perform as well as good human chess players (Holding, 1985).

Hill climbing

As noted above, an exhaustive search is ineffective with a large search space. One way to constrain the search space is to adopt a general-purpose heuristic like **hill climbing** (Newell & Simon, 1972). The hill-climbing heuristic assumes that the problem-solver only searches for steps that move the current state closer to the goal state. Computationally, this can be achieved by comparing the current state to the goal state and making some form of similarity calculation (see Chapter 2 for extensive coverage of similarity). The problem-solver considers only taking another step if that step reduces the distance or increases the similarity between the current state and the goal state. Thus, the problem space is constrained and the number of alternatives is reduced.

The best way to give an example is to consider a literal example of climbing a hill. Suppose you are building a robot that will explore another planet or an inhospitable environment. One thing the robot needs to do is to be able to climb to the top of a hill. The simplest way to achieve this is to execute commands that ask the robot to check the current altitude and only commit to another step if the altitude increases. In that way, the robot will continue to climb until no step will increase the altitude. The robot will be at the top of the hill. The only possible steps being evaluated at any given moment are those that advance the robot, and the step that is taken is the one that increases or advances the robot towards the desired goal.

Of course, as you read this you probably realize a serious limitation with hill climbing. If the hill is uneven, as shown in Figure 10.3, it is entirely possible that the robot can find itself at the top of a smaller peak that is below the main peak. In other words, the robot

Hill Climbing

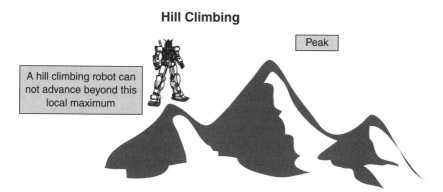

Figure 10.3 Hill climbing can be a useful problem-solving heuristic but often results in the problem of local maxima, as illustrated by this hill-climbing robot that cannot reach the true peak.

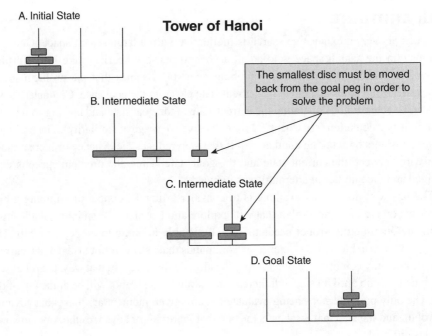

Figure 10.4 The classic "Tower of Hanoi" problem is a simple example of a problem that benefits from means end analysis, or the propensity to form subgoals.

finds itself unable to take a step that will increase its altitude despite not being at the top of the hill. If equipped with only a hill-climbing heuristic to find the top of the hill, the robot shown in Figure 10.3 is unable to make it to the true peak and instead settles on a local maximum.

Hill climbing as a general problem-solving strategy can also run into a similar problem. In cases where the solution to the problem requires first working towards a goal and then working away from the goal, this heuristic will fail to find a good solution. As an example, consider the well-known puzzle problem called the "Tower of Hanoi" (it is known by other names as well). In the simplest version of this puzzle, the problem-solver is presented with three discs of three different sizes stacked on one peg. The goal is to re-create the tower on another peg. Figure 10.4 shows an example. In this case, the initial state is as shown, with the tower built on one peg. The goal state is shown on the right, with the tower built on the rightmost peg. There are two given constraints in solving this problem. The first is that you can only move one disc at a time. The second is that you can never place a larger disc on top of a smaller disc. Figure 10.4 shows a series of intermediate steps. One of the intermediate steps shows either the smallest or the medium disc on the rightmost peg. This is the peg that will eventually contain the goal state tower. In order to continue with solving this problem, the smaller discs are first moved onto the goal peg and then moved off the goal peg in a subsequent stage in order to obey the constraints of the task and to make room for the largest peg, which is the base of the tower. The step moves away from the goal state. A strictly defined hill-climbing heuristic would have difficulty with this move because it requires moving away from the goal state. As such, hill climbing must be supplemented or replaced with another strategy.

Means end analysis

The simple example with the Tower of Hanoi suggests the need for an alternative way to reduce the problem space. One common way in which human problem-solvers reduce the problem space even further is by breaking the problem into smaller bits, and considering only one small part of the problem at a time. Newell and Simon (1972) refer to this as **means end analysis**. In means end analysis, the problem-solver breaks an ill-defined problem into several smaller well-defined problems. With the Tower of Hanoi example, the entire problem involves moving a tower of discs from one peg to another peg. But this large goal can be broken up into many smaller subgoals. For example, one subgoal requires laying the foundation on the rightmost peg with the largest disc. This subgoal can be broken up into smaller subgoals still. In order to lay the foundation, it is first necessary to solve two additional subgoals. The problem-solver needs to make sure the rightmost peg is clear. And the problem-solver needs to make sure that the largest disc has no smaller disc on top of it. By breaking the large problem up into several smaller problems, the solution can be attained by attending to and solving these smaller, more tractable problems.

The same idea applies to cooking and meal preparation. When most people are preparing a meal, they often break the large goal of the completed dish into many smaller subgoals, for example, collecting the ingredients, chopping and cutting them, and then placing the ingredients into small piles or bowls. The technical term for this is *mise en place*, which means literally, "*putting in place*". Creating the subgoals makes the problem easier to solve and the meal easier to prepare.

Means end problem-solving plays a role in the classic "hobbits and orcs" problem (Greeno, 1974; Thomas, 1974). Essentially, the problem is an expanded version of the Tower of Hanoi problem. It involves moving things from one area to another area with a set of constraints. The problem is stated below:

Three Hobbits and three Orcs arrive at a river bank, and they all wish to cross onto the other side. Fortunately, there is a boat, but unfortunately, the boat can only hold two creatures at one time. Also, there is another problem. Orcs are vicious creatures, and whenever there are more Orcs than Hobbits on one side of the river, the Orcs will immediately attack the Hobbits and eat them up. Consequently, you should be certain that you never leave more Orcs than Hobbits on any river bank. (Note that the Orcs, though vicious, can be trusted to bring the boat back from across the river!). How should the problem of ferrying everyone across the river be solved?

The Hobbits and Orcs Problem

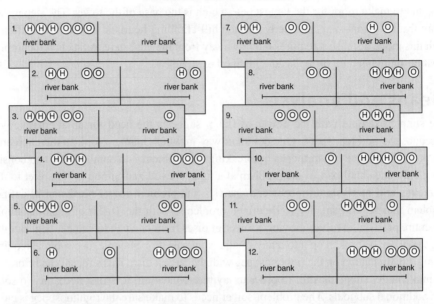

Figure 10.5 The "hobbits and orcs" problem cannot be solved via simple hill climbing. Step 1 shows the initial state (step 1, all the hobbits and orcs on the same side) and the goal state (step 12, all the hobbits and orcs at the other side). The intermediate means are steps 2–11, which show how the initial state is transformed into the goal. Problem-solvers have difficulty at steps 4–7 when some of the orcs need be moved away from the goal state.

First, ignore the most reasonable solution that would satisfy our understanding of hobbits and orcs in the Tolkien sense, that is, get the hobbits across the river and leave the orcs on the other side.

Figure 10.5 shows one possible series of steps to solve the problem. One challenging aspect for most problem-solvers is that when all of the orcs are taken to the other side, it becomes necessary to bring them back again in order to keep the appropriate balance. In other words, at step 4 it seems as if the problem is half solved – all of the orcs are on the right side of the river. From here, the solver has to work backwards partially to bring the orcs back over the river. This can be difficult for a straight hill-climbing heuristic. Means end analysis can break the problem up into smaller subgoals. Early research with this problem confirmed that participants make more errors at these positions in the problem space (Greeno, 1974; Thomas, 1974). People make more errors and take longer to choose the next move when transitioning from the position shown in step 4 to the positions in steps 5–7. In other words, hill climbing as an absolute strategy will fail for the hobbits and orcs problem. In order to reach the goal state, the problem-solver must break the problem into manageable subgoals. In addition, research examining the ability of participants to solve problems of this kind suggests problem-solvers require sufficient working memory resources in order to represent the problem variants, stages, and subgoals (Reber & Kotovsky, 1997).

Working backwards

So far, we have been thinking of problem-solving as a forward-driven series of cognitive steps. That is, we begin with an initial state and we move forward towards the goal state. Some problems, however, are better represented and solved in the opposite direction. This strategy is known as **working backwards**. For a very simple example, consider the kind of paper and pencil mazes that appear in colouring books and puzzle books for kids. There is usually a single way into the maze and a single way out. Solving the problem means finding the shortest path (and usually the only path) through the maze to the end-point. In many cases, it is more effective to work backwards from the end state. Trying to solve the problem from one direction only can lead to false paths. As another example, consider the problem posed by Sternberg and Davidson (1982):

> Water lilies on the lake will double every 24 hours. From the day the first lily appears until the lake is entirely covered it takes 60 days. When is the lake half covered?

This problem is pretty easy to solve, but it would be impossible to solve if working from a forward direction. We have no idea how large the lake is and we have no idea how many lilies it will take to fill the lake. However, if we start at the end, when the lake is completely covered, and work backwards, it is fairly simple. If they double every 24 hours, then the lake will be half covered on the 59th day. From day 59 to 60, the half-covered lake doubles to a fully covered lake. This problem is also an example of an insight problem (Metcalfe & Wiebe, 1987). Insight problems are often accompanied by a sudden flash of insight or illumination. Insight problems will be discussed later in the chapter.

THE IMPORTANCE OF PROBLEM REPRESENTATION

Many of the examples presented above emphasize heuristics and problem-solving strategies. Another way to think about problem-solving is to consider how the problem is represented. In many cases, when people solve problems, they construct a mental representation of the problem space (Newell & Simon, 1972). Many of the strategies I have discussed operate on this representation. As such, it is crucial to represent the problem correctly. Earlier in the chapter, this was discussed in the context of Posner's "bird and train" puzzle (Posner, 1973). In that case, one representation made the problem difficult or impossible to solve, but an alternative representation made the problem very simple and trivially easy to solve. In this section, I want to examine the role of problem representation in greater depth.

Choosing an appropriate representation

In Posner's "bird and train" example, the two representations were quite similar. The only difference is that one focused on the bird and the other focused on the train. Other problems require a more substantial change in representation. Consider this problem, which was first posed by Duncker (1926, 1945):

> A monk leaves the monastery at 6:00 am and gets to the mountain top by 4:00 pm. The next day he leaves the mountain top at 6:00 am and gets back home at 4:00 pm. He travels at a very irregular pace and stops often. Is there a time when he is exactly at the same spot at the same time on day one as on day two?

On the surface, this problem appears to be impossible to solve. First, the representation is very sparse and it emphasizes the irregularity of the monk's travel. We know that the monk starts and stops at the same time each day, but otherwise we don't know anything about the path that the monk takes. Second, the question itself focuses attention on exact times. The problem-solver in this case may be tempted to solve the problem for exactly when and where the monk is on day one and day two. Approached in this way, the problem cannot be solved.

However, if approached in a different way the problem is trivially easy. The simplest way to solve the problem is to represent it graphically. Figure 10.6 shows the hypothetical travel of the monk on the mountain. The y-axis shows altitude on the mountain, and the x-axis shows the time of day. On day one the monk ascends to the top. He starts at 6:00 am and he ends at 4:00 pm at the top of the mountain. And so we see an ascending line. I have drawn the line irregularly to emphasize that the pace was irregular, but this is hypothetical. We do not know the actual time/altitude ascent rate. The second line starts at the top and descends to the base. It also begins at 6:00 am and ends at 4:00 pm. And, as you can see, the two lines intersect. In fact, it is impossible to draw this graph without the lines intersecting. Any two lines that satisfy the constraints of the starting and stopping time and location will have to intersect. In other words, framing it this way emphasizes that the question and the problem are not about exactly where the monk is and when, but rather that there exists a time when he is in exactly the same spot at the same time of day on day

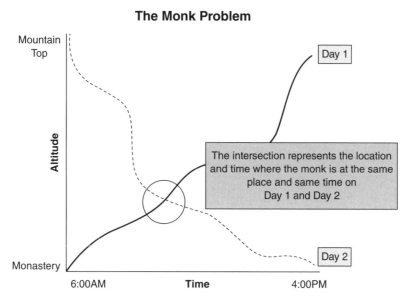

Figure 10.6 A graphical representation of the "The monk problem". The y-axis represents the altitude travelled and the x-axis represents the time of day. The circle shows the hypothetical intersection between time 1 and time 2 when the monk is in the same place and at the same time on both days.

one and day two. This spot is where the lines intersect. It can occur anywhere along the trail and along the course of the day, but it must occur.

Functional fixedness

Perhaps the most well-known example of problem representation is what is known as **Duncker's candle box** problem or the **functional fixedness** problem (Duncker, 1945). There are various versions of this problem, but the canonical version involves participants in two conditions who were presented with a series of objects and a problem to solve. The objects are shown in Figure 10.7. Participants were given a candle, a box of tacks, and a book of matches. Participants were asked to use these objects to provide a way to mount the candle so that it would illuminate the room. In one condition, the tacks and matches were removed from the boxes and placed in piles on the table, so that the participants saw empty boxes and the objects. In the other condition, which was the experimental condition or the **functional fixedness** condition, the matches were in their

The Candle Box Problem

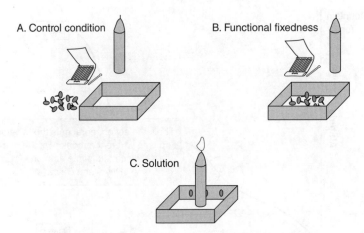

Figure 10.7 The function fixedness problem originally described by Karl Duncker (1945). Participants were given the materials either as shown in Panel A or as shown in Panel B and were asked to mount the candle to the wall so that it would illuminate the room.

box and the tacks were in their box. The correct solution, of course, is to tack one of the boxes to the wall, and tack the candle to the box. Thus the box operates as an impromptu shelf. (A word of warning, do not attempt to recreate this problem/solution in your room. As can be seen even from my simple schematic, this impromptu shelf is far too close to the wall, and would likely burn your house down. There is no way this clever solution would pass a fire code in any jurisdiction.)

In the initial study, all of the control subjects solved the task in the correct fashion. However, in the functional fixedness condition, fewer than half of the subjects were able to solve the problem correctly. Duncker's original explanation was that the function of the objects, namely the box, was fixed. When participants saw the box of tacks they were far less likely to perceive the box as a potential shelf. Its function was fixed as being a receptacle for the tacks.

BOX 10.2

Duncker's original candle box problem has been studied and examined in many contexts. Most people are quite familiar with it now, and the solution probably may not even strike us as very novel. However, the idea of using objects for something

"Life Hacks"

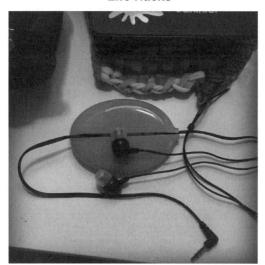

Figure 10.8 An example of a "life hack". The coin purse has been repurposed to keep headphones from being tangled.

other than their intended purpose to solve problems is something that crops up quite often in the phenomenon of "life hacks". At the time when I was writing this in 2014, it was very common to see news stories, websites, and other media showing all the clever ways in which simple household objects can be used to solve novel problems. For example, using a dustpan to fill up a bucket from a sink or using binder clips to organize the cords of your computer.

The photograph in Figure 10.8 is one that I took of my daughter's repurposing of a simple rubber change purse to store her ear buds so that the cord did not get tangled. Most of us enjoy looking at examples of these novel problem-solving attempts. For very clever life hacks, it is not uncommon to experience the sensation of satisfaction when seeing the example.

KNOWLEDGE AND ANALOGY

The preceding sections were concerned with general problem-solving heuristics and choosing the correct representation. These things work well for new problems without an obvious solution and without an obvious analogy. However, in practice many of us solve problems on a daily basis that are very similar to problems that we solved yesterday, the day before, and last week. In other words, problem-solving can be tedious. Problem-solving often involves considerable repetition and benefits from similarity between old problems and new problems. And so, effective problem-solvers typically make use of prior knowledge and analogy when solving problems.

Generally speaking, prior experience assists in solving your problems. This is especially true for experts, who may be solving many similar problems. Chapter 11 deals with expertise more explicitly, but a central component of expert-level performance is problem- solving from memory rather than from general heuristics or algorithms.

Outside of expertise, it is still fairly common to use prior experience or similar experiences when solving your problems. An excellent example was presented by Gick and Holyoak (1980). The central problem that participants were asked to solve is known as the "laser tumour problem" (Duncker, 1926). It reads as follows:

> A tumour was located in the interior of a patient's body. A doctor wanted to destroy the tumour with rays. The doctor wanted to prevent the rays from destroying healthy tissue. As a result, the high-intensity rays could not be applied to the tumour along one path. However, high-intensity rays were needed to destroy the tumour, so applying one low-intensity ray would not succeed.

Before you read any further, please take a few minutes to think about how you might solve this problem. Remember, the tumour cannot be operated on. The only way to save the patient is to destroy it with the lasers. How can this be done?

In the original study, very few participants were able to solve this problem. When I discuss this problem in my lectures, I find that approximately 5–10% of students are able to generate the correct solution (setting aside any students who may have encountered the problem in another class). Many students mention possible solutions, such as a partial operation that allows the lasers to get closer, and others answer that it cannot be done.

The correct solution is that the physician should use multiple lasers each set at a low intensity. The lasers should be pointed at the tumour as shown in Figure 10.9. Each laser is low intensity as it is directed into the body. When the lasers intersect, the intensity is additive such that the intersection point – and only the intersection point – is strong enough to destroy tissue. This allows for many low-intensity lasers to enter the body without causing damage and only reach high intensity at the precise location of the tumour. When this solution is explained to participants or students, they often mention that they did not realize they could use more than one laser. The realization they experience is known as an **insight**. The laser tumour problem is an example of an **insight problem**. Once you gain the insight into the solution, it is often accompanied by a feeling of satisfaction.

Realizing how difficult this problem is to solve, Gick and Holyoak (1980) examined the role of relevant and analogous knowledge. Prior to seeing the laser tumour problem, subjects in an experimental condition are provided with the "general and fortress" problem:

> A fortress was located in the centre of the country. Many roads radiated out from the fortress. A general wanted to capture the fortress with his army. The general wanted to prevent mines on the roads from destroying his army and neighbouring villagers. As a result, the entire army could not attack the fortress along one road. However, the entire army was needed to capture the fortress because an attack by one small group would not succeed. The general therefore divided his army into several groups. He positioned the small groups at the heads of different roads. The small groups simultaneously converged on the fortress. In this way, the army captured the fortress.

It should be clear that although these problems are different on the surface, they are analogous from a deep structure perspective. Both involve a central entity that needs to be attacked, both involve risk with sending the entire force needed, and the smaller force was not enough for the job. Participants who were given the fortress story first, and who were told that it contained a hint, were able to solve the tumour problem correctly. Additional protocol analyses indicated that most participants did use the first problem as an analogy to help solve the second problem. Even participants who were not told that the first problem could help in solving the second problem were more likely to solve the problem than those who never saw the fortress problem.

The central idea of this research is that many problems can be solved by realizing the analogy between other, already solved problems. As another example, many readers may remember a time when air passengers were able to carry full-size bottles of liquids, shampoo, etc. on to aeroplanes. In the mid-2000s, however, police in the UK foiled a terror plot in which bombers attempted to smuggle small components of an explosive device on to the plane in their liquid carry-ons. In essence, the plot was to bring aboard the plane the components of an explosive and assemble the liquid explosive on the plane. The bombers were trying to solve the problem of how to blow up a plane with a loose analogy to the "general and fortress" problem and the laser tumour problem. The analogous solution is to bring smaller amounts onto the plane and combine them into the lethal device. As a result of this foiled bombing plot, most airlines now restrict the amounts of liquid that can be carried on to a plane. Many of these restrictions have since been relaxed, but not to the point that they were prior to this attack.

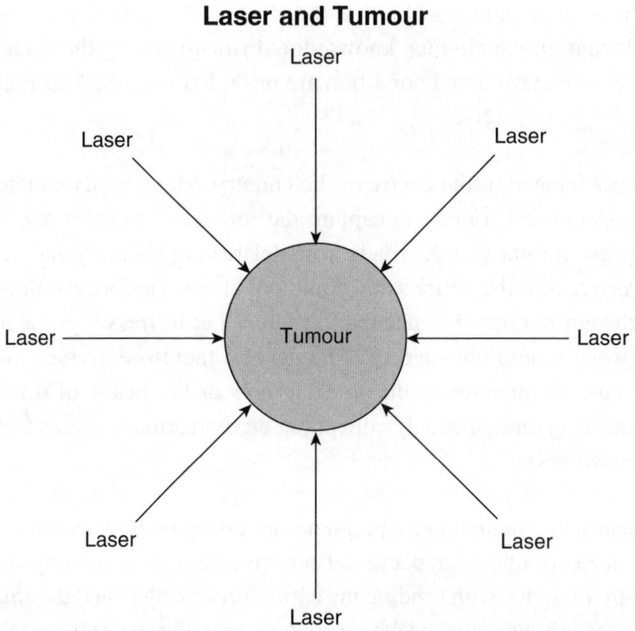

Laser and Tumour

Figure 10.9 An illustration of the laser and tumour problem. The lasers must be pointed at the tumour at a low intensity so that they intersect at the location of the tumour.

Insight problems

Some problems are difficult to solve, but when the solution is revealed, many people indicate that either they feel relieved to see the solution or, if they found the solution, they report that it happens suddenly (Metcalfe & Wiebe, 1987; Payne, Stevenson, Bowden, & Jung-Beeman, 2008). These kinds of problems are often known as **insight problems**, and they are all characterized by sudden insight. The archetypal and also apocryphal insight problem is that of Archimedes' discovery of a fluid displacement. Archimedes was a scientist, philosopher, and mathematician in ancient Greece. Although there is very little evidence that this story is factually correct, the anecdote is still interesting and informative. The story goes that a crown had been made for the king. The king had supplied the pure gold to be used. Archimedes was asked to determine whether some silver had been mixed in, which would then indicate that the manufacturer of the crown had likely stolen some of the king's gold. Archimedes had to solve the problem without damaging the crown.

While taking a bath, Archimedes noticed that the water in the tub rose when he got in. In other words, his body displaced the water. He realized that this displacement effect could be used to determine the volume of the crown. The submerged crown should displace an amount of water equal to its own volume and equal to the volume of gold that had been supplied. Archimedes realized that if the displacement was less than (or more than) expected, that cheaper metals would have been added to the crown. According to the story, when he realized this, Archimedes jumped out of the bath and ran naked through the street yelling "Eureka!" (which is from an ancient Greek expression meaning "I have found it!"). As a result, the point at which many people suddenly come upon the solution to an insight problem is often referred to as the **Eureka moment**.

The Nine Dot Problem

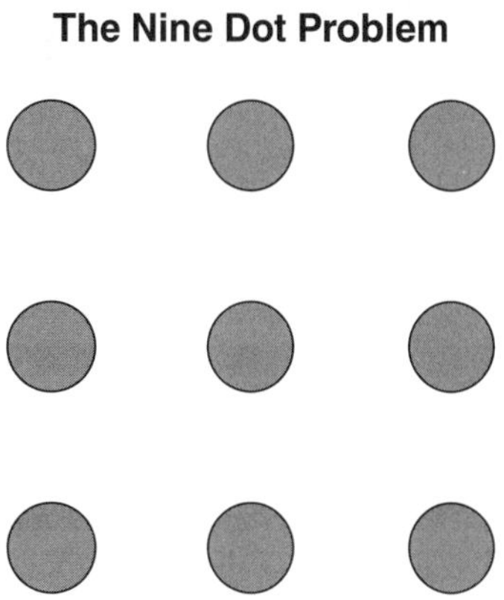

Figure 10.10 The goal of the nine dot problem is to draw four straight, continuous lines (four lines without lifting your pencil) so that the lines intersect all the dots.

An excellent example of an insight problem is what is known as the nine dot problem (Figure 10.10). Participants are presented with nine dots and are instructed to draw four lines that intersect all nine dots, without removing their pen or pencil. That is, start somewhere on the picture, draw four continuous lines and try to cover all nine dots.

The solution is shown at the end of the chapter in Figure 10.11. See if you can solve the problem yourself by replicating the puzzle on a piece of paper. If you have never solved this problem before, and you eventually arrive at the solution, did you experience a Eureka moment? If you cannot solve the problem, did you experience a Eureka moment when you read the solution at the end of the chapter? These Eureka moments are common for insight problems (Metcalfe & Wiebe, 1987).

What causes a sudden insight? The best answer seems to be that the sudden flash of insight occurs when problem-solvers engage distinct neural and cognitive processes which allow them to see connections that previously eluded them. This can take the form of enhanced semantic activation within the semantic memory system (Bowden & Jung-Beeman, 1998). There is also evidence to suggest increased activation in the right anterior superior temporal gyrus for insight problems relative to non-insight problems (Payne et al., 2008). Furthermore, additional studies have noted that roughly 1.5 seconds before arriving at a solution it is possible to detect a decrease in neural activity over the right visual cortex (Bowden, Jung-Beeman, Fleck, & Kounios, 2005; Jung-Beeman et al., 2004). It seems that the effects are not the result of emotion or a result of solving the solution, because the neural activity preceded the solutions. One possibility is that problem-solvers change the focus of their efforts just before insight solutions, allowing some information to enter into awareness (Bowden et al., 2005).

CREATIVITY

Creativity is often covered as a separate topic in the psychology of thinking. I want to cover it as a subtopic within problem-solving because so much of the research in creativity is related to problem-solving research. It seems like a natural connection.

What is creativity?

Creativity can be described both as an output and as a set of behaviours. Creative output is typically thought of as a work of art, music, or literature. But really creativity as an output can be a novel solution to a problem, a creative way to make money, or a novel engineering solution. There is much more to creativity than just the creative arts.

Creative content or creative output is best described as possessing three qualities. The first is the quality of **novelty**. Creative content is something that is novel. A creative idea is a new idea. If you create a work of art or write a song, you are making something new. If you copy a work of art or cover someone else's song, you may embellish it or add something new, but it is significantly reduced in novelty. We might argue that a new, original song is potentially more creative than the cover version. Creative content is also assumed to be relatively high in **quality**. In other words, good creative content is not just novel, it is useful as well. New music that is noteworthy is generally rated by expert peers in the marketplace as being high in quality. In other words, just being new is not enough to be considered creative. Finally, creative content is produced with **regularity**. That means that not only is the creator making new, high-quality things, but they are making them with some degree of predictive regularity. At the time that I was writing this book, the author Harper Lee, who wrote *To Kill a Mockingbird*, announced that she was going to publish a sequel. It turns out she had written a sequel long ago but had abandoned it. When it was written, *To Kill a Mockingbird* addressed aspects of race relations in the United States in a new way and Harper Lee won praise for the high quality of her writing. Her book earned its place in the canon of American literature. But it was her only book. At the time of my writing this text, not much was known about her new book. It remains to be seen whether it is of the same high quality. It would not diminish Harper Lee's standing as a great novelist if it were not, but it could enhance it if it were.

Measuring creativity

Like many psychological constructs, it may be possible to measure creativity. This may seem counterintuitive, given the emphasis on novelty in the definition of creativity. One of the original attempts to measure creativity was designed by the psychologist J. P. Guilford (Guilford, 1967). Guilford designed several tests that were rather like the insight problems described earlier. In many cases, they were problems that had a variety of solutions or no solution at all. Participants demonstrate their creativity by providing novel solutions, unusual answers, or by responding quickly to things that require some degree of creative thought. One of the most well-known examples is the **unusual uses test**. In the unusual uses test, the participant is given a list of common objects and asked to provide a set number of unusual uses for the object. They are instructed not to provide the most common use.

For example, participants might be asked to provide unusual uses for a brick. Standard uses for a brick would be as a building material or as an object to hold something down, but it is possible to imagine more unusual uses as well. A brick could be used to break a window. A brick could be used to silence an intruder. A brick could be used to create art, by pulverizing it into a fine, brick-coloured dust and then using the dust to create a pattern. A brick could be used to cool something if it is saturated and allowed to evaporate.

Another well-known measure of creativity is the **remote associate test** or RAT (Bowden & Jung-Beeman, 2004; Mednick, 1962). The remote associate test asks subjects to read three words and provide the one word that ties all three together. For example, if you are given the words "river", "note", and "blood", the answer is "bank" (a riverbank, a bank note, and a blood bank, which is a term for a medical repository for donated blood). If you are given the words "boiled", "lid", and "flower", the correct answer is "pot" (pot boiled, a pot lid, and a flower pot). These pairings vary in difficulty so that most people will find the correct word for some of the triads but other triads will be nearly impossible.

Both the unusual uses test and the remote associate test have been widely used in the psychological literature as well as in the education literature. They have been shown to correlate quite well with success in insight problems (see Duncker's candle box problem, described above). In many ways, the remote associate test has some benefits that the insight problems don't have. Insight problems are very complex and may not be solved. Furthermore, the complexity of these problems means that additional contextual variables may be introduced. For example, the subject simply may not understand the instructions. This might not mean that they are unable to solve problems or that they are lacking in creativity, but that the problem was written in a way that confuses the participant. The remote associate test avoids this problem by simplifying the response – subjects respond with a single word.

Thinking creatively

Humans have always been able to think creatively. After all, there has always existed a tradition of creative disciplines. Human ingenuity in science and engineering has been celebrated for most of our history. However, until the twentieth century, the study of creativity and most of the theories of creativity have emphasized outside influences – the influence of the divine, metaphysics, or some kind of otherworldly muse. One of the earlier attempts to understand and explain creativity was proposed by the English socialist thinker and psychologist Graham Wallas (1926). Although Wallas was working in a philosophical and Gestalt tradition, his terminology and description of the creative thinking process is still relevant. Wallas described several stages that people engage in or go through when thinking creatively.

The first of these is the **preparation stage**. In the preparation stage, you consider the problem or the decision to be made in its proper context. In other words, you evaluate all the resources you have, your talents, and any tools you may have. The second stage is the **incubation stage**. This refers to the phenomenological experience of not being able to solve a problem and yet feeling that your brain and mind continue to work at solving the problem. If you feel like a possible solution is imminent but not quite there, you are in the **intimation stage**. I used to experience this when I spent time computer programming. I would be unable to get the program to do what I wanted it to do. I would struggle and work but not succeed. Often, I would go home for the night without completing the project and wake up the next day and be able to solve it easily. This next stage is referred to as the **illumination** or **insight stage**. This is where the solution to a problem or the correct decision seems to arrive suddenly (see the discussion on insight problems above). Not coincidentally, work on insight problem-solving was very much in vogue at the time when Wallas wrote his book on creative thought. The final stage is a **verification stage**. If you feel like a creative solution has arrived suddenly in your mind, you will still need to verify it.

The idea of incubation, intimation, and illumination might have seemed to many people to argue for the existence of some kind of divine influence on creativity. From what we know about the way semantic memory is organized and the way in which different brain regions are densely interconnected in prefrontal regions, it also suggests that basic spreading activation provides a better solution and a better explanation for how insight problems seem to be solved suddenly. Many low-level activations may converge on the correct solution. It is only when the concept or concepts connected to the correct solution are activated to an appropriate threshold that the solution seems evident. This might seem to be sudden from the perspective of conscious awareness, but the activation process might still reflect gradual association.

Taking what is known about the stages of creativity, and combining it with what is known about problem-solving and the availability of standardized creativity tests, allows psychologists to examine some of the things that can influence creative thought. For example, one of the most interesting studies I read involved asking people to act out creative metaphors. It is not uncommon to hear people say things like "*think outside the box*" or to consider things "*on one hand*" and "*on the other hand*". A study by Leung and colleagues took an embodied cognition approach to investigate the functionality of these metaphors (Leung et al., 2012). They reasoned that if these metaphors have a grounding in a physiological state then placing yourself in that physiological condition might allow the metaphors to influence cognition and thinking more readily. Recall from Chapter 5 on language and thought that many conceptual metaphors have a basis in a physical reality.

Leung et al. tested this by asking their subjects to act out the metaphor. In one study, they built a large box out of PVC, pipe, and cardboard. They asked some of their subjects to stand in the box and complete a remote associate test. They asked other subjects to stand outside the box and complete the same test. In other words, half of their subjects were literally thinking outside the box. What they found was surprising: people outside the box completed more correct items on the remote associate test.

A similar test was carried out by Mehta, Zhu, and Cheema, who were interested in investigating the possibility that certain kinds of ambient noise might enhance creative thought (Mehta, Zhu, & Cheema, 2012). Many people report being able to work and think creatively in environments like a coffeehouse, or an atrium where other people are working around them. This is not an unusual claim. It is not uncommon to go into Starbucks and see people working. When I was a graduate student in the late 1990s, I completed my doctoral dissertation by writing in the café at a Wegman's store (a popular grocery chain). I found the combination of general noise combined with no identifiable conversation or music to be conducive to working. It was better than working in a very noisy environment with music, but it was also better than working in complete silence.

Mehta et al. (2012) asked their participants to carry out a number of creativity measures, like the remote associate test. Some of the participants sat in relative silence, other participants had a moderate level of ambient background noise (recordings made from a coffee restaurant) or a high level of ambient background noise played while they completed the remote associate test. Not surprisingly, participants in the moderate noise condition were able to complete more remote associate items. Subsequent studies found that the moderate levels of ambient noise increased cognitive abstraction. In other words, their explanation was that having a little extra noise caused the people in the experiment to have to work just a little bit harder on the task and that this encouraged more abstract thought.

SUMMARY

Problem-solving is a central aspect of thinking behaviour. From the simple to the complex, humans solve many problems throughout the day. When solving problems, people are actively engaging their semantic memory to look for a solution and they may note the similarity between the current problem and previously encountered problems. The beginning of the chapter laid out the components of a problem and the general stages of the process of problem-solving. If any of these parts are missing, the overall complexity of the problem may be increased.

The history of problem-solving research traditionally emphasized the strategies and heuristics used by problem-solvers to tackle novel problems. Many of these heuristics, such as hill climbing, are useful in that they provide some systematic way to move towards a solution, even for very new and unfamiliar problems. Other research has emphasized the importance of representation and how changing the way in which a problem is represented can help to provide a solution or possibly induce a state of insight. The characteristics of insight problem-solving remains an exciting area of research, and some of the most up-to-date work depends on cognitive neuroscience methods and has shown activation in frontal brain regions that corresponds to arriving at a solution (Bowden et al., 2005).

Creativity is a subtopic that relates to problem-solving. Creative contributions are those that are novel, high quality, and produced with some degree of regularity. Researchers have developed ways to explain, measure, and encourage creativity. In many ways, the stages of creativity parallel the stages of insight problem-solving and both seem to show evidence for incubation. Recent work with creativity has examined the role of context, such as an embodied metaphor and ambient noise.

Nine Dot Problem Solution

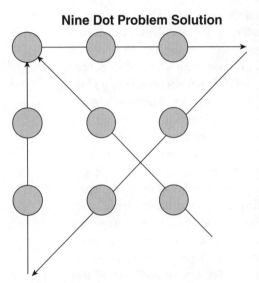

Figure 10.11 One possible solution to the nine dot problem. The lines go "outside the box". The problem is difficult because participants tend to treat the grid of nine dots as a constraint and avoid drawing lines outside this imaginary box.

The solution to the nine dot problem

The nine dot problem can be solved by literally "going outside the box". Most people see an implied square designated by the nine dots. They interpret this as a boundary and they start and stop on the dots. But by starting the line outside this imaginary box, the lines can be drawn easily. This is an example of an insight problem and is related to the constructs of functional fixedness, as described originally by Duncker (1945).

11 EXPERTISE AND EXPERT THINKING

Expertise is an advanced state of thinking and behaviour. Experts are not only highly skilled in a given domain, they are also often known explicitly for their expertise. They may be defined by it, and quite often they make a living at it. Expertise is something that many people can obtain, but not everyone will. Expertise is related to skill and practice, but expertise goes beyond merely being skilled. An expert is someone who is extremely skilled.

You are probably very skilled at some things without even realizing it. You are, relatively speaking, probably highly skilled in terms of reading in your native language. You spend many years learning to read. You practise and are frequently tested and assessed. By secondary school and university, you can read quickly and can extract the details from a passage of text. Of course, it does not really feel like expertise because it is something that you do without much thought or consideration. Most people you know probably have reading skills that are comparable, and so your individual skill with reading does not stand out or seem remarkable. That is, you are highly skilled at reading in your native language, but this skill does not constitute expertise.

However, there may be other areas in which you are an expert. Perhaps you have mastered and excelled at playing an instrument, or have competed at an elite level in a sport. If so, you may be an expert in these fields. And if you are using this text in conjunction with a course that is being taught at a college or university, the professor who is teaching the class is very likely to be an expert in their field of study. In general, however, most of us are not experts. We may have attained mastery in some areas, but have probably not achieved the more elite level of expertise. This chapter discusses what an expert is, what expertise is, and how expertise develops. The second half of the chapter discusses the effects of expertise on cognition.

DEFINING EXPERTISE

What is expertise?

K. Anders Ericsson is an expert on experts. His work on deliberate practice will be discussed later in this chapter. In a recent overview of expertise, he provides the following definition of how one might distinguish real expertise from skilled, competent performance:

> Real expertise must pass three tests. First, it must lead to performance that is consistently superior to that of the expert's peers. Second, real expertise produces concrete results. Brain surgeons, for example, not only must be skillful with their scalpels but also must have successful outcomes with their patients. A chess player must be able to win matches in tournaments. Finally, true expertise can be replicated and measured in the lab. (Ericsson, Prietula, & Cokely, 2007: 2)

Ericsson specifies three aspects of true expertise: **superior performance**, **concrete results**, and **replicable performance**. A good piano accompanist may be able to produce consistently good performances, but may not be superior in their field. Conversely, someone who has achieved a high honour once and faded may also not be a true expert. All experts are high performers, but not all high performers can be considered experts in their fields. Erickson's definition focuses on expert output. Thus, one good definition of an expert is someone who is able to produce superior performance, achieve concrete results, and is able to replicate that performance in a variety of circumstances.

Experts are highly trained

An expert is someone who has studied and practised in a specific domain until they have received a recognizable status in their field. Medical experts are a great example. In the USA and in Canada, for example, an **attending physician** would be an expert in her area of specialization because she has attended medical school for several years, put in several years as an intern, a resident, and possibly in a fellowship after that. Attending physicians work in a hospital or clinic, admit patients, and supervise other medical residents. By the time she has taken up a position as an attending physician at a hospital, she is likely to have accumulated at least a decade of extensive training and clinical experience. As a result, she is known in the field as an expert. People come to her for expert opinion. She is able to train others in her field of expertise.

Defining experts in terms of the amount of training they have received and the degree to which they have accumulated dedicated practice in their field is a fundamental definition of expertise.

Experts think like experts

A third way to define expertise is in terms of how the expert's cognition and performance differs from that of novices. Experts, for example, will need less time to make a decision about a salient stimulus. For example, the medical expert will be able to arrive at a correct diagnosis much more quickly than a novice or an intermediate-level physician. An expert may also require less information to make a decision because they will be able to fill in perceptual gaps with their extensive knowledge. Relative to novices, experts will be much better able to perceive the deep structure of a problem and ignore irrelevant surface detail. Think of some of the problems that were discussed in Chapter 10, where the initial representation was made difficult to solve because of the way the problem was represented. An expert will be able to solve problems in their area of expertise much more effectively because access to memory will facilitate choosing the correct problem representation.

To summarize, experts and expertise can be defined in at least three ways. The first focuses on people who produce superior performance, the second focuses on the amount and quality of training that the person has, and the third focuses on how the expert thinks differently from the novice. All are important parts of the definition and all are important in understanding expertise. Below I discuss expert training and a widely known maxim about expertise that relates to the number of hours of dedicated practice. I then discuss critiques of that maxim, and alternative ways to describe expertise. Later sections will cover the differences in thinking and performance between expert and novice thinking and cognition.

THE ROLE OF DELIBERATE PRACTICE

In the example above regarding medical expertise, the physician in question has accumulated nearly a decade of extensive training before she becomes an attending physician. It is difficult to know exactly how many hours of training she put in, but consider how many hours the average person works in a day. If you spend 40 hours a week working and training, that's over 2,000 hours a year. In five years, you will spend around 10,000 hours dedicated to doing something. Our physician probably put in far more than that on some days and probably fewer hours on other days, given the number of hours physicians spend in residency and the number of years required to become an attending physician. Yet by the time a physician has completed the requisite training and has spent a few years as an attending physician, she has more than surpassed 10,000 hours of practice.

The 10,000 hour rule

The aggregate of all of this extensive practice has been described by some psychologists as the "**10,000 hour rule**". Broadly speaking, this maxim suggests that expertise in a field is characterized by the achievement of approximately 10,000 hours of deliberate practice. The general idea comes from research by Anders Ericsson (Ericsson, Krampe, & Tesch-Römer, 1993), and the rule serves as a useful guideline for understanding how much training goes into becoming an expert. It also serves as a benchmark to distinguish experts from skilled non-experts. It is a useful rule of thumb, but is not an algorithm for expertise. That is, 10,000 hours of doing something will not necessarily make you an expert at it. Or, as Ericsson et al. put it, "the belief that a sufficient amount of experience or practice leads to maximal performance appears incorrect" (1993: 366).

Empirical support for the 10,000 rule

In an influential paper, Ericsson and colleagues estimated that people who have achieved expertise in a given field were generally likely to have spent at least 20 hours a week over the course of 10 years dedicated to practising and mastering the skills that are needed to become an expert (Ericsson et al., 1993). Although this may seem fairly intuitive to us now, owing to the degree to which their maxim has entered the popular lexicon, their paper was a sizeable departure from the psychology of expertise at the time. Expertise was typically defined as being a result of natural ability; the role of practice was still not well understood. Practice was generally regarded as being necessary for skill acquisition, but its role in defining expertise was unclear.

Ericsson et al. arrived at this conclusion by studying existing experts in diverse fields. For example, they asked university violin teachers to nominate who they thought were the best violinists in the programme. Another study examined the best piano students at an elite conservatory in Berlin. Extensive interviews and protocol analyses were carried out and the subjects were asked about when they began their training, when they practised, how much they practised, how they practised, and the kind of training they received. What Ericsson et al. found was that the musicians with the highest level of achievement were those who had spent close to 20 hours or more per week devoted to **deliberate and focused practice** on their instruments. This differed from the practice habits of those who were identified as amateurs or intermediates. Whereas by their mid-20s experts had accumulated over 10,000 hours of practice, amateurs had accumulated only about 3,000 hours. The same pattern seemed to emerge when Ericsson et al. looked at other studies of expert performance. In short, there was a clear pattern of extensive, deliberate practice totalling or exceeding 10,000 hours that was present in expert performers, but not in players and performers who were not in the elite group.

Later work by Ericsson and others generalized the results and findings into many other domains (Charness, Tuffiash, Krampe, Reingold, & Vasyukova, 2005; Ericsson, 2004, 2008; Ericsson et al., 2007). This research sought to emphasize the role of deliberate practice in the achievement of expertise. Or, put another way, this research argued that experts are trained and developed, and not just born. Basic talent, personality, good fortune, and luck are still very important, but this research showed that, all of these factors aside, true expertise will not develop unless the person practises deliberately and trains extensively.

However, it was not the intent of Ericsson and others to suggest that 10,000 hours was a magic number, or a formula for expert success. This is a rule of thumb and characterizes a necessary, but not sufficient, condition for expertise to develop. Unfortunately, the notion that 10,000 hours of practice is required for expert-level performance has sometimes been viewed as a threshold and as an algorithm for success. Below, I discuss the shortcomings of this approach and several critiques of the deliberate practice hypothesis.

Critiques of the 10,000 hours rule

The notion of the 10,000 hours rule has entered the public consciousness more recently with the publication of popular science writer Malcolm Gladwell's book *Outliers* (Gladwell, 2008). Gladwell's book covers both science and biography and it profiles several well-known experts' development and rise to prominence. For example, the book discusses the lives and work of people like Bill Gates, J. Robert Oppenheimer, the Beatles, and others who have become remarkably successful. Although the book touches on several themes, including the role of luck and fortune, it also discusses Ericsson's work on extensive deliberate practice and refers to the "10,000 hour rule". As an example, Gladwell discusses the early working days of the Beatles, who spent many years and hours playing and performing in Hamburg, Germany, so much so that over the course of four years, they accumulated about 10,000 hours by the time they returned to England. Others, such as Bill Gates and even Gladwell himself as a writer, are shown to have put in at least 10,000 hours of practice.

The popularity of this book resulted in the possible misconception that 10,000 hours is a formula for expertise. This is an oversimplification, as Ericsson's work early on indicated that practice plays a role and is not the only prerequisite. More recent meta-analytic work has challenged the 10,000 rule as well. A paper by Macnamara, Hambrick, and Oswald (2014) examined over 9,000 research papers about practice relating to acquiring skills. Using a meta-analytic design, they looked more carefully at 88 specific papers that collected and recorded data about practice times. This included work with chess players, musicians, sportsmen and women, and professional expertise, and across the different studies and papers represented data from over 11,000 subjects, which is an extensive meta-analysis. Although the effects of practice were noted in all of these studies, Macnamara et al. found that the contribution of deliberate practice was much lower than expected, and that it varied by domain. Figure 11.1 shows the proportional role of deliberate practice for each of five different areas of expertise. For games (like chess), practice accounts for 26% of the variance, but for other domains, like professional expertise, the contribution is less than 1%. That is, deliberate practice was not an explanatory

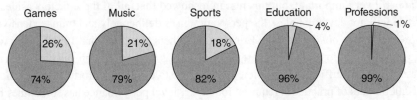

Figure 11.1 Proportion of performance accounted for by deliberate practice in several fields (adapted from Macnamara et al., 2014).

factor for variance in performance in professional expertise. Macnamara et al. concluded that deliberate practice is important, but is not as important as has been argued.

In conclusion, the work of Ericsson and colleagues in the early 1990s challenged a long-held notion that talent was a critical factor of expertise development. More recent work suggests that while deliberate practice is still important, it is only one of many factors that are important for expert-level performance and it may play a negligible role for experts in some fields, especially those with a less well-defined concept of what constitutes deliberate practice.

THE EFFECTS OF EXPERTISE ON COGNITION

In this section, I will examine some of the many effects of expertise on cognition. This approach aims to understand how experts differ from non-experts in terms of basic cognition and thinking. Of course, it is obvious that experts will be better than novices at doing the things that they are experts in. But expertise may bring improvements in the cognitive processes that underlie the area of expertise. So in order to understand how experts perform better than novices, it is important to look at the cognition involved in expertise.

Memory

A well-known and well-studied effect of expertise on thinking is the improved memory that experts show for facts within their domain of expertise. In many ways, the modern study and understanding of expertise began with research into experts' superior memory. In a very general sense, it should seem obvious that experts have superior memory within their own domain. For example, someone who spends considerable time following a baseball team or baseball in general will often know a lot more about players' statistics, general facts, and rules of the game than someone who does not follow baseball. If you have ever tried to have a conversation with someone who is a dedicated fan of a sports team when you are only a casual fan, it can be difficult and maybe even frustrating to keep up because they remember so many more things about the sport.

BOX 11.1

Consider this fictional example of expertise and exceptional memory. In the Harry Potter series, when Harry first goes to pick out his wand from Olivander, he is surprised at how quickly Olivander remembers everything about every wand he has ever sold (Rowling, 1997). And of course, he recognizes that the wand that chose Harry (remember, the wand chooses the wizard) was deeply connected to the wand used by Voldemort.

"I remember every single wand I've ever sold, Mr. Potter. It so happens that the phoenix whose tail feather is in your wand, gave another feather — just one other. It is very curious indeed that you should be destined for this wand when its brother gave you that scar." (Rowling, 1997: 65)

The implication is that Olivander is an expert wand maker and seller, and he relies on his extensive memory for detail to make this observation.

These are simple, illustrative examples, but the relationship between expertise and memory has been investigated more systematically. The initial studies on expertise and memory were conducted with experts in chess. Chess has often been the domain of study of expertise because the game has a finite set of pieces, a strict rule structure, an incredibly large configuration of positions, and, most importantly, it is possible to determine experts from novices. Expert chess players can attain a player rating, which is an objective measure of their expertise.

Experts clearly play better chess than novices. That's why an expert will generally win against a novice. Early in the history of cognitive science, De Groot published a now famous book about how experts seem to choose smarter moves (De Groot, 1965). In one study, he showed a chess position to Grand Master players and candidate master players (candidate masters are good but not great). He asked them to think aloud as they tried to find the best next move for the white position. On average, the Grand Masters found the correct move more quickly. The analysis of their thinking-aloud protocols suggested a similar search process, so the source of their expertise must be related to the efficiency of memory recall rather than their reasoning in general.

Examples of Legal and Random Chess Positions

Real Game Positions   Random Positions

Figure 11.2 An example of chess pieces in legal positions from a game and in random positions that do not correspond to any game configurations.

Later work compared the results of expert chess players and novice chess players with respect to memory. For example, a study by Chase and Simon (1973) used a very clever technique to determine the source of experts' superior performance and memory. Novice subjects and players with different ratings, all the way up to Grand Master, were shown depictions of chess boards like the one shown in Figure 11.2. On the left-hand side, the pieces are arranged in a configuration that resembles a common positioning in the middle of the game. This is important, because although there are many possible positions, there is a finite number of legal positions based on the strict movement patterns of each piece. Certain configurations have a high probability of occurring in a common game between two experienced players. In fact, experienced chess players study configurations of famous games in much the same way that experienced musicians will watch other musicians play the same piece, or experienced gymnasts will watch other gymnasts' routines and become familiar with them. In other words, highly experienced chess players know a great deal about common game configurations, and are likely to know many of them from memory.

The right-hand side of Figure 11.2 shows pieces on a chessboard in a random configuration. Unless you have never played chess before, a close inspection of this configuration should strike you as unnatural. For example, notice that both of the white bishops appear on black squares. In chess, the white player would have one bishop on white squares and one bishop on black squares. It is impossible to have both of your bishops on the same colour square. To anyone other than a complete novice, this board configuration is meaningless. There is no way this configuration of pieces could ever appear in a real game. In other words, considering both of the configurations shown in Figure 11.2, the one on the left should have considerable meaning to expert players because it should bear similarity to configurations they have studied and encountered in real games. The configuration on the right should not have the same effect. But to novice players, although the configuration on the right might be noticed as being illegal, it may not be that much different from the configuration on the left. Unless you have a strong repository of chess memory, the one on the left should not invoke any special memory advantage.

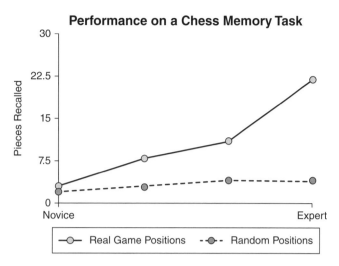

Figure 11.3 Performance differences between expert and novice chess players when pieces are in legal positions (solid line) or in random positions (dashed line).

Returning to Chase and Simon's experiment, participants were shown the configuration for 10 seconds or less, and were then asked to reconstruct them from memory. If you want to get an idea of how difficult this is, study one of the configurations in Figure 11.2 for 10 seconds, cover it up, and try to draw it on a sheet of paper without looking. More than likely, unless you are a chess expert, you will fail to get most of the pieces in the right position. Not surprisingly, that's the kind of performance that novice chess players showed in the study. Interestingly, experts were able to re-create the boards quite well. Figure 11.3 shows a hypothetical example of the difference between novices and experts in terms of their ability to correctly recall and re-create the chessboard. The y-axis shows the number of pieces correctly recalled, and the x-axis shows the player rating, which is an index of expertise in this case. The solid line clearly shows that as player rating increases, so too does performance. The experts are remembering the positions correctly. But the interesting part of this study is shown by the other line on the graph. The dotted line is nearly flat. This is the performance by players when they saw one of the random configurations. Regardless of their level of expertise, participants did not perform well when they were asked to re-create a chessboard with random configurations. Experts performed no better than novice and intermediate players when random configurations were used.

The implication is clear. Expertise in chess is founded upon many years and many hours of direct experience with game positions. This is supplemented with additional study of chess positions and game configurations. Experts have a considerable store of real, in-progress game positions that they use to play the game. And so they can re-create the game position boards not so much by memorizing the game board they were just presented with, but rather by matching that game board to patterns stored in memory.

As an analogy, consider being presented with a list of 10 familiar words to learn, along with a list of random letter strings. You will be able to recall the list of words much better that the letter strings because the words have meaning and map onto patterns stored in your lexical memory. The random letter strings have no advantage. Just like the random chess pieces.

Chase and Simon (1973) argue that this is part of the basis of player expertise. The extensive schema for these positions is how and why expert players are able to select the correct move so quickly and so efficiently. Chase and Simon argue that experts create larger chunks of chess-relevant information, rather than individual pieces, which seems to be the focus of novices. Put another way, novices are focusing on individual letters (pieces) whereas experts focus on words (larger chunks). Some recent work supports this claim by examining chess expertise and tracking expert and novice eye movements (Reingold & Charness, 2005). In general, experts have been found to have much larger visual spans while processing structured, legal positions but not when processing random chess positions. In addition, experts made fewer fixations over all. They fixated between related pieces, rather than on individual pieces. This is consistent with the notion of structured representations and larger chucks of chess memory that may relate to internalized moves and positions from previously played and studied games.

Perceptual and recognition effects

Another fundamental difference between experts and non-experts is that experts show distinct perceptual advantages over non-experts in their domain of expertise. Collectors can be experts within their domain of expertise. I have a small collection of interesting antique coins – coins that I have found over many years. Anytime I see an old or unusual coin in circulation, I keep it in my collection. It is only an amateur collection. I do not have any idea of the value of these coins, and probably most of them are worth little more than the face value. I cannot tell the difference between one that is in good condition or bad condition, and I cannot really tell the difference between small changes that were made to a coin's face in different years of circulation. Unless I consult a guide, I am unable to notice fine distinctions between antique coins of value and those with little additional value. I am an amateur coin collector.

However, consider someone who has an extensive coin collection or who is a dealer. This person is likely to have spent many more hours acquiring coins, handling and scrutinizing them, and learning about the fine-grained differences between coins that have similar surface characteristics. An expert coin collector is able to determine whether or not one US quarter from 1923 is worth collecting and has a greater value than another US quarter from 1923. This person knows about mint markings and the composition of metals in the coins themselves. As an amateur collector, I might add both of them to my collection without care. An expert coin collector might put both of them in his collection, but might also know which one is worth more than the other and which one merits special care.

I used another example like this in a chapter on the role of verbal analysis and similarity in classification (Minda & Miles, 2010), but the domain was sport fishing rather than coin collecting. Consider the differences between a novice and an expert angler. A young angler first learning to fish must learn to tell the difference between fish species that are legal to catch and those which are not. Or, they may need to learn to tell the difference between the different species so that they can tell whether or not they have caught their limit of rainbow trout, or smallmouth bass, etc. To the novice, the differences can be subtle, so they may need to use a fish identification guide that points out the critical features necessary for identification. In Ontario, where I live, the Ministry of Natural Resources publishes an annual sport fishing guide that includes this information, along with pictures, so that anglers know how to tell one fish species from another. Very few experienced anglers need to rely on the critical features listed in the identification guide. Most experienced anglers know immediately what kind of fish they have caught. They can identify the difference between a brown trout and a rainbow trout because they know what the brown trout looks like, they know where it is going to be found, they know when they are likely to catch one species or the other. All of this information allows the expert to quickly identify a subspecies whereas the novice will take longer, may have to use diagnostic rules, and may even have to consult a guide. In short, the expert's identification is fast, effortless, and memory-driven whereas the novice's identification is slower, more laborious, and is rule-driven.

This kind of expert-level perception has been studied more systematically in the area of bird recognition and fish identification. Bird watching (**birding**) is a hobby and recreational pastime that is enjoyed by many people with different levels of expertise. I am not an experienced birder. I can identify a few birds by sight, but for the most part I group birds into several very big and broadly defined categories: small birds in the backyard, hawks and birds of prey, waterbirds, and game birds. This is a very coarse description and is not an expert-level analysis. But I know several people who are expert birders. People who engage in birding as a hobby often look to acquire a list of all of the different kinds of birds they have identified. This is referred to as a "life list". As a result, they spend a lot of time looking at birds, identifying them, and classifying them.

An interesting study by Johnson and Mervis (Johnson & Mervis, 1997) looked at how experts differ from novices in terms of identification and attribute generation for species that were within their range of expertise. Their participants included a range of experienced and intermediate bird and fish identification experts (from biology departments, the Audubon society, local aquariums, etc.) as well as university undergraduates who were not experts in either field. In several experiments, participants were asked to identify pictures, to generate exemplars and attributes when given a category name, and to identify silhouettes of birds and fish. Although it was expected that experts would generate more responses, what was interesting was that the experts seemed to show a preference for responding at the subordinate level. That is, whereas novices generated more names and more attributes at the basic level, experts demonstrated that their preferred level of identification and classification was at the subordinate level. In other words, experts seemed to show a basic-level category advantage within their level of expertise for objects or animals at the subordinate level. Whereas most people intuitively name objects at the basic level (see Chapters 4 and 5 for a description of the basic level), experts do the same thing but at the subordinate level.

Medical experts also show expertise-related advantages. In an early study by Lesgold and colleagues (1981), novice (residents) and experienced radiologists were shown pictures of an x-ray and were asked to identify anomalies and to generate a think-aloud protocol as they did so. Not surprisingly, experts were quicker to notice the anomalies. The more interesting aspect of the study was the result that experts were able to describe far more basic anatomy in the x-ray compared to novice participants. This implies that experts will spend less time on the surface characteristics of the image and will be better able to notice the anomalies. In other words, these experts had a considerable store of previously seen images of lung x-rays and so did not need much time to process the basic anatomy. They can essentially fill in the details from memory (Myles-Worsley, Johnston, & Simons, 1988).

In general, this work on expertise and perceptual identification suggests a **conceptual advantage** for experts that helps to drive the perceptual identification advantage. Experts have richer conceptual structure and have better differentiated concepts. This allows the expert to fill in general, category-level detail from memory so that they can process features and make identifications at more precise, subordinate levels. The suggestion that these identification advantages are a result of experts' conceptual structure prompts an investigation into expert advantages in classification and expert/novice differences in similarity judgements.

Similarity

Chapter 2 discussed the psychology of similarity. One of the things that was mentioned was that experts are more likely to be able to appreciate similarity in terms of deep features rather than surface features. As an example of the difference between these two kinds of features, consider three simple objects: a red apple, a green apple, and a red rubber ball that is the same size as the apples. You might identify the red apple as either a Gala apple or a Red Delicious apple or something similar. You might identify the green apple as something like a Granny Smith apple. And the red rubber ball would be like something you would use to play handball. Now imagine that these three stimuli are arranged in a forced choice classification task. This task was described in Chapter 2 in the section on assessing similarity. In this case, the red apple is the target, and you have to choose which is more similar, the green apple or the red ball.

On the surface, the target stimulus is more similar to the red ball than it is to the green apple. They are the same size, they are the same colour, and they are the same shape. However, most of us would rate the similarity between the target apple and the green apple as being higher. Although they are not the same colour, they are the same size and shape, but, more importantly, they share deep feature similarity. They are the same on the inside. They belong to the same class or category. Because we have experience with apples and balls, we recognize this as being the stronger pairing. A completely naïve subject (or a computer with sparse semantics) might still choose the apple and ball comparison on the basis of surface features.

In general, the literature has supported the conclusion that experts are better able to perceive and use deep features when compared to novices. An influential paper by Chi and colleagues (1981) explored the interaction between expertise, problem-solving, and similarity. They noticed that some existing literature suggested that experts can quickly classify and categorize problems on the basis of solution-relevant features. For example, they noted that university students can categorize algebra word problems into types and categories, and this classification occurs very quickly. The implication is that upon reading the problem, a student with experience can perceive the deeper structure of the problem. To investigate this idea within the context of professional expertise, Chi et al. studied the ability of physics experts and novices to quickly classify physics problems. In order to classify and group problems, it is necessary for the classifier to make a judgement about how similar one problem is to other problems. If experts are better able to perceive and use deep features, then they should group problems together on the basis of deep, solution-relevant features whereas novices should group problems together on the basis of surface features.

Their initial study utilized a sorting procedure. They contacted several advanced PhD students from the physics department at Carnegie Mellon University and several undergraduates who had minimal experience with physics (having studied one course in introductory physics). Because of the amount of time spent on studying physics, the assumption was made that the advanced PhD students were considered experts. The participants were then given 24 problems that came from a standard textbook on the fundamentals of physics. Participants were instructed to sort the problems into groups based on similarities of the solution. They were not allowed to use any writing material and were not asked to actually solve the problem.

Figure 11.4 shows an example of several of the problems that they used. The panel on the left shows a grouping by novices. Novices group problem 10 and 11 together because both show a disk with some velocity. Novices mention things like "angular velocity,

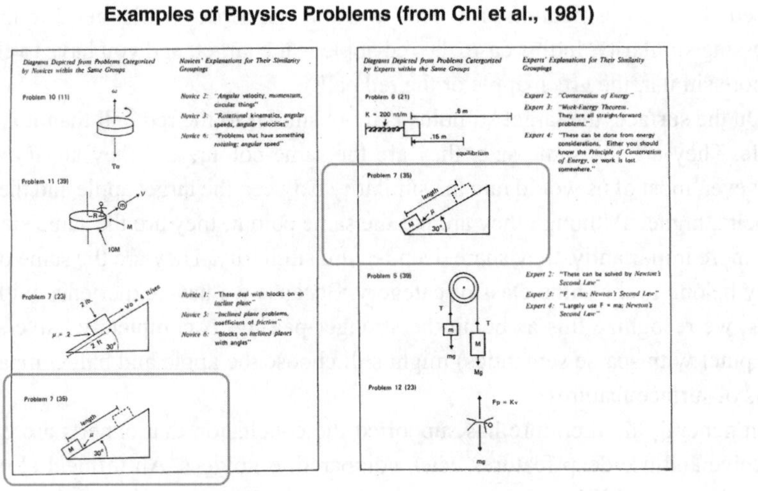

Examples of Physics Problems (from Chi et al., 1981)

Figure 11.4 Examples of grouping of physics problems by novice and expert participants. The figure shows the results from Chi et al., 1981.

momentum, circular things" as justifications for their grouping. Novices also grouped together problems 7(23) and 7(35), which showed blocks on an inclined plane, and mentioned things like "these deal with blocks on an inclined plane" as a justification. In the panel on the right are some groupings made by experts. Notice that experts put together problem 6(21) and problem 7(35). On the surface, these problems look very different. Furthermore, notice that problem 7(35) was grouped with inclined planes by the novices but not by the experts. The experts seem to rely on the basic principles of physics that are involved in solving the problem in order to make their grouping. One expert says "Work-energy theorem. They are all straightforward problems". What this means is that novices, although they may be able solve the problems, group them together on the basis of how the problems look on the surface. Experts are able to ignore the surface characteristics and group the problems together based on the conceptual, deep understanding of how the problems would be solved.

Other studies in the same paper replicated and confirmed this finding. For example, one study asked participants to elaborate on their problem-solving schemas. As expected, novice schemas were relatively more sparse and emphasized surface features (things like blocks, planes, length, etc.). In contrast, representations of expert schemas included principles of motion, conservation of energy, Newtonian laws, etc. Taken together, Chi et al.'s (1981) study reinforced the notion of expert-level advantages in similarity and the influence of expert conceptual structure on problem-solving. More importantly, this paper set the stage for much of the modern work on expertise in professional domains.

Classification

The relationship among similarity, classification, and expertise was explored in even more depth in a fascinating paper by Doug Medin and colleagues (Medin et al., 1997). We discussed this paper in Chapter 6 when discussing how people make inferences and inductions about things they are familiar with. In this chapter, I want to emphasize the role of expertise.

Building on Chi et al.'s (1981) demonstration of experts' tendency to perceive and use deep, solution-relevant features in their sorting and classification, Medin et al. (1997) reasoned that subtle differences between types of expert should result in differences in the way in which experts classify at subordinate levels. In other words, they speculated that experts form categories on the basis of goals that are relevant to their individual expertise.

Medin et al. examined the classification and reasoning abilities of three kinds of experts with trees. The first group were landscape designers/architects. These were individuals who worked with clients and municipalities to design and plan landscapes. They needed to be experts in trees, they needed to know what kind of trees to plant in different circumstances and scenarios. They needed to know what kind of trees were likely to require additional maintenance. They needed to know how fast trees grow, and whether or not trees would create additional landscape waste (like a black walnut tree that drops walnuts all over the ground). A second group of experts were municipal park maintenance workers. These were professional arborists employed by a city to look after and tend the many trees on city property. This study was carried out in Evanston, Illinois, and between Evanston and Chicago there are an enormous number of parks and old trees. These experts needed to know how to care for trees: how to trim them, how to remove trees that were in an undesirable category, and whether or not it was better to treat a sick tree or remove it. The final group of experts were botanists and taxonomists at the university. These experts were skilled at knowing the scientific taxonomy of how trees in one subspecies relate to trees in other subspecies.

Medin et al. (1997) employed a sorting task similar to that used by Chi et al. (1981). Participants were given cards with 48 trees names typed on them. The researchers used the names, rather than pictures, in order to avoid any possible bias of surface features. Participants were asked to sort the cards into as many piles as seemed necessary. They were asked to examine their sorting, and re-sort them if they were not sure. All participants were given ample time to complete the sorting task. Participants also gave justifications for the piles they created.

The key result from the first study is shown in Figure 11.5. This shows the different kinds of justifications provided, along with the portion of participants in each expert subgroup that used that type of justification in their sorting. Expert taxonomists used primarily taxonomic information in order to sort the trees, and also used some morphological information. This should be expected because expert taxonomists are experts in taxonomy,

Justification by Experts for Sorting Trees

Types of Justification	Taxonomist	Maintenance Worker	Landscaper
Taxonomic	1.00	0.90	0.90
Morphological	0.25	0.80	0.40
Weed	0.00	0.60	1.00
Landscape Utility	0.00	0.10	0.80
Aesthetic	0.00	0.40	0.60
Size	0.00	0.20	0.60
Distribution	0.00	0.20	0.40
Native/Non-native	0.00	0.10	0.50

Figure 11.5 A summary of different justifications by experts for how they sorted trees in the experiment conducted by Medin et al. (1997).

and they sort the trees accordingly. The expert maintenance workers, however, provided many more justifications. They used many cases of taxonomy and morphology, but also a sizeable number of the maintenance workers' sorting strategies relied on "weed trees" as a justification, as well as fewer mentions of size, distribution, etc. The landscape architects again relied on taxonomy, but most of their sortings also relied on whether or not trees were considered as weeds. In addition, many landscapers sorted on "landscape utility".

Medin et al. (1997) interpreted these results as evidence that experts produce and rely on **goal-derived categories**. The primary goal of tree classification for taxonomists is a taxonomic sort. Maintenance workers also resonate with broad taxonomic differences. Landscapers, on the other hand, intuitively group trees into categories on the basis of how they will be used in a landscape setting. Landscapers may have a salient, but idiosyncratic category of weed trees (these might be trees like walnut trees, or shrub-like trees) and also have salient idiosyncratic categories that represent different landscape utilities, aesthetic value, etc.

Medin et al. (1997) also showed that the three different kinds of experts still retain the same fundamental knowledge about trees. Although they tended to classify and sort the trees on the basis of deep features related to specific goals, when asked to do a categorical induction task, all three groups relied on taxonomic structure. The induction task was similar to the kind of induction tasks we discussed in Chapter 6. Experts were told that a tree of one kind has a novel property and then were asked which one of two alternative trees was most likely to have that same property. Although the expert taxonomists performed the best in this task, all three groups relied on taxonomy in order to make their inductions. Interestingly, the landscape architects, who had previously shown heavy reliance on goal-oriented categories like "weed" and "landscape utility", did not rely on those goal-oriented categories to make inductive inferences. The landscape architects were flexible in their classification and conceptual understanding of trees. Their spontaneous grouping reflected their training and goals, but their reasoning reflected their knowledge of tree biology. Flexibility like this is a characteristic of expert thinking.

A recent study from my own lab demonstrated a similar kind of expertise in medicine (Devantier et al., 2009). Physicians perform many different tasks during an encounter with the patient. They make a diagnosis, they may prescribe a treatment, and they may manage the patient's health. In many cases, diagnosis and treatment can take a backseat to management. For some conditions, such as diabetes for example, the patient sees their physician to help them manage their disease rather than make a diagnosis. We wondered if expert physicians formed patient management categories that were analogous to the kinds of goal-oriented categories that tree experts formed or that expert physicists might form.

We asked a group of endocrinologists (the expert group), medical residents (intermediate group), and med students (novice group) to engage in a forced choice task using hypothetical patient profiles. Figure 11.6 shows an example. Participants in the task were asked to choose which one of two patients was the best match with the target patient profile. One match was a **surface-feature match** and the other match was a **deep-feature match** based on patient management. At the top of Figure 11.6, the one target shows a patient named Mrs Davis, who is 75 and has type II diabetes, which she has had for the past 10 years. She lives alone. It mentions retinopathy, blindness, and information about her treatment and medication. Two possible matches are shown below. One possible match is Mr Harris, who is a 60-year-old widower who has just been diagnosed with diabetes. He has severe, crippling arthritis. The other possible match (shown on the right) is Mrs Martin, who is 74 and has had diabetes for two years. The profile also mentions renal failure and retinopathy.

Before reading any further, take a moment to look at the three profiles in Figure 11.6 and decide which one of the two possible matches goes best with the target. Think about why you have made that choice.

The target, Mrs Davis, has several pieces of information that allow for classification into different kinds of categories. For example, the fact that she is 75 years old and female and has had diabetes for 10 years might suggest a category of patient who has been managing the disease for a while. The mention of retinopathy indicates that the diabetes is serious. However, another crucial piece of information is that the severe retinopathy has left her blind, and because she lives alone she is unable to check her own sugar level or to administer insulin if needed. An expert who has treated many diabetes patients might

Patient Profiles Demonstrating Surface and Deep Features

Target

> Mrs. Davis is 75 and has had Type II DM for the past 10 years. She has severe retinopathy and is nearly blind in both eyes. Because she lives alone she has been unable to check her sugars for the past year. She is currently taking metformin 1000 mg twice daily as well as glyburide 5 mg twice daily. To her knowledge she has had no hypoglycemic reactions.

Possible Match 1

> Mr. Harris is a 60 year old type II widower with severe crippling rheumatoid arthritis involving the small joints of both hands as well as his knees and feet. He has just been diagnosed with type II diabetes based on an elevated fasting glucose and a HgA1c of over 10%.

Possible Match 2

> Mrs. Martin is 74 and has been a type II diabetic for the past 8 years. She also has HTN with chronic renal failure and a creatinine of 220 mmol/L and mild retinopathy. She used to be on oral hypoglycemics but because of her renal failure she has been placed on insulin which she is tolerating well.

Figure 11.6 An example of three patient profiles from a paper on medical classification by Devantier et al. (2009).

recognize this as a crucial aspect to this patient's management. Experts are likely to have an existing category or concept of patients who need home care in order to deal with problems like this. If an expert recognizes these deep features and has a category like this in mind, then the expert might be likely to choose Mr Harris as the best match and as the most similar. Mr Harris, although being younger, male, and only recently diagnosed, also has a different condition that would interfere with his ability to check his sugars and administer insulin. He has arthritis. The other possible match (Mrs Martin) would be a surface-feature match because the strong similarities are related to age, gender, and disease history. Although both Mrs Davis and Mrs Martin have retinopathy, the impact of the retinopathy differs significantly. Mrs Martin's retinopathy is mild, and does not impair her ability to treat her disease. In other words, Mr Harris represents a deep-feature, expert-level match. Mrs Martin represents a surface-feature, novice match.

We asked participants in each of the groups to view a series of these forced choice classification tasks, to choose one of the possible matches, and to provide a justification for their choice. As we predicted, experts and intermediates were significantly more likely to choose the deep-feature match when compared to med students. This suggests that experts are sensitive to deep-feature characteristics and are able to spontaneously group patients into management-like categories. Interestingly, the intermediate participants only showed an expert advantage for forced choice triads where the deep-feature match was related to patient management. On a subset of the forced choice triads, the deep-feature match was related to endocrinological aspects of the disease. The only group of experts who were able to perceive this set of deep features were the expert endocrinologists. For this subset of items, intermediates performed equivalently with novices.

The implications of this research with respect to expertise suggests that clinical expertise and time with patients is necessary to be able to perceive and use deep-feature categories related to patient management. All of the medical students in our sample had studied diabetes and understood the characteristics of the disease, but with no direct clinical experience, they had not acquired the necessary exposure to patients and how to best manage them. The intermediates were in the midst of their medical residency, and as a result had begun to acquire experience in managing patients. But these same intermediates had not taken part in the required fellowship in order to become an endocrinologist. Only the endocrinology experts had enough experience and practice with the biological intricacies of diabetes in order to make the deep-feature responses for those trials.

EXPERTISE IN MEDICAL DIAGNOSIS

I have touched on the notion of medical expertise at several points in this chapter. Medical expertise is relevant to cognitive processes like memory, decision-making, problem-solving, and classification. This section devotes more attention to this topic.

The study of medical expertise is in many ways similar to the study of expertise in other fields. However, unlike the study of expertise in chess, physics, or even tree experts, medical expertise is the result of fairly standardized training and clinical experience. Medicine carries with it the prospect of great risk when errors are concerned. This is not to diminish the kind of errors that may undermine a successful chess match, or may undermine a successful landscape plan, but only to emphasize that many psychologists have studied medical thinking and reasoning as a way to reduce the negative consequences of medical error.

In most countries, students training to become physicians study for four years as undergraduates and are then admitted to medical school. Medical trainees at most schools spend considerable time studying basic anatomy, biochemistry, physiology, and other biomedical fields. Afterwards, students engage in internships, and then a residency. The residency is the part of the physician's training that involves the most clinical experience. Although earlier in this chapter we suggested that the so-called "10,000 hour rule" is not a hard-and-fast rule, it should be noted that several years of a residency combined with time at medical school is likely to give a young physician close to 10,000 hours of training. Many residency programmes involve long shifts and many hours a week. This is necessary because physicians need clinical experience more than anything else to be able to practise medicine effectively.

Characteristics of expert medical reasoning

One of the hallmarks of medical reasoning is the degree to which many medical experts rely on **similarity** and **exemplar memory** rather than biomedical knowledge or textbook knowledge during a diagnostic encounter. Rather than engaging in specific-to-general reasoning – that is, mapping the specifics of a patient to the general characteristics of a disease category – many researchers have argued that experienced physicians engage in specific-to-specific reasoning (Patel, Arocha, & Zhang, 2005) – that is, they map the characteristics of a current patient onto remembered exemplars of previous patients. Geoff Norman and Lee Brooks, over the course of many studies, demonstrated that diagnosis by physicians looking at x-rays, dermatological slides, and electrocardiograms, rely on specific similarity to previously seen instances more than anything else (Brooks et al., 1991; Norman, 2005; Norman & Brooks, 1997; Norman, Coblentz, Brooks, & Babcock, 1992). Furthermore, they noted that when many of these medical experts made an error, it was likely to be influenced by patient history. Norman and Brooks argued that expert physicians do not typically engage in what they referred to as **analytic reasoning** when making a diagnosis. For Norman and Brooks, analytic reasoning is consistent with System 2 thinking, and is consistent with the specific-to-general diagnostic process. Norman and Brooks suggest that medical experts generate diagnostic hypotheses on the basis of a comparison of the current patient exemplar with retrieval of highly similar, previously seen cases.

This kind of exemplar-based reasoning is consistent with reasoning seen in other areas as well. For example, in Chapter 10 on problem-solving, we discussed several papers that emphasized the role that instance and analogical transfer play in solving problems (Gick & Holyoak, 1980, 1983). The laser and tumour problem was solved much more quickly by participants who had read the description of the general and fortress problem. With respect to medical expertise, the suggestion is that experts have accumulated extensive clinical knowledge and they rely on the clinical knowledge to make their diagnoses, rather than rule knowledge or prototypical knowledge. The research discussed earlier by Devantier et al. (2009) is consistent with this idea as well.

The suggestion that medical experts rely on exemplar retrieval and extensive clinical experience to generate diagnostic hypotheses rather than rules and prototypes highlights a potential problem in the way in which physicians are trained. Typically, medical training emphasizes basic biomedical facts: biochemistry, anatomy, etc. Medical training does not generally emphasize exemplar retrieval. It does not generally emphasize problem-solving by analogy. And as the research by Devantier points out, it is not until the later stages of medical residency that physicians begin to acquire the requisite exemplar knowledge. So how do medical experts incorporate their initial medical school training in basic science with their clinical experience?

One possibility is **knowledge encapsulation**, which refers to the integration of basic biomedical concepts with clinical propositions into a single representation (Boshuizen & Schmidt, 1992). In other words, as physicians gain experience, they integrate the basic knowledge that was acquired during medical school with features and facts about each clinical case that they encounter. Because the clinical features are the most frequently encountered features and serve as the entry into this knowledge representation, the biomedical propositions are subsumed. In other words, medical experts think and classify at the level of remembered instances and exemplars, but do not lose access to the basic biomedical facts. In some ways, this is analogous or similar to the kind of reasoning shown by the landscape architects in the tree classification study (Medin et al., 1997). As discussed earlier, they tended to group trees together on the basis of how they interacted with them rather than on the basis of their taxonomic relatedness. But they did not lose access to that knowledge, and were able to switch to taxonomic relationships when engaging in a categorical induction task. With encapsulated knowledge, the suggestion is that the preferred level of identification and reasoning is goal-relevant, and clinically-relevant. As such, experienced physicians tend to heavily weight the degree to which a current patient reminds them of previous patients. But this does not mean that they have lost access to basic biomedical features.

Boshuizen and Schmidt wrote an excellent paper on encapsulated knowledge in medicine and have noted that as expertise increases, physicians tend to make diagnoses and produce diagnostic explanations at high levels of generality (Boshuizen & Schmidt, 1992). Interestingly, as expertise in medicine increases, doctors' responses reflect highly abstract knowledge, rather than the emphasis on specific subordinate levels, as is seen in bird identification and fish identification. This does not mean that medical experts are operating at a superordinate level, but it does mean that the biological aspects enter in only at the highest levels. The suggestion from Boshuizen and Schmidt is that medical diagnosis is a result of encapsulated knowledge possibly related to individual exemplar comparisons as described by Brooks and colleagues (1991).

The knowledge encapsulation hypothesis also explains a curious phenomenon observed in medicine. Medical experts are often prone to what is known as the **intermediate effect** (Boshuizen & Schmidt, 1992; Patel, Glaser, & Arocha, 2000; Patel et al., 2005; Rikers, Schmidt, & Moulaert, 2005). The intermediate effect is found when performance does not increase monotonically with expertise. Figure 11.7 shows an example of the intermediate effect. The dashed line shows a hypothetical performance acquisition process in which increasing experience leads to correspondingly better performance. But the intermediate effect (solid line) shows a decrease in performance relative to what should be expected. Although this is not seen in every aspect of performance, it suggests that the knowledge

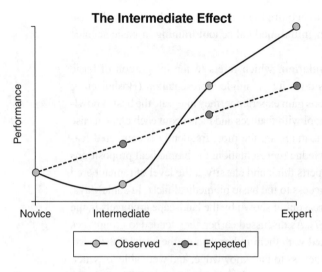

The Intermediate Effect

Performance

Novice   Intermediate   Expert

—○— Observed   ··●·· Expected

Figure 11.7 A hypothetical example showing the intermediate effect in medical expertise. The actual performance acquisition curve is not monotonic.

base of novices is fairly sparse and dominated by biomedical fact. The knowledge base of experts is rich and dominated by clinical experience. The degradation seen at the intermediate level reflects the inadequacy of the basic biomedical knowledge combined with minimal clinical experience. Boshuizen and others have suggested that this may be the point at which knowledge encapsulation occurs. Intermediates have started to move away from a reliance on basic science, but have not encapsulated the basic science with clinical experience. These intermediates may be very good at making a diagnosis, but may not be able to integrate knowledge between the two domains.

Interestingly, Devantier et al. (2009) found that the intermediate effect disappeared when the participants were asked to make forced choice judgements on patient management cases, but the intermediate effect persisted when the forced choice items reflected more complex knowledge. It is possible that for these intermediates, management information has been encapsulated, but endocrinological knowledge has not yet encapsulated with clinical experience.

The impact of research on medical education

As discussed, medical experts are characterized by their reliance on exemplar memory as well as their knowledge of diagnostic prototypes and diagnostic rules. Over the course of several years, students must acquire the rudimentary scientific knowledge and incorporate it with clinical expertise in order to become effective processors of medicine. Some have suggested that medical experts rely on encapsulated knowledge in order to make decisions and arrive at conclusions quickly. This may reflect a reliance on System 1 rather than System 2 thinking. And indeed, the degree to which diagnostic errors are made may reflect a reliance on System 1. This tendency has resulted in some tension within the medical expertise and medical training field. Some researchers, such as Pat Crosskerry, are champions of an approach known as the **default interventionist approach** (Crosskerry, 2003). The default interventionist approach assumes that System 1 is the fast default approach to most cognition. Physicians who rely on exemplar retrieval and instance memory are relying on System 1 and, as a result, might commit errors if they arrive at a diagnosis too quickly. Crosskerry (2003) suggests training physicians to intervene by slowing down to monitor performance, and to allow System 2 to produce a more deliberative response. This does not mean that exemplar information should be discarded, but rather that the deliberative practitioner takes the time to look for possible cognitive errors.

On the other hand, researchers like Geoff Norman emphasize the importance of instance memory and exemplar retrieval and suggest that slowing down and attempting to intervene with System 2 might undermine the effects of acquired expertise (Norman, 2005). In many ways, Norman's approach is fairly consistent with other aspects of the expertise literature and shares many similarities with the role of memory in chess performance and the reliance on deep-feature categories in physics expertise. When I was writing this text, both of these approaches received considerable attention.

SUMMARY

This chapter attempts to answer the questions of what an expert is, how expertise develops, and what kind of cognitive advantages are most closely associated with expertise. It should be clear that there is no single answer to any of these questions. Expertise can be defined as a function of the time spent in deliberate practice. This has given rise to the so-called 10,000 hour rule. And this seems to characterize many kinds of skilled performers. For other kinds of expertise, however, the 10,000 hour rule does not seem to hold. At the very least, it may be a necessary component of expertise in some skills, but is by no means a sufficient predictor of expertise.

Expertise brings with it changes in the way people perform. Experts rely on schemas and consolidated memories. In medical expertise, physicians seem to rely on encapsulated knowledge. With respect to playing chess, experts seem to rely on chunks of knowledge related to games they have played or studied. With respect to skilled professions, experts seem to rely on groupings that emphasize very specific goals related to how they interact with the objects of their expertise. Across many domains, it seems clear that experts rely on rich associations between concepts and across different levels of a conceptual hierarchy. Experts in bird identification can simultaneously access basic-, subordinate-, and superordinate-level information. Experts in tree identification can work flexibly with goal-oriented categories and taxonomic categories. Experts in medical diagnosis can arrive at a diagnosis via specific item similarity without losing access to deep, biomedical knowledge. It is this activation of different levels in a semantic network in parallel that seems to be one of the true hallmarks of cognitive expertise.

REFERENCES

Anderson, J. R. (1990). *The Adaptive Character of Thought*. Hillsdale, NJ: Lawrence Erlbaum.

Anderson, R. C., & Pichert, J. W. (1978). Recall of previously unrecallable information following a shift in perspective. *Journal of Verbal Learning & Verbal Behavior*, *17*(1), 1–12.

Armstrong, S. L., Gleitman, L. R., & Gleitman, H. (1983). What some concepts might not be. *Cognition*, *13*, 263–308.

Ashby, F. G., Isen, A., & Turken, A. U. (1999). A neuropsychological theory of positive affect and its influence on cognition. *Psychological Review*, *106*, 529–550.

Attneave, F. (1950). Dimensions of similarity. *The American Journal of Psychology*, *63*(4), 516–556.

Baas, M., De Dreu, C. K. W., & Nijstad, B. A. (2008). A meta-analysis of 25 years of mood-creativity research: hedonic tone, activation, or regulatory focus? *Psychological Bulletin*, *134*(6), 779–806.

Baddeley, A. D. (2003). Working memory: looking back and looking forward. *Nature Reviews Neuroscience*, *4*(10), 829–839.

Baddeley, A. D. (2012). Working memory: theories, models, and controversies. *Annual Review of Psychology*, *63*(1), 1–29.

Baddeley, A. D., & Hitch, G. (2004). Developments in the concept of working memory. *Neuropsychology*, *4*, 485–493.

Baron, J. (2007). *Thinking and Deciding* (4th edn). Cambridge, UK: Cambridge University Press.

Baumann, N., & Kuhl, J. (2005). How to resist temptation: the effects of external control versus autonomy support on self-regulatory dynamics. *Journal of Personality*, *73*(2), 443–470.

Baumeister, R. F. (2014). Self-regulation, ego depletion, and inhibition. *Neuropsychologia*, *65*, 313–319.

Baumeister, R. F., Bratslavsky, E., Muraven, M., & Tice, D. M. (1998). Ego depletion: is the active self a limited resource? *Journal of Personality and Social Psychology*, *74*(5), 1252.

Baumeister, R. F., Vohs, K. D., & Tice, D. M. (2007). The strength model of self-control. *Current Directions in Psychological Science*, *16*, 351–355.

Berlin, B., & Kay, P. (1969). *Basic Color Terms: Their Universality and Evolution*. Berkeley, CA: University of California Press.

Bever, T. G. (1970). The cognitive basis for linguistic structures. In J. R. Hayes (ed.), *Cognition and the Development of Language* (pp. 279–362). New York: John Wiley & Sons.

Biederman, I. (1987). Recognition-by-components: a theory of human image understanding. *Psychological Review*, *2*, 115–147.

Boroditsky, L. (2001). Does language shape thought? Mandarin and English speakers' conceptions of time. *Cognitive Psychology*, *43*(1), 1–22.

Boshuizen, H. P. A., & Schmidt, H. G. (1992). On the role of biomedical knowledge in clinical reasoning by experts, intermediates and novices. *Cognitive Science, 16*, 153–184.

Bowden, E. M., & Jung-Beeman, M. (1998). Getting the right idea: semantic activation in the right hemisphere may help solve insight problems. *Psychological Science, 9*, 435–440.

Bowden, E. M., & Jung-Beeman, M. (2004). Normative data for 144 compound remote associate problems. *Behavior Research Methods, Instruments, & Computers, 35*(4), 634–639.

Bowden, E. M., Jung-Beeman, M., Fleck, J., & Kounios, J. (2005). New approaches to demystifying insight. *TRENDS in Cognitive Sciences, 9*(7), 322–328.

Bransford, J. D., & Johnson, M. K. (1973). Considerations of some problems of comprehension. In W. G. Chase (ed.), *Visual Information Processing* (pp. 383–438). New York: Academic Press.

Brooks, L. R., Norman, G. R., & Allen, S. W. (1991). Role of specific similarity in a medical diagnostic task. *Journal of Experimental Psychology: General, 120*, 278–287.

Bruner, J. S., Goodnow, J. J., & Austin, G. A. (1956). *A Study of Thinking.* New York: Wiley.

Charness, N., Tuffiash, M., Krampe, R., Reingold, E., & Vasyukova, E. (2005). The role of deliberate practice in chess expertise. *Applied Cognitive Psychology, 19*(2), 151–165.

Chase, W. G., & Simon, H. A. (1973). Perception in chess. *Cognitive Psychology, 4*(1), 55–81.

Chater, N., & Oaksford, M. (1999). Ten years of the rational analysis of cognition. *TRENDS in Cognitive Sciences, 3*(2), 57–65.

Cheng, P. W., & Holyoak, K. J. (1985). Pragmatic reasoning schemas. *Cognitive Psychology, 17*(4), 391–416.

Chi, M. T. H., Feltovich, P. J., & Glaser, R. (1981). Categorization and representation of physics problems by experts and novices. *Cognitive Science, 5*, 121–152.

Chi, M. T. H., Glaser, R., & Rees, E. (1982). Expertise in problem solving. In R. J. Sternberg (ed.), *Advances in the Psychology of Human Intelligence* (pp. 7–75). Hillsdale, NJ: Lawrence Erlbaum.

Collins, A. M., & Loftus, E. F. (1975). A spreading-activation theory of semantic processing. *Psychological Review, 82*(6), 407.

Collins, A. M., & Quillian, M. R. (1969). Retrieval time from semantic memory. *Journal of Verbal Learning & Verbal Behavior, 8*(2), 240–247.

Collins, A. M., & Quillian, M. R. (1970). Does category size affect categorization time? *Journal of Verbal Learning & Verbal Behavior, 9*(4), 432–438.

Craik, F., & Tulving, E. (1975). Depth of processing and the retention of words in episodic memory. *Journal of Experimental Psychology: General, 104*, 268–294.

Crosskerry, P. (2003). The importance of cognitive errors in diagnosis and strategies to minimize them. *Academic Medicine, 78*(8), 775–780.

De Groot, A. D. (1965). *Thought and Choice in Chess.* The Hague, Netherlands: Mouton.

Descartes, R. (1637/2001). *Discourse on Method.* Vol. XXXIV, Part 1. The Harvard Classics. New York: P.F. Collier & Son, 1909–14; Bartleby.com.

Devantier, S. L., Minda, J. P., Goldszmidt, M., & Haddara, W. (2009). Categorizing patients in a forced-choice triad task: the integration of context in patient management. *PLoS ONE, 4*(6), e5881.

Dreisbach, G., & Goschke, T. (2004). How positive affect modulates cognitive control: reduced perseveration at the cost of increased distractibility. *Journal of Experimental Psychology: Learning, Memory and Cognition, 30*(2), 343–353.

Duncker, K. (1926). A qualitative (experimental and theoretical) study of productive thinking (solving comprehensible problems). *Pedagogical Seminary and Journal of Genetic Psychology, 33*, 1–67.

Duncker, K. (1945). On problem solving. *Psychological Monographs, 58*, 1–120.

Ericsson, K. A. (2004). Deliberate practice and the acquisition and maintenance of expert performance in medicine and related domains. *Academic Medicine*, *79*, S70–S81.

Ericsson, K. A. (2008). Deliberate practice and acquisition of expert performance: a general overview. *Academic Emergency Medicine*, *15*, 988–994.

Ericsson, K. A., & Simon, H. A. (1993). *Protocol analysis: Verbal reports as data*. Cambridge, MA: MIT Press.

Ericsson, K. A., Krampe, R. T., & Tesch-Römer, C. (1993). The role of deliberate practice in the acquisition of expert performance. *Psychological Review*, *100*, 363–406.

Ericsson, K. A., Prietula, M. J., & Cokely, E. T. (2007). The making of an expert. *Harvard Business Review*, *85*(7/8), 114.

Evans, J. S. B. T. (2003). In two minds: dual-process accounts of reasoning. *TRENDS in Cognitive Sciences*, *7*(10), 454–459.

Evans, J. S. B. T. (2005). Deductive reasoning. In K. J. Holyoak & R. G. Morrison (eds.), *The Cambridge Handbook of Thinking and Reasoning* (pp. 169–184). Cambridge, UK: Cambridge University Press.

Evans, J. S. B. T. (2008). Dual-processing accounts of reasoning, judgment, and social cognition. *Annual Review of Psychology*, *59*(1), 255–278.

Evans, J. S. B. T., & Stanovich, K. E. (2013). Dual-process theories of higher cognition: advancing the debate. *Perspectives on Psychological Science*, *8*(3), 223–241.

Förster, J., & Higgins, E. T. (2005). How global versus local perception fits regulatory focus. *Psychological Science*, *16*, 631–636.

Frazier, L., & Rayner, K. (1982). Making and correcting errors during sentence comprehension: eye movements in the analysis of structurally ambiguous sentences. *Cognitive Psychology*, *14*, 178–210.

Frisch, von, K. (1967). *The Dance Language and Orientation of Bees*. Cambridge, MA: Belknap Press of Harvard University Press.

Gable, P. A., & Harmon-Jones, E. (2010). The blues broaden, but the nasty narrows: attentional consequences of negative affects low and high in motivational intensity. *Psychological Science*, *2*, 211–215 .

Gailliot, M. T., Baumeister, R. F., DeWall, C. N., Maner, J. K., Plant, E. A., Tice, D. M., et al. (2007). Self-control relies on glucose as a limited energy source: willpower is more than a metaphor. *Journal of Personality and Social Psychology*, *92*(2), 325–336.

Gasper, K., & Clore, G. L. (2002). Attending to the big picture: mood and global versus local processing of visual information. *Psychological Science*, *13*(1), 34–40.

Gathercole, S. E. (1999). Cognitive approaches to the development of short-term memory. *TRENDS in Cognitive Sciences*, *3*(11), 410–419.

Gawronski, B., & Bodenhausen, G. V. (2006). Effects of varying levels of expertise on the basic level of categorization. *Psychological Bulletin*, *132*(5), 692–731.

Gawronski, B., Peters, K. R., Brochu, P. M., & Strack, F. (2008). Effects of varying levels of expertise on the basic level of categorization. *Personality and Social Psychology Bulletin*, *34*(5), 648–665.

Gentner, D. (1983). Structure-mapping: a theoretical framework for analogy. *Cognitive Science*, *7*(2), 155–170.

Gick, M., & Holyoak, K. J. (1980). Analogical problem solving. *Cognitive Psychology*, *12*, 306–355.

Gick, M., & Holyoak, K. J. (1983). Schema induction and analogical transfer. *Cognitive Psychology*, *15*, 1–38.

Gigerenzer, G. (1996). On narrow norms and vague heuristics: a reply to Kahneman and Tversky (1996). *Psychological Review, 103*, 529–598.

Gigerenzer, G., Hell, W., & Blank, H. (1988). Presentation and content: the use of base rates as a continuous variable. *Journal of Experimental Psychology: Human Perception and Performance, 14*, 513–525.

Gigerenzer, G., Gaissmaier, W., Kurz-Milcke, E., Schwartz, L. M., & Woloshin, S. (2008). Helping doctors and patients make sense of health statistics. *Psychological Science in Public Interest, 8*, 53–96.

Gigerenzer, G., Hertwig, R., & Pachur, T. (2011). *Heuristics: The Foundations of Adaptive Behavior.* Oxford: Oxford University Press.

Gladwell, M. (2008). *Outliers: The Story of Success.* New York: Little, Brown, and Company.

Gobet, F., & Simon, H. A. (1996). Recall of rapidly presented random chess positions is a function of skill. *Psychonomic Bulletin & Review, 3*, 159.

Goldszmidt, M., Minda, J. P., & Bordage, G. (2013). Developing a unified list of physicians' reasoning tasks during clinical encounters. *Academic Medicine, 88*, 1–8.

Goodman, N. (1983). *Fact, Fiction, and Forecast.* Cambridge, MA: Harvard University Press.

Graham, L. O. (1992, August). Invisible man. *New York Magazine.*

Greeno, J. G. (1974). Hobbits and Orcs: acquisition of a sequential concept. *Cognitive Psychology, 6*, 270–292.

Griffiths, T. L., & Tenenbaum, J. B. (2006). Optimal predictions in everyday cognition. *Psychological Science, 17*(9), 767–773.

Griggs, R. A., & Cox, J. R. (1983). The effects of problem content and negation on Wason's selection task. *The Quarterly Journal of Experimental Psychology Section A, 35*(3), 519–533.

Guilford, J. P. (1967). *The Nature of Human Intelligence.* New York: McGraw-Hill.

Harel, A., & Bentin, S. (2013). Are all types of expertise created equal? Car experts use different spatial frequency scales for subordinate categorization of cars and faces. *PLoS ONE, 8*(6), e67024.

Heider, E.R. (1972). Universals in color naming and memory. *Journal of Experimental Psychology, 93*(1), 10.

Heit, E., & Hahn, U. (2001). Diversity-based reasoning in children. *Cognitive Psychology, 43*(4), 243–273.

Henle, M. (1962). On the relation between logic and thinking. *Psychological Review, 69*(4), 366–378.

Hertwig, R., & Gigerenzer, G. (1999). The "conjunction fallacy" revisited: how intelligent inferences look like reasoning errors. *Journal of Behavioral Decision Making, 12*, 275–305.

Higgins, E. T. (1997). Beyond pleasure and pain. *American Psychologist, 52*(12), 1280–1300.

Higgins, E. T. (2000). Making a good decision: value from fit. *American Psychologist, 55*, 1217–1230.

Hintzman, D. L. (1986). "Schema abstraction" in a multiple-trace memory model. *Psychological Review, 93*, 411–428.

Hintzman, D. L., & Ludlam, G. (1980). Differential forgetting of prototypes and old instances: simulation by an exemplar-based classification model. *Memory & Cognition, 8*, 378–382.

Hockett, C. F. (1960). The origin of speech. *Scientific American, 203*, 89–97.

Hodgman, M. J., & Garrard, A. R. (2012). A review of acetaminophen poisoning. *Critical Care Clinics, 28*(4), 499–516.

Holding, D. H. (1985). *The Psychology of Chess Skill.* Hillsdale, NJ: Lawrence Erlbaum.

Hu, J. C. (2014). What do talking apes really tell us? *Slate.com.* Retrieved August 2014.

Imai, S. (1977). Pattern similarity and cognitive transformations. *Acta Psychologica, 41*(6), 433–447.

Isen, A., Shalker, T. E., Clark, M., & Karp, L. (1978). Affect, accessibility of material in memory, and behavior: a cognitive loop? *Journal of Personality and Social Psychology, 36*(1), 1–12.

Isen, A., Johnson, M. M., Mertz, E., & Robinson, G. F. (1985). The influence of positive affect on the unusualness of word associations. *Journal of Personality and Social Psychology, 48*(6), 1413–1426.

Isen, A. M., Daubman, K. A., & Nowicki, G. P. (1987). Positive affect facilitates creative problem solving. *Journal of Personality and Social Psychology, 52*(6), 1122–1131.

James, W. (1890). *The Principles of Psychology*. New York, NY: H. Holt and Co.

Johnson, K. E., & Mervis, C. B. (1997). Effects of varying levels of expertise on the basic level of categorization. *Journal of Experimental Psychology: General, 126*, 248–277.

Johnson-Laird, P. (1999). Deductive reasoning. *Annual Review of Psychology, 50*, 109–135.

Johnson, K. E., & Mervis, C. B. (1997). Effects of varying levels of expertise on the basic level of categorization. *Journal of Experimental Psychology: General, 126*, 248–277.

Jung-Beeman, M., Bowden, E. M., Haberman, J., Frymiare, J. L., Arambel-Liu, S., Greenblatt, R., et al. (2004). Neural activity when people solve verbal problems with insight. *PLoS Biology, 2*(4), e97.

Kahneman, D. (2011). *Thinking Fast and Slow*. New York: Straus and Giroux.

Kahneman, D., Knetsch, J. L., & Thaler, R. H. (1991). Anomalies: the endowment effect, loss aversion, and status quo bias. *The Journal of Economic Perspectives, 5*(1), 193–206.

Kahneman, D., & Tversky, A. (1973). On the psychology of prediction. *Psychological Review, 80*(4), 237–251.

Kahneman, D., & Tversky, A. (1979). Prospect theory: an analysis of decision under risk. *Econometrica, 47*, 263–291.

Kahneman, D., & Tversky, A. (1984). Choices, values, and frames. *American Psychologist, 39*(4), 341–350.

Kane, M. J., Hambrick, D. Z., Tuholski, S. W., Wilhelm, O., Payne, T. W., & Engle, R. W. (2004). The generality of working memory capacity: a latent-variable approach to verbal and visuospatial memory span and reasoning. *Journal of Experimental Psychology: General, 133*(2), 189–217.

Kempton, W. (1986). Two theories of home heat control. *Cognitive Science, 10*, 75–90.

Kintsch, W. (1994). Text comprehension, memory, and learning. *American Psychologist, 49*, 249–303.

Knowlton, B. J., Ramus, S. J., & Squire, L. R. (1992). Intact artificial grammar learning in amnesia: dissociation of classification learning and explicit memory for specific instances. *Psychological Science, 3*, 172–179.

Knowlton, B. J., & Squire, L. R. (1993). The learning of categories: parallel brain systems for item memory and category knowledge. *Science, 262*(5140), 1747–1749.

Kruschke, J. K. (2011). Models of attentional learning. In E. M. Porthos & A. J. Wills (eds.), *Formal Approaches in Categorization* (pp. 1–14). Cambridge, UK: Cambridge University Press.

Lakoff, G. (1987). *Women, Fire and Dangerous Things*. Chicago, IL: The University of Chicago Press.

Lakoff, G., & Johnson, M. (1980). *Metaphors We Live By*. Chicago, IL: The University of Chicago Press.

Lesgold, A. M., Feltovich, P. J., Glaser, R., & Wang, Y. (1981). *The Acquisition of Perceptual Diagnostic Skill in Radiology* (Technical Report No. PDS-1). Pittsburgh, PA: Learning Research and Development Center, University of Pittsburgh.

Leung, A. K. Y., Kim, S., Polman, E., Ong, L. S., Qiu, L., Goncalo, J. A., & Sanchez-Burks, J. (2012). Embodied metaphors and creative "acts." *Psychological Science, 23*, 502–509.

Lewandowsky, S. (2011). Working memory capacity and categorization: individual differences and modeling. *Journal of Experimental Psychology: Learning, Memory and Cognition, 37,* 720–738.

Lo, Y., Sides, A., Rozelle, J., & Osherson, D. (2002). Evidential diversity and premise probability in young children's inductive judgment. *Cognitive Science, 26*(2), 181–206.

Loftus, E. F., & Palmer, J. C. (1974). Reconstruction of automobile destruction: an example of the interaction between language and memory. *Journal of Verbal Learning & Verbal Behavior, 13*(5), 585–589.

Lopez, A. (1995). The diversity principle in the testing of arguments. *Memory & Cognition, 23,* 374–382.

Lundeberg, M. A., & Fox, P. W. (1991). Do laboratory findings on test expectancy generalize to classroom outcomes? *Review of Educational Research, 61*(1), 94–106.

MacDonald, M. C., Pearlmutter, N. J., & Seidenberg, M. S. (1994). Syntactic ambiguity resolution as lexical ambiguity resolution. *Psychological Review, 101,* 676–703.

Macnamara, B. N., Hambrick, D. Z., & Oswald, F. L. (2014). Deliberate practice and performance in music, games, sports, education, and professions: a meta-analysis. *Psychological Science, 25*(8), 1608–1618.

Maddox, W. T., Baldwin, G. C., & Markman, A. B. (2006). A test of the regulatory fit hypothesis in perceptual classification learning. *Memory & Cognition, 34,* 1377–1397.

Malt, B. C., & Smith, E. E. (1982). The role of familiarity in determining typicality. *Memory & Cognition, 10,* 69–75.

Malt, B. C., Sloman, S. A., Gennari, S., Shi, M., & Wang, Y. (1999). Knowing versus naming: similarity and the linguistic categorization of artifacts. *Journal of Memory and Language, 40*(2), 230–262.

Markman, A. B., Maddox, W. T., Worthy, D. A., & Baldwin, G. C. (2007). Using regulatory focus to explore implicit and explicit processing in concept learning. *Journal of Consciousness Studies, 14,* 132–155.

Masicampo, E. J., & Baumeister, R. F. (2008). Toward a physiology of dual-process reasoning and judgment: lemonade, willpower, and expensive rule-based analysis. *Psychological Science, 19*(3), 255–260.

McBeath, M. K., Shaffer, D. M., & Kaiser, M. K. (1995). How baseball outfielders determine where to run to catch fly balls. *Science, 268,* 569–573.

McCloskey, M., & Glucksberg, S. (1979). Decision processes in verifying category membership statements: implications for models of semantic memory. *Cognitive Psychology, 11,* 1–37.

Medin, D. L., & Schaffer, M. M. (1978). Context theory of classification learning. *Psychological Review, 85,* 207–238.

Medin, D. L., & Schwanenflugel, P. J. (1981). Linear separability in classification learning. *Journal of Experimental Psychology: Human Learning and Memory, 7,* 355–368.

Medin, D. L., Lynch, E. B., Coley, J. D., & Atran, S. (1997). Categorization and reasoning among tree experts: do all roads lead to Rome? *Cognitive Psychology, 32,* 49–96.

Medin, D. L., Coley, J. D., Storms, G., & Hayes, B. L. (2003). A relevance theory of induction. *Psychonomic Bulletin & Review, 10*(3), 517–532.

Mednick, S. (1962). The associative basis of the creative process. *Psychological Review, 69*(3), 220–232.

Mehta, R., Zhu, R. J., & Cheema, A. (2012). Is noise always bad? Exploring the effects of ambient noise on creative cognition. *Journal of Consumer Research, 39*(4), 784–799.

Merriam, E. P., Thase, M. E., Haas, G. L., Keshavan, M. S., & Sweeney, J. A. (1999). Prefrontal cortical dysfunction in depression determined by Wisconsin card sorting test performance. *The American Journal of Psychiatry, 156,* 780–782.

Metcalfe, J., & Wiebe, D. (1987). Intuition in insight and noninsight problem solving. *Memory & Cognition*, *15*, 238–246.

Miles, S. J., Matsuki, K., & Minda, J. P. (2014). Continuous executive function disruption interferes with application of an information integration categorization strategy. *Attention, Perception & Psychophysics*, *76*(5), 1318–1334.

Minda, J. P., & Miles, S. J. (2010). The influence of verbal and nonverbal processing on category learning. In B. H. Ross (ed.), *The Psychology of Learning and Motivation* (Vol. 52, pp. 117–162). New York: The Psychology of Learning and Motivation.

Minda, J. P., & Rabi, R. (2015). Ego depletion interferes with rule-defined category learning but not non-rule-defined category learning. *Frontiers in Psychology*, *6*(35), 1–40.

Minda, J. P., & Smith, J. D. (2001). Prototypes in category learning: the effects of category size, category structure, and stimulus complexity. *Journal of Experimental Psychology: Learning, Memory and Cognition*, *27*(3), 775–799.

Minda, J. P., & Smith, J. D. (2011). Prototype models of categorization: basic formulation, predictions, and limitations. In E. M. Pothos & A. J. Wills (eds.), *Formal Approaches in Categorization* (pp. 40–64). Cambridge, UK: Cambridge University Press.

Mischel, W., & Ebbesen, E. B. (1970). Attention in delay of gratification. *Journal of Personality and Social Psychology*, *16*(2), 329–337.

Miyake, A., Friedman, N. P., Emerson, M. J., Witzki, A. H., & Howerter, A. (2000). The unity and diversity of executive functions and their contributions to complex "frontal lobe" tasks: a latent variable analysis. *Cognitive Psychology*, *41*(1), 49–100.

Morris, B. (2014). The Rate of Domestic Violence Arrests Among NFL Players. *A Five Thirty Eight List Apart: For People Who Make Websites*. Retrieved from http://fivethirtyeight.com/datalab/the-rate-of-domestic-violence-arrests-among-nfl-players/

Murphy, G. L. (2002). *The Big Book of Concepts*. Cambridge, MA: MIT Press.

Murphy, G. L., & Medin, D. L. (1985). The role of theories in conceptual coherence. *Psychological Review*, *92*, 289–316.

Murphy, G. L., Hampton, J. A., & Milovanovic, G. S. (2012). Journal of memory and language. *Journal of Memory and Language*, *67*(4), 521–539.

Myles-Worsley, M., Johnston, W. A., & Simons, M. A. (1988). The influence of expertise on X-ray image processing. *Journal of Experimental Psychology: Learning, Memory and Cognition*, *14*(3), 553–557.

Nadler, R. T. D., Rabi, R. R., & Minda, J. P. (2010). Better mood and better performance: learning rule-described categories is enhanced by positive mood. *Psychological Science*, *21*, 1770–1776.

Newell, A., & Simon, H. A. (1972). *Human Problem Solving*. Englewood Cliffs, NJ: Prentice-Hall.

Nickerson, R. S. (1998). Confirmation bias: a ubiquitous phenomenon in many guises. *Review of General Psychology*, *2*, 175–220.

Nisbett, R. E., & Miyamoto, Y. (2005). The influence of culture: holistic versus analytic perception. *TRENDS in Cognitive Sciences*, *9*, 467–473.

Nisbett, R. E., Peng, K., Choi, I., & Norenzayan, A. (2001). Culture and systems of thought: holistic versus analytic cognition. *Psychological Review*, *108*, 291–310.

Nokes, T. J., Schunn, C. D., & Chi, M. T. H. (2010). Problem solving and human expertise. *International Encyclopedia of Education*, *5*, 265–272.

Norman, G. R. (2005). Research in clinical reasoning: past history and current trends. *Medical Education*, *39*(4), 418–427.

Norman, G. R., & Brooks, L. R. (1997). The non-analytical basis of clinical reasoning. *Advances in Health Sciences Education*, *2*, 173–184.

Norman, G. R., Coblentz, C. L., Brooks, L. R., & Babcock, C. J. (1992). Expertise in visual diagnosis: a review of the literature. *Academic Medicine, 67*, s78–s83.

Nosofsky, R. M. (1986). Attention, similarity, and the identification-categorization relationship. *Journal of Experimental Psychology: General, 115*, 39–57.

Nosofsky, R. M. (1987). Attention and learning processes in the identification and categorization of integral stimuli. *Journal of Experimental Psychology: Learning, Memory and Cognition, 13*, 87–108.

Nosofsky, R. M. (1992). Exemplars, prototypes, and similarity rules. In A. F. Healy, S. J. Kosslyn, & R. M. Shiffrin (eds.), *From Learning Theory to Connectionist Theory: Essays in Honor of William K. Estes* (Vol. 1, pp. 149–167). Hillsdale, NJ: Lawrence Erlbaum.

Nosofsky, R. M. (2011). The generalized context model: an exemplar model of classification. In E. M. Pothos & A. J. Wills (eds.), *Formal Approaches in Categorization* (pp. 18–39). Cambridge, UK: Cambridge University Press.

Oaksford, M., Morris, F., Grainger, B., & Williams, J. M. G. (1996). Mood, reasoning, and central executive processes. *Journal of Experimental Psychology: Learning, Memory and Cognition, 22*(2), 476–492.

Oberauer, K. (2009). Design for a working memory. *Psychology of Learning and Motivation, 51*, 45–100.

Ophir, E., Nass, C., & Wagner, A. (2009). Cognitive control in media multitaskers. *Proceedings of the National Academy of Sciences, 106*(37), 15583.

Osherson, D. N., Smith, E. E., Wilkie, O., Lopez, A., & Shafir, E. (1990). Category-based induction. *Psychological Review, 97*, 185–200.

Pashler, H. (1994). Dual-task interference in simple tasks – data and theory. *Psychological Bulletin, 116*, 220–244.

Patel, V. L., Glaser, R., & Arocha, J. F. (2000). Cognition and expertise: acquisition of medical competence. *Clinical and Investigative Medicine, 23*, 256–260.

Patel, V. L., Arocha, J. F., & Zhang, J. (2005). Thinking and reasoning in medicine. In K. J. Holyoak & R. G. Morrison (eds.), *The Cambridge Handbook of Thinking and Reasoning* (pp. 727–750). Cambridge, UK: Cambridge University Press.

Payne, L., Stevenson, J., Bowden, E. M., & Jung-Beeman, M. (2008). The origins of insight in resting-state brain activity. *Neuropsychologia, 46*, 281–291.

Pinker, S. (2011). *The Better Angels of Our Nature: Why Violence Has Declined*. New York: Viking.

Posner, M. I. (1973). *Cognition: An Introduction*. New York: Foresman.

Posner, M. I., & Keele, S. (1968). On the genesis of abstract ideas. *Journal of Experimental Psychology, 77*, 353–363.

Quine, W. V. (1969). Natural kinds. In N. Rescher (ed.), *Essays in Honor of Carl G. Hempel.* (pp. 42–56). Dordrecht: D. Reidel.

Rabi, R., & Minda, J. P. (2014). Rule-based category learning in children: the role of age and executive functioning. *PLoS ONE, 9*(1), e85316.

Reber, P. J., & Kotovsky, K. (1997). Implicit learning in problem solving: the role of working memory capacity. *Journal of Experimental Psychology: General, 126*, 178–203.

Reber, P., Stark, C., & Squire, L. R. (1998a). Contrasting cortical activity associated with category memory and recognition memory. *Learning & Memory, 5*, 420–428.

Reber, P., Stark, C., & Squire, L. R. (1998b). Cortical areas supporting category learning identified using functional MRI. *Proceedings of the National Academy of Sciences, 95*, 747–750.

Reingold, E., & Charness, N. (2005). Perception in chess: evidence from eye movements. In G. Underwood (ed.), *Cognitive Processes in Eye Guidance* (pp. 325–354). Oxford: Oxford University Press.

Rikers, R. M., Schmidt, H. G., & Moulaert, V. (2005). Biomedical knowledge: encapsulated or two worlds apart? *Applied Cognitive Psychology*, *19*(2), 223–231.

Rips, L. J. (1975). Inductive judgments about natural categories. *Journal of Verbal Learning & Verbal Behavior*, *14*(6), 665–681.

Rips, L. J. (1989). Similarity, typicality, and categorization. In S. Vosniadou & A. Ortony (eds.), *Similarity and Analogical Reasoning* (pp. 21–59). Cambridge, UK: Cambridge University Press.

Roediger, H. L., III. (2008). A typology of memory terms. In R. Menzel (ed.), *Learning Theory and Behavior. Vol. 1 of Learning and Memory: A Comprehensive Reference* (pp. 11–24). Oxford: Elsevier.

Roediger, H. L., III, & McDermott, K. B. (1995). Creating false memories: remembering words not presented in lists. *Journal of Experimental Psychology: Learning, Memory and Cognition*, *21*(4), 803.

Roediger, H. L., III, Marsh, J. E., & Lee, C. S. (2002). Varieties of memory. In D. L. Medin & H. Pashler (eds.), *Stevens' Handbook of Experimental Psychology. Vol. 2 Memory and Cognitive Processes* (3rd edn, pp. 1–42). New York: John Wiley & Sons.

Roney, C. J. R., Higgins, E. T., & Shah, J. (1995). Goals and framing: how outcome focus influences motivation and emotion. *Personality and Social Psychology Bulletin*, *21*(11), 1151–1160.

Rosch, E., & Mervis, C. B. (1975). Family resemblances: studies in the internal structure of categories. *Cognitive Psychology*, *7*, 573–605.

Rosch, E., Mervis, C. B., Gray, W., Johnson, D., & Boyes-Braem, P. (1976). Basic objects in natural categories. *Cognitive Psychology*, *8*, 382–439.

Rowling, J. K. (1997). *Harry Potter and the Philosopher's Stone*. London: Bloomsbury.

Saunders, B., & van Brakel, J. (1997). Are there nontrivial constraints on colour categorization? *Behavioral and Brain Sciences*, *20*, 167–228.

Schacter, D. L. (1999). The seven sins of memory: insights from psychology and cognitive neuroscience. *American Psychologist*, *54*(3), 182.

Schmeichel, B. J. (2007). Attention control, memory updating, and emotion regulation temporarily reduce the capacity for executive control. *Journal of Experimental Psychology: General*, *136*(2), 241–255.

Shafir, E., Simonson, I., & Tversky, A. (1993). Reason-based choice. *Cognition*, *49*(1), 11–36.

Shafir, E., Smith, E. E., & Osherson, D. N. (1990). Typicality and reasoning fallacies. *Memory & Cognition*, *18*(3), 229–239.

Shah, P., & Miyake, A. (1996). The separability of working memory resources for spatial thinking and language processing: an individual differences approach. *Journal of Experimental Psychology: General*, *125*, 4–27.

Shepard, R. N. (1987). Toward a universal law of generalization for psychological science. *Science*, *237*, 1317–1323.

Simon, H. A. (1957). *Models of Man: Social and Rational: Mathematical Essays on Rational Human Behavior in Society Setting*. New York: Wiley.

Simon, H. A. (1972). Theories of bounded rationality. In C. B. McGuire & R. Radner (eds.), *Decisions and Organization* (pp. 161–176). Amsterdam: North-Holland.

Simons, D. J., & Chabris, C. F. (1999). Gorillas in our midst: sustained inattentional blindness for dynamic events. *Perception*, *28*(9), 1059–1074.

Simons, D. J., & Levin, D. T. (1997). Change blindness. *TRENDS in Cognitive Sciences*, *1*(7), 261–267.

Simons, D. J., & Levin, D. T. (1998). Failure to detect changes to people during a real-world interaction. *Psychonomic Bulletin & Review*, *5*(4), 644–649.

Sloman, S. A. (1993). Feature-based induction. *Cognitive Psychology*, *25*, 231–280.

Sloman, S. A. (1996). The empirical case for two systems of reasoning. *Psychological Bulletin*, *119*(1), 3–22.

Sloman, S. A., & Lagnado, D. A. (2005). The problem of induction. In R. G. Morrison & K. J. Holyoak (eds.), *The Cambridge Handbook of Thinking and Reasoning* (pp. 95–116). Cambridge, UK: Cambridge University Press.

Sloman, S. A., Love, B. C., & Ahn, W.-K. (1998). Feature centrality and conceptual coherence. *Cognitive Science*, *22*(2), 189–228.

Smith, E. E., & Medin, D. L. (1981). *Categories and Concepts*. Cambridge, MA: Harvard University Press.

Smith, E. E., Shoben, E. J., & Rips, L. J. (1974). Structure and process in semantic memory: a featural model for semantic decisions. *Psychological Review*, *18*, 214–241.

Smith, J. D. (2002). Exemplar theory's predicted typicality gradient can be tested and disconfirmed. *Psychological Science*, *13*(5), 437–442.

Smith, J. D., & Minda, J. P. (1998). Prototypes in the mist: the early epochs of category learning. *Journal of Experimental Psychology: Learning, Memory and Cognition*, *24*(6), 1411–1436.

Smith, J. D., & Minda, J. P. (2002). Distinguishing prototype-based and exemplar-based processes in dot-pattern category learning. *Journal of Experimental Psychology: Learning, Memory and Cognition*, *28*(4), 800–811.

Smith, J. D., Tracy, J. I., & Murray, M. J. (1993). Depression and category learning. *Journal of Experimental Psychology: General*, *122*, 331–346.

Smith, J. D., Murray, M. J., & Minda, J. P. (1997). Straight talk about linear separability. *Journal of Experimental Psychology: Learning, Memory and Cognition*, *23*(3), 659–680.

Smith, J. D., Redford, J. S., & Haas, S. M. (2008). Prototype abstraction by monkeys (Macaca mulatta). *Journal of Experimental Psychology: General*, *137*(2), 390–401.

Soja, N. N., Carey, S., & Spelke, E. S. (1991). Ontological categories guide young children's inductions of word meaning: object terms and substance terms. *Cognition*, *38*, 179–211.

Sternberg, R. J., & Davidson, R. J. (1982). The mind of the puzzler. *Psychology Today*, *16*, 37–44.

Sweller, J. (1988). Cognitive load during problem solving: effects on learning. *Cognitive Science*, *12*, 257–285.

Tanaka, J., & Taylor, M. J. (1991). Object categories and expertise: is the basic level in the eye of the beholder? *Cognitive Psychology*, *23*, 457–482.

Tarr, M. J. (1995). Rotating objects to recognize them: A case study on the role of viewpoint dependency in the recognition of three-dimensional objects. *Psychonomic Bulletin & Review*, *2*, 55–82.

Tarr, M. J., Williams, P., Hayward, W., & Gauthier, I. (1998). Three-dimensional object recognition is viewpoint dependent. *Nature Neuroscience*, *1*(4), 275–277.

Thaler, R. (1980). Toward a positive theory of consumer choice. *Journal of Economic Behavior & Organization*, *1*(1), 39–60.

Thaler, R. (1985). Mental accounting and consumer choice. *Marketing Science*, *4*(3), 199–214.

Thomas, J. C. (1974). An analysis of behavior in the Hobbits–Orcs problem. *Cognitive Psychology*, *6*, 257–269.

Thompson-Schill, S., Ramscar, M., & Chrysikou, E. G. (2009). Cognition without control: when a little frontal lobe goes a long way. *Current Directions in Psychological Science*, *18*(5), 259–269.

Tulving, E. (1972). Episodic and semantic memory. In E. Tulving & W. Donaldson (eds.), *Organization of Memory* (Vol. 381, p. 403). New York: Academic Press.

Tulving, E. (1983). *Elements of Episodic Memory*. New York: Oxford University Press.

Tulving, E. (2002). Episodic memory: from brain to mind. *Annual Review of Psychology*, *53*, 1–25.

Tversky, A. (1977). Features of similarity. *Psychological Review*, *84*(4), 327–352.

Tversky, A., & Gati, I. (1982). Similarity, separability, and the triangle inequality. *Psychological Review*, *89*(2), 123–154.

Tversky, A., & Kahneman, D. (1973). Availability: a heuristic for judging frequency and probability. *Cognitive Psychology*, *5*(2), 207–232.

Tversky, A., & Kahneman, D. (1974). Judgment under uncertainty: heuristics and biases. *Science*, *185*(4157), 1124–1131.

Tversky, A., & Kahneman, D. (1981). The framing of decisions and the psychology of choice. *Science*, *211*(4481), 453–458.

Tversky, A., & Kahneman, D. (1983). Extensional versus intuitive reasoning: the conjunction fallacy in probability judgment. *Psychological Review*, *90*, 293–315.

Tversky, B. (1973). Encoding processes in recognition and recall. *Cognitive Psychology*, *5*(3), 275–287.

Vohs, K. D., Baumeister, R. F., Schmeichel, B. J., Twenge, J. M., Nelson, N. M., & Tice, D. M. (2008). Making choices impairs subsequent self-control: a limited-resource account of decision making, self-regulation, and active initiative. *Journal of Personality and Social Psychology*, *94*(5), 883–898.

Vohs, K. D., Glass, B. D., Maddox, W. T., & Markman, A. B. (2011). Ego depletion is not just fatigue: evidence from a total sleep deprivation experiment. *Social Psychological and Personality Science*, *2*(2), 166–173.

von Hecker, U., & Meiser, T. (2005). Defocused attention in depressed mood: evidence from source monitoring. *Emotion*, *5*(4), 456.

Voytovich, A. E., Rippey, R. M., & Suffredini, A. (1985). Premature conclusions in diagnostic reasoning. *Academic Medicine*, *60*(4), 302–307.

Wallas, G. (1926). *The Art of Thought*. J. Cape: London.

Wason, P. C. (1960). On the failure to eliminate hypotheses in a conceptual task. *Quarterly Journal of Experimental Psychology*, *12*(3), 129–140.

Wason, P. C. (1966). Reasoning. In B. M. Foss (ed.), *New Horizons in Psychology I* (pp. 106–137). Harmondsworth: Penguin.

Wason, P. C., & Evans, J. (1975). Dual processes in reasoning? *Cognition*, *3*(2), 141–154.

Wertheimer, M. (1959). *Productive Thinking*. Chicago, IL: The University of Chicago Press.

Whorf, B. (1956). *Language, Thought, and Reality: Selected Writings of Benjamin Lee Whorf*. Cambridge, MA: MIT Press.

Wittgenstein, L. (1953). *Philosophical Investigations*. Blackwell Publishing: Oxford.

Zelazo, P. D. (2004). The development of conscious control in childhood. *TRENDS in Cognitive Sciences*, *8*, 12–17.

INDEX

tip of the tongue phenomenon, 50
To Kill a Mockingbird, 212
total feedback, 83, 84
Tower of Hanoi problem, 200–1
Tracy, J.I., 157
trait focus, 153
transformational model, 31–3
transience, 50
trees, 117–18, 231–3, 235, 237, 239
triangle inequality, 29–30
Tulving, Endel, 43, 46, 48–9
Tversky, Amos, 28, 29–31, 36–7, 118–20, 127, 173, 175, 179, 182–5
Tversky, Barbara, 48
two doors problem, 128, 142–3
Tylenol, 61
typicality effects, 45, 68, 70, 72

uncertainty, 165, 178–80
universal affirmatives, 129–30
universal cognitive metaphors, 90–1
universal law of stimulus generalization, 106
universal negatives, 131
unusual uses test, 213

ventral striatum, 148
verbal fluency, 158
verification stage, problem-solving, 214
violence, 37–8
visual cortex, 211
visuospatial sketchpad, 41, 42–3
von Hecker, U., 157

Wagner, A., 7
Wallas, Graham, 214
Wason card selection tasks, 138–40, 156
well-defined problems, 190, 192, 193, 195
Wertheimer, Max, 11–12, 196
Whorf, Benjamin, 92–4
Wisconsin card sorting task, 157
within-category similarity, 70–2
Wittgenstein, Ludwig, 67, 72
working backwards strategy, 203
working memory, 14, 35, 40–2, 83, 139, 147–8, 160, 166, 197, 203

x-ray images, 53, 54, 228, 236

Zhu, R.J., 215